MW00782726

ROLL WITH IT

Refiguring American Music

A series edited by Ronald Radano and Josh Kun

Charles McGovern, contributing editor

ROLL WITH IT

Brass Bands
in the Streets of
New Orleans

MATT SAKAKEENY

With artwork by
WILLIE BIRCH

Duke University Press   Durham and London   2013

Library of Congress Cataloging-in-Publication Data
Sakakeeny, Matt, 1971–
Roll with it : brass bands in the streets of New Orleans /
Matt Sakakeeny ; with images by Willie Birch.
pages cm — (Refiguring American music)
Includes bibliographical references and index.
ISBN 978-0-8223-5552-6 (cloth : alk. paper)
ISBN 978-0-8223-5567-0 (pbk. : alk. paper)
1. Brass bands—Louisiana—New Orleans.
2. African American musicians—Louisiana—New Orleans.
3. Brass instrument players—Louisiana—New Orleans.
I. Birch, Willie. II. Title. III. Series: Refiguring American music.
ML1311.7.L8S34 2013
785.06509763′35—dc23
2013013827

Duke University Press gratefully acknowledges the support of the AMS 75 PAYS Endowment of the American Musicological Society, funded in part by the National Endowment
for the Humanities and the Andrew W. Mellon Foundation, which provided funds toward
the publication of this book. Tulane University also provided funds to commission the
artwork used in the book.

"Roll With It" is a song composed by Tyrus Chapman and Glen Andrews of the Rebirth Brass Band.

*The paintings in this book were not selected to illustrate the writing. The artwork and words
are meant to be an artistic pairing. All pieces were created between 2000–2008, using charcoal and
acrylic on paper. The pieces dating from 2003–2004 were created when Birch was artist-in-residence
at the New Orleans Jazz and Heritage Foundation.*

Frontispiece. *The Gang's All Here.* 2000. 60″ × 48″. © WILLIE BIRCH.

CONTENTS

LIST OF ARTWORK

ALL IMAGES BY WILLIE BIRCH

P.1 *Tuba Player on Villere Street.* 2003. 63″ × 48″. © WILLIE BIRCH.

CROSSING THE THRESHOLD

On a sunny Sunday afternoon in November 2006 I stand with a few hundred others outside a New Orleans barroom, waiting for the Prince of Wales Social Aid and Pleasure Club to start their annual second line parade.[1] Prince of Wales is one of fifty or so clubs that organize these parades, in which the members dress in matching outfits and dance through their neighborhoods to the beat of a brass band. Throughout the year Prince of Wales holds meetings and fund-raisers at a neighborhood bar called the Rock Bottom Lounge, in the Uptown neighborhood where I have lived since 1997, all building up to this day.

My eyes are fixed on eight men in their twenties and thirties leaning against the brick wall of the Rock Bottom, in a strip of shade underneath the roof overhang. They mill about, in no particular hurry, until the tallest of them picks up a street-worn tuba from the sidewalk and the others gather around him with their instruments: two trumpets, two trombones, a saxophone, bass drum, and snare drum. When the first note is sounded, the doors of the Rock Bottom fly open and the Prince of Wales strut out one by one. This is the moment club members anticipate all year; they call it "crossing the threshold" or "coming out the door." Men appear first in double-breasted red suits, gold fedoras, and matching shoes made of alligator leather, and then the Lady Wales dance out in contrasting gold pantsuits with red berets, in each hand a large feathered fan with the words "PRINCE OF WALES, est. 1928." The parade marshal blows his whistle, the musicians fall in step behind the club, and suddenly we are off.

The band and club members make up what is known as the first line, while the rest of us marching behind, and along the sides, make up the second line. Together we move through the backstreets, maneuvering through parked cars. Roving vendors wheel ice chests and yell "Ice cold beer. Get your water," while others set up "car bars" on the roofs of pickup trucks parked at designated stops. Plumes of marijuana smoke fill the air. The Prince of Wales take up the center of the street, flanked by rows of men holding rope to clear their path. Young boys and girls crawl into the open space to dance, and the crowd on the other side of the rope pauses to cheer them on.

The band plays one song after another without pause for several blocks; the groove will not stop, cannot stay put, is restless and elastic. The sound beckons people out of their houses, and as we make our way past my house the parade is expanding. What can appear to be a uniform mass of bodies is actually rather diverse: Janine, a black pharmacist who owns the fully renovated house next door, dances next to Rock, another neighbor who lives in a run-down house with no electricity; white and black anthropologists, professional photographers, and journalists intermingle with others here for the "free concert." And these identifications with race, class, and occupation can tell only so much about where we fit in the collective. Gerald Platenburg, one of the most active and visible dancers at the second line, works as an executive chef at a hotel restaurant; he is also a member of a Social Aid and Pleasure Club called Nine Times and, along with his fellow club members, is the author of a book called *Coming Out the Door for the Ninth Ward*. Gerald's dancing is a perfect analogy of his identity: he is always in motion.

The music draws us together. Our pace is set by the bass drum, snare drum, and tuba, and we determine our degree of involvement based on our proximity to the band. Along the perimeter, black motorcyclists wearing matching leather jackets have room to roam, and riders on horseback seem to prance out of crevices in the urban landscape. Behind the band, in the loose crowd of marchers, a man confined to a wheelchair dances by tilting his chair backward and spinning in circles. In the immediate vicinity of the

Prince of Wales the action is more concentrated and intense. Gerald is dancing so close to the musicians that he has to duck under trombonist Jerome
Jones's slide to avoid getting hit.

When we turn onto busy Magazine Street, police on motorcycle and
horse patrols have blocked off the traffic. Gerald makes use of the extra
space to twirl and jump while tourists pour out of local shops to catch a
glimpse. He likes to dance alongside the band in what he calls the "side-
show": "dancing on the sidewalk, jumping on cars, or on the railing of the
project, sliding on poles, and just going wild," he wrote in his book. "The
music just possesses me."[2]

The author and educator Kalamu ya Salaam observed:

> The best dancers have a way of merging jerking with gliding. . . . They
> sometimes seem to be floating down the street, legs and arms all curves,
> no angles. Then suddenly, they seize up like they've been hit by live wire,
> or they drop to the ground so fast you think something's wrong. But then
> another moment later and they're back just floating again like nothing
> even happened.

Those of us whose dancing skills are more limited are also welcome as long
as we participate: "Whatever you do, you just do it. . . . You don't have to
have any talent or skill and you don't have to ask permission. Just join in
and try to stay on the beat."[3]

The second line is all about participation, and sound is organizing our
movement, working to bring us into synchrony. Some sounds are meant
to be disruptive: second liners jump in the air and smack street signs with
open hands, and hip-hop blares from the open windows of cars parked
along the parade route. Other sounds are meant to augment the intensity
of the music: the parade marshal directs the flow with rhythmic bursts of a
whistle he wears around his neck, while a couple men hold cowbells or an
empty bottle of Wild Irish Rose above their heads, banging out syncopated
rhythms with a drumstick.

Underneath it all, forming the subterranean layer of the soundscape,
is the music of the Hot 8 Brass Band. The band is a perpetual-motion machine, except not a machine but an assemblage of human beings who hold
instruments in their hands and use them like tools to get people moving.[4]
The Hot 8 switches to a new song, the tempo rises, and those of us nearest

the action whoop and shout in recognition. When the procession turns onto Louisiana Avenue, the band is playing an original song from the 2005 album *Rock with the Hot 8*, and some of us chant the refrain:

> *It's real*
> *We ain't talking no shit*
> *Everybody jump when the Hot 8 hit!*

Bennie Pete anchors the parade with booming bass notes. He is an imposing presence, six-feet-six, over 350 pounds. That is why he was chosen to play the biggest brass instrument, back in sixth grade when he was already wearing a size 9 men's shoe and had a 38-inch waist. "I was just like I am now, I was sticking out," he told me when we first met in 2006. The band director took one look at him and assigned him the tuba. Now he is in his thirties, and everyone recognizes Bennie for his tuba playing. "Hey, Big Tuba!" they greet him when he's taking a break between songs.

Technically Bennie's instrument is not a tuba but a sousaphone, and though the term *tuba* is used more often — as evidenced by the nicknames "Big Tuba," "Tuba Fats," and "Tuba Phil" — the distinction is telling. In the 1890s the bandmaster John Philip Sousa commissioned the new instrument because the tuba was too cumbersome to march with, and of course it is not possible to march with a string bass, so the sousaphone was key to enabling the mobility of marching bands. Because the development of the New Orleans brass band tradition occurred in dialogue with emerging styles of black popular music (traditional jazz, swing, bebop, R&B, soul, funk, hip-hop) that increasingly emphasized the lower spectrum, the sousaphone came to be featured more prominently in musical arrangements and came to distinguish black brass band music in New Orleans from other styles and places.[5] So while Bennie anchors the syncopated grooves of the rhythm section with short melodic fragments, or "riffs," that are associated with funk and hip-hop, he can move people, literally, in ways that James Brown or Jay-Z could not.

The dense web of rhythm created by the adjunct percussionists is occasionally interrupted by a sputtering drumroll from Dinerral Shavers, a small man in an oversized white T-shirt with a silver cross medallion and a snare drum strap over his shoulders. Dinerral's powerful arms are working overtime, but his eyes never look down; he is constantly scanning the action around him while keeping in step with Bennie and bass drummer Harry

P.2 *Like Father Like Son*. 2001. 57″ × 42″. © WILLIE BIRCH.

Cook to keep the crowd moving. The rhythm section—Bennie, Dinerral, and Harry—is responsible for maintaining synchrony and maximizing intensity, and even at leisurely tempos their rhythmic activity has a way of "up-tempoing slow music," as Gerald described it to me.

About a month after the Prince of Wales parade, at a concert at the House of Blues nightclub, I witnessed Dinerral's ingenuity in bringing together martial rhythms, the syncopated shuffle of traditional New Orleans brass bands, and hip-hop beats. The show was billed as a "Brass Band Blowout" and was sponsored by KMEZ-FM ("Old School and Today's R&B"), and in between bands DJ Captain Charles kept the audience dancing with a seamless mix of contemporary hip-hop (e.g., Beyoncé's "Irreplaceable") and local music (e.g., Lil' Rascals Brass Band's "Knock with Me—Rock with Me"). Though the crowd was made up mostly of black New Orleanians familiar with brass band music, in any stationary setting the physical separation between audience and performer and the deafening sound system have the potential to limit participation and encourage passive spectatorship. Onstage Dinerral works to overcome his surroundings, augmenting his drum setup with a tambourine, cowbell, wood block, and cymbal in order to replicate the second line. This level of multitasking creates complex polyrhythmic grooves, broken up by short blasts, like the one near the beginning of Dinerral's song "Get Up," when a space is left for him to play a drumroll that doubles in rhythmic value and rises in volume before landing with a *crash!* of the cymbal. "Cold style. Like an octopus," is how trombonist Jerome Jones summed up Dinerral's approach.

Since seeing the Hot 8 at the Prince of Wales parade I had reached out to Bennie, asking if I could interview him for a radio segment I was producing. He obliged, appearing precisely at the arranged time, positioning himself in front of a microphone, leaning back in an office chair, and flashing a modest smile while no doubt sizing me up.

In a high, genial voice he spoke for two and a half hours, unraveling an epic narrative of nomadic connections between seemingly detached events. He spoke with gratitude about the pleasure he brought to audiences on the street and onstage. ("It's just like a 'feel-good' music," is how he described the New Orleans brass band tradition.) He spoke with modest pride about the Hot 8's original hip-hop–inflected compositions that have expanded the traditional repertoire of brass band music. ("We try to mix it up a little bit.") He spoke with anger of the gap between the cultural capital of the brass band as an icon of New Orleans culture and the economic capital doled out by nightclubs, festivals, and Social Aid and Pleasure Clubs. ("I'm just tired of being a damn good cheap act.") And he spoke with pain about the loss of three of his band members, including trombonist Joseph Williams, who was gunned down by police officers in 2004 at the age of twenty-two, and of the difficulty of performing at their funerals. ("I felt I had to play, no matter how bad I felt—sad, hurt, wanting to cry, crying—I had to play because I owed him that.")

What I could not have known at the time was that Bennie was leading me into topical areas—the power of the brass band to move people, the debates over tradition and innovation, the promises and pitfalls of the cultural economy, the power of music as a mediating voice in interpersonal and structural violence—that would provide the core themes of this book. I also could not have known that, within a few weeks, Dinerral would become the fourth member of the Hot 8 to die too young, when he took a bullet apparently intended for his stepson, Thaddeus, leaving behind a wife and a son, a mother and three sisters, and a band of young men who had grown up with him and loved him.

So it was that two months after first seeing Dinerral perform, I was watching Bennie Pete and dozens of musicians from every brass band in the city lead a funeral procession in his honor. In a New Orleans jazz funeral, friends and family of the dead march from the church to the burial site, their bodily movement and emotional state governed by the musicians. First, the procession moves slowly and deliberately to the sounds of sacred dirges; then, at a significant location, traditionally the place of burial, the band strikes up an up-tempo spiritual and the mournful march is transformed into a festive parade. The music that structures the funeral is virtually all instrumental, performed on trumpets, trombones, saxophone or clarinet, tuba, bass drum, and snare drum.[6] The sound is intended to communicate to the living and to the dead without recourse to language.

The intensity of emotion at a jazz funeral, especially for a young musician, underscores its status as the most sacred, profound, and traditional form of local black culture. And yet playing for funerals is a routine activity for all brass band musicians, a momentous event that closely resembles mundane events of little consequence. Whatever emotional distress the various members of the Hot 8 were under after sending off Dinerral, they had to put it behind them and go about their usual business, playing a birthday party at a daiquiri bar before sundown.

The experiences of New Orleans musicians like those in the Hot 8 Brass Band say something about the vitality of local black culture. They also say something about the insecurities of life for many in urban centers across the United States at the start of the twenty-first century, a perilous state of unending limbo that has been described as *precarity*.[7] There is much to celebrate here in the way that these young men use tradition to provide people with a sense of community through music, their success in reconfiguring tradition to resonate with contemporary experience, and their ability to accumulate status and earn a living by playing music in diverse contexts. But there is also much to condemn in the way they remain vulnerable to various forms of risk. This book follows these musicians as they mobilize across these two sides of the same coin. As a song by the Rebirth Brass Band repeats over and over, the lesson is to "roll with it."

FORWARD MOTION

In the summer of 1997 I was working as a sound engineer for the Smithsonian, traveling up and down the Mississippi River on assignment with the PBS documentary *River of Song* when our crew arrived in New Orleans. Though this was the final destination in our travelogue of the Mississippi, I cannot say I fully grasped the magnitude of New Orleans's reputation as a musical city. That was about to change because I had just accepted a job with a public radio program based in the French Quarter and would relocate to New Orleans in a few months. In retrospect, the trip was kind of a teaser for a new life I was about to begin and an initiation into the domain of local culture that would become an integral part of this life.

For one of the scenes we recorded a concert by the Soul Rebels at Joe's Cozy Corner in the Tremé neighborhood. I remember lugging audio equipment through the cramped front barroom at Joe's and into the back room that served as a makeshift performance area, with two folding tables, a space in the rear for the band, and room for dancing in between. Cramped in a corner, rubbing shoulders with an energetic crowd, steadying the table that held the recording equipment while someone climbed up to dance, I was feeling a mix of shock and excitement that I would soon be living in a place where such an event was even possible, let alone routine. Out front, Joe and two other bartenders served drinks to patrons who saw no particular reason to get up off their stools and venture back to listen.

I was twenty-six and going through the kinds of transitions typical for that age. A short, long-haired, white guitarist from Worcester, Massachusetts, a ragged postindustrial city, I had grown up playing rock music and then attended conservatory to study classical guitar and audio engineering. My embrace of "serious" music may have been subconsciously motivated by my grandfather and namesake, Mitri Sakakeeny, a Syrian American who worked in the textile mills as a child and followed a lifelong path to middle-class assimilation. Regardless, an internship in Europe making recordings of elite musicians sent me packing, first to make documentaries at the Smithsonian Museum of American History and then as an engineer and producer for the weekly radio program *American Routes*. After moving to New Orleans with my girlfriend Alex, I spent six years familiarizing myself with the local music scene, going to shows and recording interviews with musicians by the program's creator and host, Nick Spitzer.

I have vague, unprocessed memories of encountering brass bands in those years. The sound of the brass band ensemble permeates daily life in New Orleans to a degree that, like many New Orleanians, I took it for granted. Out running errands on a Saturday morning, Alex and I might stop at an intersection so a jazz funeral procession could pass by, the mourners marching in step to the tap of the snare drum, the thud of the bass drum, and the boom of the tuba. When a tricked-out Monte Carlo with shiny chrome hubcaps drove down our street, there was nothing unusual about the sound of trumpets, trombones, and saxophones blaring out of its open windows. And when we got married in 2000, it was common sense to have a brass band lead us on a ceremonial parade through the French Quarter. In 2002 I recorded a jazz funeral for Harold Dejan, which left an indelible impression on me, solidifying my recognition of the power of local culture and brass band music. Still, if you had told me then that I would spend years of my life researching and writing a book about brass band musicians, their performances, and their experiences, I would have laughed.

I came to black music by way of blues guitar playing, listening sessions at *American Routes*, and excursions to fife-and-drum picnics in the Mississippi hill country, jook joints on the outskirts of Memphis, zydeco dances in the bayou, and habitual outings in my adopted hometown. There was more

to it, though, for my attraction to black music was motivated by a fascina-
tion with race, informed by the racial polarization I witnessed in my actual
hometown as well as my father's liberal musings on morality and injustice
from the perspective of an ethnic minority, of which my classes in public
schools and conservatory taught me little. In 2001 I decided to go back to
school at Tulane University, initially researching the music of Mardi Gras
Indians and then writing a thesis on J&M Studios, where virtually every New
Orleans rhythm and blues and soul record was made. I found New Orleans
music equally as exotic as classical music: radically different, of course, and
far more socially inclusive, but with a comparable learning curve regarding the role of music in creating a sense of shared identity and retaining a
cultural connection between the past and the present. Then there were the
associations with marginalization and resistance, which, after reading authors such as Amiri Baraka, Albert Murray, Samuel Floyd, Charles Keil, and
Ronald Radano, I began to detect not only in the words of spirituals, soul,
and hip-hop but also in the pleasurable and seemingly innocuous social
dance music that surrounded me.[1]

In 2003 I entered a PhD program in the anthropological study of music
at Columbia University that led me to reexamine my experiences in New
Orleans. New Orleans music is not only a form of expressive culture; it is
also a site where competing social, political, and economic vectors intersect;
New Orleans musicians cannot be reduced to a collective of tradition-bearers
once their individual experiences are accounted for; and New Orleans as an
inscrutable place is nevertheless a thoroughly American urban center with
all of the poverty, racial marginalization, segregation, and other problems
that characterize postindustrial cities. In my last year of study, just as I was
preparing grant applications to fund fieldwork in New Orleans, Hurricane
Katrina struck, challenging me to contextualize local culture within much
larger political structures. It was then that the brass band parade presented
itself as a point of intersection for my main interests: race, power, and music.

This was by no means an ethnographic "discovery" of a hidden cultural
tradition; to the contrary, New Orleans brass bands have been popularized
through recordings, festival appearances, and concert tours and have been
the subject of continuous scholarly study and media reportage.[2] It was precisely the music's ubiquity and magnetism that drew me in; the brass band
is a sonic identifier of the city, a musical icon that is indelibly linked to race
and to place, and the sound is always there, waiting around every corner.

Upon returning to New Orleans in August 2006, I began talking with brass band musicians, attending parades and concerts, and eventually collaborating on public programs, and it was through these encounters that my ideas about New Orleans music were most profoundly revised and expanded.

The protagonists of this book are a dozen or so people who happen to spend their time, make their living, and articulate their experiences playing music. These musicians share qualities that evidence their collective identity. They are all black, they are all men, and most came of age in the post–civil rights period (sometimes referred to as the "hip-hop generation"). So in one, very limited sense, this book is an addition to a long line of studies of expressive cultural practices among urban black men in the United States.[3] However, I align my research with recent critical race studies that stand as a challenge to an intellectual lineage of "ghetto" studies projecting a "culture of poverty" and a hapless "underclass," which have circulated widely in public discourse. Beginning at the level of the microsocial—the words and actions of musicians I have interacted with—I then evaluate how their experiences relate to macroeconomic and political forces.

These musicians are from New Orleans and are members of three of the city's most prominent brass bands: Rebirth, the Soul Rebels, and the Hot 8. As such, they share qualities that evidence their collective culture. In furthering the parading tradition, they are ambassadors of a legacy that stretches back to the emergence of jazz at the turn of the twentieth century, and further, to slave dances in Congo Square near the French Quarter. Because the brass band parade has become a traveling symbol of local black culture, musicians have marched off the backstreets and into concert halls, festival grounds, and recording studios. In another sense, then, this book extends the study of New Orleans as an exceptional place and of music as the ultimate barometer of the city's uniqueness.[4] Where else, I wondered that first time I saw the Soul Rebels at Joe's Cozy Corner, do young black Americans continue to play instruments and dance to live music as a thoroughly unremarkable part of their everyday activities? Virtually nowhere, I reckoned, and still do.

Yet my investment in the idea of New Orleans exceptionalism has changed character over time. The experiences of New Orleans musicians offer a localized case study of the national and global transaction of black culture that is part of an equally deep and dark history of struggle for human rights and equal citizenship. Their stories speak not only to the power of local culture but also to the uneven terrain that characterizes U.S. urban centers in the post–civil rights period, particularly for black men. Their status as dual citizens—exceptional icons celebrated as culture-bearers and unremarkable subjects whose lives and livelihoods are forever at risk— makes them ideally positioned to diagnose relations of power.

As the foundation upon which my study rested began to shift— problematized by scholarship, politicized by tragedy, and humanized by intimacy—my research became less directed, more improvisational, and messier. I could no longer confine my "data" within a theoretical frame-work (expressive culture in a particular place) while other frameworks (race, class, economics of culture, transformation of tradition, interpersonal violence, urban restructuring) kept intervening, redirecting, and reframing my course of study. This topical expansiveness came about as a result of a narrowing in subject focus: the handful of people I interacted with consis-tently, the diverse experiences that they shared with me, and their public lives as working musicians formed the central organizing principle of the book. Because brass band musicians in New Orleans are virtually all men, I have focused on their experiences in relation to public discourse and media representations of urban black men as a "problem" category, but women are present and active at every turn: at home, in church, as members of so-cial clubs, as community leaders, in performance venues, and occasionally onstage.[5] These people became the frame, and within the frame there was nothing resembling a still life, for we were all in perpetual motion.

During the period of most intensive fieldwork, from 2006 to 2008, I caught people at parades and concerts, conducting research that often inter-sected with my work in radio. Though I was no longer working for *American Routes* regularly, in November 2006 I produced a segment on brass bands that led to my first recorded interviews with the bandleaders Bennie Pete of the Hot 8, Philip Frazier of Rebirth, and Lumar LeBlanc of the Soul Rebels. Soon after, I also reached out to bass drummer Keith Frazier of Rebirth to set up an interview, and by the end of the year I was helping snare drum-mer Derrick Tabb to launch an afterschool music program, Roots of Music. When my advisor Michael Taussig came to visit we were able to attend a jazz funeral, a second line parade, a nightclub concert, and a parade exhibition at Harrah's Casino in the space of two days.

When drummer Dinerral Shavers was murdered in December 2006, I decided to file a report for the National Public Radio program *All Things*

Considered, nervously phoning his bandleader Bennie to ask if he would be willing to share his reaction to Dinerral's killing with a radio audience. On a Wednesday night in the empty *American Routes* studios, Bennie and Hot 8 trombonist Jerome Jones allowed me to tap into the raw emotions of a tragic moment. I don't know how to describe the feeling in that room, but listening back to the recording I can recapture some of the intensity in the intonation, timbre, pitch, and cadence of their voices and the silence of the pauses. When discussion turned to the preparations for Saturday's funeral, Bennie took a long time to respond, sighing and rubbing his eyes with fatigue before answering in a soft, low voice: "I don't know. It's still unknown to me, man. It's still like it ain't real. It never really sinked in with us."

Our conversation that night wound through what would become the central themes of this book—agency, subjectivity, mobility—by way of another: *voice*. Voice can refer to the act of talking or singing; it can describe the sound made by musicians through their instruments; and it can serve as a symbol of subjectivity, of the basic capacity to have a voice and the basic right to use it. When talking with me about playing a jazz funeral for his friend and bandmate, Bennie necessarily uses his voice to communicate words and emotions. What he is describing is another sort of voice: speaking to his lost friend through music without language or music in which language is but one of several layers of semantic content. Finally, voice is invoked as a metaphor for agency; when Bennie leads a procession of predominantly black New Orleanians through public spaces where lynchings, race riots, segregation, and gentrification have all taken place, the actions of musicians and marchers "give voice" to these submerged histories. Throughout the pages that follow, these multiple meanings of voice are shown to be inseparable. In a performance such as that of the spiritual "Just a Closer Walk with Thee" at Dinerral's jazz funeral, each voice is present: the second line marchers sing the sacred text over the sound of instruments in a ritual procession that symbolizes a communal voice.[6]

What can this polyphony of voices tell us about race, power, and music? Brass band musicians are agents in the public sphere who utilize voices and instruments as technologies for producing subjectivity, identity, and culture. Their musical practices are forms of social action, and when evaluated as such they offer insight into *agency* as the exercise of, or against, power. Parades and musical events are mobilized by people committing verifiable acts, people "exerting some degree of control over the social relations in which one is enmeshed," writes the sociologist William Sewell Jr. of agency, "which in turn implies the ability to transform those social relations to some degree."[7] The anthropologist Sherry Ortner suggests that ethnographers studying living people have particular insight into the "dynamic, powerful, and sometimes transformative relationship between the practices of real people and the structures of society, culture, and history."[8] Music is one way that the people in this study came to know themselves as New Orleanians, black Americans, and cultural icons.

The actions and voicings of musicians led me to reconceive my study as about *subjectivity*. I mean this less in the romantic philosophical sense of musicians as creative individuals, or the classic folkloric sense of musicians as undifferentiated carriers of culture, than in the contemporary anthropological sense of individuals as subjects and agents of power, the "vulnerable, failing, and aspirational human beings" whom the anthropologists João Biehl, Byron Good, and Arthur Kleinman assess as "at once a product and an agent of history."[9] The contributors to their book *Subjectivity: Ethnographic Investigations* put forth a series of "cultural analyses that make visible differences of interests, access, power, needs, desires, and philosophical perspectives" among individuals situated within hierarchies of power.[10]

Human agency and subjectivity are measurable in voices material and metaphorical, musical and verbal, including my own voice as a scholar, journalist, client, and curator of New Orleans music. As is typical of anthropological and ethnomusicological studies, my voice resonates loudest when retelling and reframing the stories of others that arose in fieldwork, but in this case the field encompasses a diverse set of engagements—radio segments, public programs, class visits, and performances—that constitute my daily life in New Orleans.

Also in this network are fellow anthropologists and researchers who share an engagement with local culture and collaborate on events and programs. When I met Helen Regis in 2006 at the parade described in the prologue I was already familiar with her research on Social Aid and Pleasure Clubs such as Prince of Wales. At a parade later in the season, Helen (an anthropologist at Louisiana State University) introduced me to Rachel Breunlin (an anthropologist at the University of New Orleans), and the following year we coordinated a mixed panel at the Society for the Anthropology of North America conference in New Orleans. The panelists were Hot 8's bandleader Bennie Pete, Social Aid and Pleasure Club Task Force members Tamara Jackson and Troy Materre, and House of Dance and Feathers museum curator Ronald W. Lewis. Rachel, who codirects the Neighborhood

Story Project, and Helen, who helped found the Porch, a cultural organization in the Seventh Ward neighborhood, worked to make the event a true collaboration. They also provided me with a model for public engagement, shrinking the distance that can characterize ethnographic relationships in the field.[11] Rachel asked Bennie to have the Hot 8 play at her wedding on the same weekend as the conference, and after my wife and daughter and I socialized with the band, they played a raucous celebration with Rachel and her husband, Dan, dancing with Troy and Gerald and the other members of the Nine Times.[12]

By this time I had finished my dissertation and taken a job in the Department of Music at Tulane University, ending any semblance of compartmentalization in my work, home, and social lives. At Tulane I invite musicians to give workshops and lead class discussions on campus, and I offer service learning courses that put my students in contact with young musicians at the Roots of Music afterschool program. As a cultural intermediary, I am sometimes called upon to hire bands for gigs, including academic conferences, or interview musicians at public programs. The thing I do most often is attend second line parades and brass band concerts with family, friends, and an endless stream of guests (including not a small number of ethnomusicologists and anthropologists).[13] These are not excursions peripheral to my work but rather are integral to it, appearing in these pages alongside the kinds of rituals that dominate the anthropological record, such as the funeral procession for Harold Dejan, the bandleader for the Olympia Brass Band who passed away at age ninety-three in 2002 (episode 1.1), or a performance by the Free Agents Brass Band at a back-a-town bar (episode 3.1).

These are each *events* that take place in a resonant public sphere, including what the anthropologist Sally Falk Moore terms "diagnostic events" that "reveal ongoing contests and conflicts and competitions and the efforts to prevent, suppress, or repress these."[14] Throughout her studies of Tanzania, Moore draws attention to the actions of individuals in relation to larger structures, so that her observations of events as "part of the cultural construction of part of a society at a particular time" are then situated within and against "larger processual implications of the local moment."[15] Hurricane Katrina was, of course, a diagnostic event that directly impacted everyone in this book, but the full significance of Katrina can be measured only in context, which for those most vulnerable to devastation has been shaped by histories of enslavement, segregation, disempowerment, and curtailed free-

1.2 *Mule Leading Funeral Procession.* 2005. 72″ × 99″. © WILLIE BIRCH.

doms. The election of Barack Obama as the first black American president in November 2008 was a global event that instantaneously revised these histories and was detectable at the microlevel in the congratulatory exchanges and boastful T-shirts seen along the parade routes. A parade or a funeral is itself a diagnostic event linked to the past, emerging in the present, and shaping the future.

In events specifically chosen to diagnose power relations, I track the *mobility* of musicians practicing various forms of agency.[16] Just as *voice* is a keyword with literal and metaphorical meanings, mobility can refer to both physical and symbolic movement. The objective of the brass band musician is to mobilize audiences to march and dance, and this work requires them to traverse social landscapes such as the bureaucracy of client-patron relations, the opportunities and burdens of being a tradition-bearer, and the threat of urban violence. A career as a brass band musician offers young black men the potential for social mobility, but the path is unpredictable and littered with obstacles; the trick is to generate momentum within structures that constrain; to maximize mobility in the "tight spaces" that the Black Studies scholar Houston A. Baker Jr. identifies as characteristic of the black experience.[17] In tight spaces, musicians direct audiences and one another to roll with it.

By following musicians as they move and propel the movements of others, and by observing the traps and dead-ends that cause dreaded stagnation, I witnessed them navigating across terrains that are traditionally segregated in subdisciplines of anthropology and ethnomusicology and I began to ask more critical and expansive questions: How is race lived? What can the unprecedented crisis of Hurricane Katrina reveal about the historical consistency of vulnerability, and where does music reside within these histories? How do deeply rooted traditions remain relevant in the dislocated spaces of modernity? Which musicians are most active in mobilizing tradition, and which have been demobilized through violence, addiction, incarceration, or other constraints?

The brass band parade—in each of its forms, from the traditional jazz funeral, to the community second line parade, to staged exhibitions—is my model for contextualizing the mobilizations of individuals. Parades reside at the center of this book, but that center is not fixed; parades are always traveling restlessly forward or entrancingly round and round in circles, going back and forth over the "same" streets for a hundred-plus years but never remaining static because the people, the music, and even the landscapes change. Everything stays in motion, unless halted by death or interrupted by destruction or something more mundane, and even these hiccups create emergences that revise existing formations. New meanings are elicited with each step.

What makes brass band parades so foundational to my research is not what they reveal about an isolated area but the way they intersect with many areas, collecting people together whether or not they share experiences and orientations. The parade is an event made up of other successive and overlapping events, such as the performance of a particular song, the chant of a refrain, the display of a dance step, or the passing of a site endowed with local significance. My engagement with musicians—moving alongside them, at their pace, across territorial boundaries—became my template for writing.

The ideal language and structure of this book would be a mimetic replication of a brass band parade. Stretching across four chapters and further subdivided into compact episodes, the rhythm of the text moves at different paces, in a continuous flow of activity with breaks, interruptions, deviations, reversals, and shifts in velocity. Topical areas such as voice, agency, subjectivity, and mobility have only been glossed here because I will reapproach these themes from different routes, sometimes pausing to linger and other times decelerating just enough to make a connection before moving on.

On the streets and in these pages, intensities and intimacies vary according to proximity. The toppling force of violent death and its sublime memorialization in the music of the jazz funeral is meant to shock readers out of complacency, placing you at the epicenter of the event, adjacent to the musicians, where the musical and emotional intensity makes bodies vibrate. Other stories are recounted from the perimeter, where interactions are more casual, fleeting, and unstructured. Participants orient themselves differently to the parade, and the way I situate myself is modeled on the complex politics of participation that I experienced on the street.

Words, as the literary critic Walter Benjamin idealized them, have the potential to rub up so closely against their referent that readers experience what is being represented through their senses.[18] The episodes in this book adopt different narrative strategies that correspond to specific people, practices, and topics.[19] For some scholars, this experiential mode of narrative storytelling may limit the potential to generate exportable theory, and I have purposefully curtailed theoretical abstractions and relegated many citations to footnotes, limiting references to those who assisted me in understanding interactions on the ground.[20] The voices of musicians commingle with the voices of academics without differentiation or segmentation, brought into semblance through writing.[21]

Interspersed throughout is the artwork of Willie Birch. As we discuss in the afterword, my writing tools are comparable to Birch's methods as a visual artist; composition, scale, contrast, and perspective are used not simply to depict parades but as a model for injecting rhythm and motion into a two-dimensional drawing. "Through perspective," he explained, "I'm going to force you to enter this piece and I'm going to allow you to release around the edge." Rather than representing the real, Willie and I are both intentionally creating other manifestations of the real. His are different from mine—in fact, for the most part, the subjects of my research do not appear in his drawings, and his musician-subjects tend to be older than those I concentrate on—but we both apprehend our subject material as a methodological model for our creative work.

If we have succeeded you might imagine that you are in a parade, sensing the music's effect in uniting bodies, interacting with others with diverse orientations, feeling pleasure or suffering, inclusion or isolation, empowerment or vulnerability. And moving, always moving.

1.1 *Jazz Funeral for Big Moose.* 2004. 85″ × 84″. © WILLIE BIRCH.

CHAPTER 1

ONWARD AND UPWARD

EPISODE 1.1: A Funeral Fit for a Duke

Harold "Duke" Dejan was born in New Orleans's historic Tremé neighborhood in 1909, just after the dawn of jazz. His first music lesson was with his neighbor Albert Nicholas, the great clarinetist among the first generation of jazz musicians, and his first job was at the College Inn on Rampart Street, next door to Tom Anderson's saloon, where Nicholas and Louis Armstrong played together. It was the early 1920s, jazz was becoming an international phenomenon, and both Armstrong and Nicholas would leave for Chicago to launch careers as ambassadors of black music to the world. Dejan meanwhile would go on to cultivate a thoroughly local musical ensemble and gain a relative degree of notoriety as the founder of the city's most prominent group in the 1960s and 1970s, Dejan's Olympia Brass Band.

As young men, each of these musicians solidified his status in the community by performing in musical funerals and parades, cultural displays that occupied public space with the sights, sounds, and physical presence of people subject to segregationist laws intended to limit their movements. "I really felt that I was somebody," Armstrong wrote in his autobiography. "When I played with the Tuxedo Brass Band I just felt as proud as though I had been hired by John Philip Sousa or Arthur Pryor."[1]

Over the course of the twentieth century, the brass band parade became recognized not only as a proud communal tradition among black New Orleanians but also as a traveling symbol of their rich heritage for a global audience of admirers. By the end of Dejan's life, in a radically different era defined by the events of September 11, the cultural capital of the brass band tradition had given him a degree of social mobility that, while nothing in comparison to Armstrong's, allowed him to travel the world, be recognized as a local celebrity, purchase his own home, and tool about in a Lincoln Continental with the personalized license plate "Duke D."

A week after he passed away at the age of ninety-three on the Saturday afternoon of July 13, 2002, Harold Dejan was memorialized with a traditional jazz funeral befitting a musician of his age and stature, attended by thousands and accompanied by media coverage from the *Times-Picayune* newspaper and all the local network television stations. The artist Willie Birch was there, "looking for imagery," as he later put it, and he created a piece in honor of Dejan titled *In the Sweet Bye and Bye* that graces the cover of this book. The full scope of the prestige accorded to the brass band parade and to Dejan himself is also indicated by my presence at his funeral. At the time, I was a radio producer assigned the task of recording the procession for broadcast on the public radio program *American Routes*. Alongside the host, Nick Spitzer, I marched with my microphone on a boom pole and my headphones atop my head in what I perceived as another day at the office.

The event begins with Dejan's casket carried out of the Charbonnet-Labat Funeral Home and placed in a horse-drawn carriage, followed in precise order by those who make up the first line: parade marshals wearing black suits and hats and carrying feathered fans with pictures of Dejan in the center; funeral directors clearing a path for the cortege to pass through ("Open up, please, off to the side, please"); Dejan's pastor; his family; and the Olympia band playing the slow dirge "What a Friend We Have in Jesus."[2]

The first line turns onto Claiborne Avenue, the main thoroughfare cutting through the Tremé neighborhood adjacent to the French Quarter in the Downtown district. The second line of black and white New Orleanians, tourists, reporters, and photographers falls in behind and alongside the mourners. We march beside the concrete decks of Interstate 10 that tower over the street. As vehicles zing by overhead, the procession moves slowly and solemnly for several blocks, the band gradually ratcheting up the tempo with the traditional Baptist spirituals "Bye and Bye" and "I'll Fly Away," each faster than the one before. Thirty musicians march in honor of their former bandleader, wearing the traditional uniform of "black and whites": short-sleeve white work shirt, black pants and shoes, and a visored cap bearing the band's name in gold lettering. The back row of bass drum, snare drum, and tuba provides rhythmic and harmonic consistency, while the trumpets, trombones, clarinets, and saxophones in the front line play the melody and improvise simultaneously, creating a thick contrapuntal texture that has been a hallmark of New Orleans brass band music for over a century.

At first recognition of the melody, we clap along to the beat. Some have brought their own cowbells and tambourines. The rhythm ripples through concentric circles of bodies. More and more sway to the strike of the bass drum in a freestyle choreography of communal motion. I take off my headphones to find that I too am swaying. Anthony "Tuba Fats" Lacen, a respected musical elder performing in the funeral of his former bandleader, leads the crowd in the refrain. In unison we sing:

I'll fly away, oh Glory, I'll fly away
When I die, Hallelujah bye and bye, I'll fly away

The cemetery is several miles away, so the funeral organizers decide to "cut the body loose" at the intersection of Claiborne and Esplanade Avenues and then proceed to the cemetery by car. As we near the overpass, the band switches to "Lord, Lord, Lord" at a fast march tempo and the dancers move with more force, undaunted by the heat of the midday summer sun. When we make the turn under massive decks of the interstate, police sirens melt into the soundscape of instruments and singing. The band plays the most recognizable musical phrase in the brass band repertoire, known as the "Joe Avery riff," a four-note trumpet call from the 1950s standard "Joe Avery's Blues." After each statement by the trumpets—"DA-DA-DAAA-DA!"—the crowd punctuates the riff by yelling "HEY!"[3] Call-and-response phrasing, what the musicologist Samuel Floyd calls "the master trope" of black music, highlights the lack of separation between audience and performer.[4] "Joe Avery" is a gesture of inclusion, because if you do not yell "HEY" along with the musicians and everyone else, you are not participating.

The trumpet calls and we respond; "Joe Avery" comes only when the musicians want to intensify their dialogue with the second liners. The participatory nature of the second line multiplies its affective power as first and second lines commingle, the sound emanating from all of us. The brass band organizes the extramusical sounds and accounts for the environmental effects in order to provide sonic structure, continuity, and coherence. The musicians set the pace so that under the overpass, when our bodies are closest together, we share a responsibility to move in sync, to land our feet on the ground when the beat hits or risk disrupting the flow. The earth shakes with the collective thud of feet and bass drums. The music is based on improvisation, intended to produce unrestrained emotions, and yet the formula for this degree of participation is necessarily controlled and even somewhat rigid in its adherence to certain tempos and repertoires and, in a particularly iconic practice, the summoning of a minute musical phrase. Participation is generated by musicians who initiate chants, call-and-response textures, collective improvisations, and polyrhythmic grooves at specific tempos, while the rest of us determine our degree of involvement based on our proximity to the band.

I once asked a photographer how to avoid disrupting the parade while taking pictures; his suggestion was to distance myself from the dancers surrounding the band and roam along the perimeter. "The energy radiates from the center, from the sousaphone," he told me, his metaphor underscoring the fundamental role of the band as the energy that fuels movement. Gerald Platenburg, a second line dancer, described the "bass horn" as "the quarterback of a second line." The desire to take a photo, converse with a friend, or fully participate in the parade poses the problem of where to situate yourself—among those in the first line, in the more sparsely populated area behind them, or along the sidewalks—and the bell of the sousaphone is literally at the center of the decision-making process.

"DA-DA-DAAA-DA!" "HEY!"

The band plays their final chord, and the merriment continues a cappella for several minutes. When the collective excitement dissipates, the hearse leads the cortege to the burial site and the second line disperses. "There was something special about Mr. Dejan, boy," Willie Birch later recalled of the funeral. "It felt so peaceful, man, it felt so spiritual."

EPISODE 1.2: An Eventful History

In the first years of the twentieth century, when Harold Dejan was born, the New Orleans brass band was not perceived as a tradition of distinction and a career as a brass band musician was not equated with prestige. Up until that time there had been little to differentiate bands in New Orleans from those throughout the United States, initially brought by European militaries and Christian missionaries and then popularized by the bandmasters Patrick Gilmore and John Philip Sousa.[5] In antebellum New Orleans, bands of Europeans and Americans were a routine presence at every major holiday, funeral, or commemoration, and after the Civil War bands made up of people of color became a sizable presence as well. Reports suggest that these ensembles, though ethnically and racially distinct, were otherwise roughly comparable: the musicians all wore Prussian-style military uniforms, marched in closed formations, and performed stock arrangements of the latest marches, European dances, and popular songs. The black bands would not have identified themselves as such, for they were made up predominantly of Creoles with mixed European and African ancestry who were generally musically literate and otherwise fluent in Eurocentric methods, and who adopted names (the Excelsior, the Imperial, the Superior) that captured some of the grandeur previously reserved for the white bands.

Harold Dejan's parents were Creoles who grew up in the Downtown district that included the French Quarter, Marigny, and Tremé neighborhoods, where Italian, Spanish, and especially French were spoken, across from the Uptown district on the other side of Canal Street, where English-speaking Anglo-Protestants and black Americans were concentrated.[6] While Dejan does not appear to have come from a particularly musical family, he grew up around dynasties such as the Barbarins and their patriarch, Isidore Barbarin, a cornetist with the Onward Brass Band and father of four professional brass band musicians (Paul, Louis, Lucien, and William) and grandfather to guitarist Danny Barker, born in the French Quarter in the same year as Dejan.

Between the time when Isidore was indoctrinated into brass bands in the late 1800s and Harold Dejan and Danny Barker first picked up instruments in the 1910s, radical social, political, and musical changes had transformed their lives and livelihoods. In 1892 Homer Plessy, a Creole New Orleanian, was arrested for sitting in the white car of a segregated train, leading to a landmark Supreme Court decision that institutionalized segregation, stripped blacks of their rights, and had the local consequence of legally classifying Creoles and black Americans together.[7] From a strictly musical perspective, the subsequent interactions—sometimes contested—between black American, Creole, and European immigrant musicians caused an efflorescence akin to a chemical reaction brought about by the synthesis of multiple elements: jazz. From a broader perspective, the public performance of social dance music within a hierarchical order that imposed humility and deference was an act of political significance. Dancing to "good-time music," in the words of the cultural critic Albert Murray, "is the direct opposite of resignation, retreat, or defeat," nowhere more evident than in the jazz funerals and second line parades that literally marched across the segregated spaces of New Orleans.[8]

Funerals and parades led by bands of all races and ethnicities serve the essential function of regulating the movement of crowds, of "keeping together in time" as wind bands have done since Crusaders first encountered Saracen armies seven centuries ago. But as Rob Boonzajer Flaes writes in *Brass Unbound: Secret Children of the Colonial Brass Band*, community brass bands never lost their association with "the brightly polished expression of a Western sense of beauty and order, the resounding proof of Western military, religious, and cultural superiority."[9] By leading processionals in the same streets where lynchings and race riots occurred, bands made up of black musicians turned this association on its head.[10] The musicologist Thomas Brothers writes in his book *Louis Armstrong's New Orleans* that the second line parade, as a "public display of African American vernacular culture," was implicitly a "symbolic act of resistance to Jim Crow."[11] As laws and codes sought to segregate public accommodations into black and white spaces, parades defied segregation in their volume and plenitude.

The ways that the music oriented black New Orleanians toward one another connected the black brass band parade of the post-Reconstruction period not only to European-derived marching bands but also to another, entirely different antebellum musical event. Until the 1840s slaves were permitted to congregate and sell goods on Sunday afternoons in Congo Square, a grassy expanse on the perimeter of the French Quarter, where they also sang and danced in the form of a ring shout.

In an essay linking the slave dances in Congo Square to the development of brass band parades, Samuel Floyd locates "all of the defining elements of black music" in the ring shout, including "call-and-response devices; additive rhythms and polyrhythms; . . . timbral distortions of various kinds; musical individuality within collectivity; . . . and the metronomic foundational pulse that underlies all Afro-American music."[12] The most detailed account of Congo Square, from an 1819 journal entry by the architect Benjamin Henry Latrobe, makes reference to several of these characteristics. The many drummers, whose sound Latrobe compared to "horses trampling on a wooden floor," were likely creating the complex polyrhythms that characterize ritual drumming in West Africa and the Americas.[13] While one group of women was "respond[ing] to the Song of their leader" in call-and-response fashion, others were "walk[ing], by way of dancing, round the music in the Center," creating what Floyd would recognize as "an activity in which music and dance commingled, merged, and fused to become a single distinctive cultural ritual."[14] The historian Michael Gomez writes that the ring shout helped to strengthen communication among slaves, "[bringing] them together, transcending cultural barriers and hastening the creation of a pan-African cultural mix with numerous points of intersection."[15]

In historical relation to the black brass band parades of freemen and their descendants, the ring shout is the foundational ritual of community recognition and value through participatory music making in what the historian Gwendolyn Midlo Hall refers to as "the most African city in the United States."[16] It would be crude and essentialist to draw a direct link from the music at Harold Dejan's jazz funeral back to ring shout dances at Congo Square, and it would be equally problematic to ignore the ongoing persistence and dynamic vitality of outdoor festival traditions among black New Orleanians subject to varying forms of bondage. In the time of Jim Crow rule, Isidore Barbarin witnessed Joe "King" Oliver, Louis Armstrong, and other jazz musicians transform the brass band through improvisation, syncopation, and the addition of repertoire including ragtime, blues, and spirituals; Harold Dejan updated the Olympia with rhythm and blues music that was the soundtrack of the civil rights movement; and the Dirty Dozen and Rebirth brass bands brought the music into dialogue with funk and hip-hop as the hopes attached to the movement receded in the last quarter of the twentieth century. These musicians and their contemporaries maintained

the participatory, inclusive character of brass band music not through
preservation but through recalibra-
tion, retuning tradition to be consonant with the experiences of younger
generations.

Dejan was an agent in mobilizing
musical traditions, racial identities,
and social locations from the Jazz Age
up through the birth of the hip-hop
generation. He was partly responsible
for the prestige that the New Orleans
brass band accumulated over the
course of his lifetime. In turn, his own
status as a cultural practitioner was
enhanced both in terms of economic
capital and what the sociologist Pierre
Bourdieu identified as symbolic capital, such as cultural capital and social
capital, which bestows status on indi-

viduals within a group.[17] This broad understanding of value as the accrual
of material and immaterial wealth, accumulating like puddles of water on
uneven pavement, reappears throughout this book in stories of the haves,
the have-nots, and the in-betweens. The noble Duke's jazz funeral, like his
flashy yet respectable Lincoln Continental, was a sign of individual and collective wealth: a memorial for a prominent community member honored
with a spectacular funeral procession and a reaffirmation of a tradition that
was now known around the globe. A durable tradition, the brass band is by
no means static; it has been continually redirected by powerful innovators
who have deployed specific yet adaptable musical practices in public events
situated within shifting political infrastructures. Along the way, musicians
have enhanced the prestige of the brass band tradition and the music, in
turn, has bestowed social and economic capital upon them.

EPISODE 1.3: Second Lining with Rebirth

On the Sunday afternoon of February 25, 2007, I march with the Tremé Sidewalk Steppers Social Aid and Pleasure Club, the Rebirth Brass Band, and about five hundred other participants through the Tremé neighborhood. The Sidewalk Steppers are one of dozens of neighborhood clubs in New Orleans that organize yearly parades called second lines. The name of the second line parade and the practice itself derive from the jazz funeral, but while funerals are necessarily scheduled with some haste and proceed from a church or funeral home to a burial site, the dates and routes of second line parades are planned with much preparation and anticipation. Each week, except in the summer months, parades are routed through the many neighborhoods where clubs are based, making designated stops at the houses of club members and other significant neighborhood sites, typically barrooms. The events surrounding Hurricane Katrina mark the time that has passed since Harold Dejan's funeral, even as the Steppers' return to the streets underscores the persistence of the parading tradition.

The Steppers are a relatively young club, with most members in their

1.2 *The Revolution Got Soul, Soul, Soul* (3 PIECES). 2004. 25″ × 60″.
© WILLIE BIRCH.

thirties and forties, and their style is thoroughly modern and in step with
black aesthetics in Atlanta, Chicago, Houston, or Los Angeles. In January
2001, when I first attended a Steppers parade, the members and musicians
were dressed in camouflage military fatigues, combat boots, and black face
paint. The aesthetics were inspired, in part, by the local rapper Soulja Slim
and other "souljas" popular during the heyday of southern gangsta rap in the
late 1990s and early twenty-first century. In 2007 the members were wearing
gold lamé suits with black fans and feather boas and they were augmenting
the traditional buck jump and high-step dance moves with more contemporary ones like the crawl.

The Steppers exit their clubhouse in the Tremé dancing to the Rebirth
Brass Band. Since forming in the early 1980s, Rebirth has gained an international reputation as the primary innovators of the brass band tradition.
This has allowed the core members — Philip Frazier (tuba), Keith Frazier
(bass drum), Derrick Tabb (snare), Vincent Broussard (saxophone), Stafford
Agee and Corey Henry (trombone), and Glen Andrews and Derrick Shezbie (trumpet) — to perform full time, putting them in an elite group of local
musicians who consistently earn money and respect.[18] I have seen Rebirth
bring an audience at Madison Square Garden to their feet, and I have stood
among the throngs at the Maple Leaf Bar on Tuesday nights, the most renowned weekly gig on the New Orleans musical calendar, and I have spent
many Sunday afternoons parading with the band, grateful that their success has not enticed them to leave the streets. This distinguishes Rebirth
and other black brass bands from a handful of white bands — ranging from
the traditional Storyville Stompers to the progressive Nightcrawlers — that
play in a variety of settings but are not hired for community parades such
as this one.[19]

The bandleader Philip Frazier and his younger brother, Keith, came up
through the tradition, learning from the Olympia, Dirty Dozen, and other
established bands. They have created a signature sound by perpetuating certain conventions learned from their predecessors and altering others to keep
tradition relevant to new generations. The Steppers parade begins with an
original song, "You Don't Want to Go to War," recorded as a collaboration
with rapper Soulja Slim for the 2001 album *Hot Venom*. From this point
forward every aspect of tempo and rhythm, melody and repertoire, improvisation and repetition is strategically executed with the purpose of mov-

ing audiences. The band orients the participants within a collective whose membership is both fixed (the musicians and club members) and fluctuating (the second liners entering and exiting the procession). As the Steppers parade winds through the backstreets of the Tremé, Rebirth assesses the crowd's response and modifies their performance—including fluctuations in tempo, beat, and choice of repertoire—to maximize crowd participation.

Bodily movement and audience participation are heightened by specific tempos set by the band. "I think it really does go back to second line dancing," Keith explained to me the first time I interviewed him, in April 2007. "We want the beat to stay at a certain tempo [in order for] people to get up and dance." In the 1970s the Dirty Dozen became the most influential brass band, in part, by increasing the tempo to match the funk songs and dance styles of the period, and Rebirth stays in this range of about 100 to 124 beats per minute. "If it drops below that it gets kind of boring, and people start standing around," said Keith.

Another practice designed to maintain a high degree of audience participation is to sequence songs continuously, without pause. When we met in November 2006, Philip told me, "We try to play continuous to keep everybody going, to keep the energy rolling." Instead of structuring a performance around songs with breaks between them, the music proceeds without interruption, with fluctuations in tempo. "We might be playing a song at this tempo," said Philip, snapping his fingers quickly, "and right in the middle of the song I might break it down to a slow pace," he added, snapping slower. "I think it mess with they mind, they heart, they soul. Even me, myself, when I be playing and I slow a song down in the middle of a fast song and then pick it back up, it's like a rush." There is not a single tempo that generates audience participation in brass band performance, but a range of tempos for musicians to move between at different moments.

A successful second line parade is an act of reciprocity: in a circular dialogue, musicians respond to audiences responding to their music. Musicians make choices in the moment, improvising in the broadest sense of the term. "We don't want to play any songs straight," Philip said, "we want to keep it spontaneous":

> You hear a little bit of melody, then you hear something else going on. Try to figure, "What is that going on?" It's like confusion, but good confu-

sion, like "I know this! Man, they playing like it's constructed, then they playing like it's not constructed. Is they reading off a paper? No, they ain't reading off a paper but I know what they doing and I can feel it."

In order to create "good confusion," Philip will make repertoire changes instantaneously, sometimes by calling out a different song but more often by simply nodding his head or raising his eyebrows as he begins playing a tuba line from Rebirth's extensive catalogue. "We never talk, there's no communication, you just have to know what's going to happen," said Keith. "That's why I say New Orleans brass band music is one of the most improvisational type musics you have." At the Sidewalk Steppers parade, some songs last for several blocks, while others are quickly dropped when the musicians take note of dancers drifting into conversation or club members pausing to sip beer, pose for a picture, or wipe the sweat from their brow.

In any second line parade there are moments when traditional conventions in repertoire and tempo are observed. Every parade honors fallen club members, musicians, and other significant figures by pausing at the deceased's home or place of business and staging a miniature jazz funeral, typically made up of a single dirge followed by an upbeat hymn. During the Steppers parade, a ceremony of this sort helped me understand how musical sound facilitates relations between people, providing a sense of place in which the social is enmeshed with the political and the present is entangled with the past.

Back in the Tremé, people are chanting "Here comes the Sidewalk! Here comes the Sidewalk!" over "Paul Barbarin's Second Line," an upbeat standard from the 1950s, when the members stop outside a boarded-up bar and Rebirth abruptly switches to a slow dirge. The tempo and volume drop dramatically. The Steppers huddle together near the band. Tears stream down some of the men's faces. They call the band closer and the crowd encircles them, hushed by a change in the atmosphere initiated by musical dynamics.

What is the significance of this truncated jazz funeral, and why does it generate such intense sorrow within an otherwise exuberant event? Answers are not immediately available, and for the moment I can only summon generalizations: the musicians continually assess their surroundings and work to regulate the movement of the parade as they mobilize us across space. When the dirge ends, the huddle breaks up, and as we turn onto South Robertson, a narrow street lined with tightly packed houses, Rebirth signals that the parade has resumed by seamlessly segueing to a new song that is faster but remains relatively restrained. Philip later explained to me that alterations in repertoire and tempo are based on complex criteria, including crowd response and the physical effects of the built environment:

> When you get to a certain intersection or a certain street where there's an opening, if the street is really wide, you know that's more dancing room for everybody, you want to keep everybody upbeat. When you get to a street where it's more closed, and the parade might slow down at a pace, you slow it down because you know everybody's trying to get through that small street.

In the narrow streets of the Tremé, even the up-tempo songs are dialed back to keep the large crowds under control. However, when the parade passes the Candlelight Lounge and turns again so that we now face the overpass of Interstate 10, the tempo is rising. In the temporal and spatial progression of a parade, the arrival here, "under the bridge," as locals refer to it, represents the emotional peak, when the scale of intensity is tipped. Philip said, "When you get under a overpass, because of the acoustics, you know the band's going to be loud anyway, and the crowd knows that's going to be like some wild, rowdy stuff and you want to get everybody hyped."

On this day, hundreds of people are gathered at the interstate, anticipating the arrival of the Steppers and Rebirth. Underneath the highway, the parade suddenly doubles in size, and the ecstatic collision intensifies when Rebirth transitions to one of their fastest and loudest songs. The front line points their horns upward and the back row pushes the rhythm harder as the sound blooms and the parade participants jump high in the air while singing in unison, "re-birth! re-birth!" Since Katrina, the band's name has taken on added meaning, just as the band's sound has come to define the distinctiveness and the resiliency of the city, nowhere more so than under the overpass. Among the dancing bodies, I spot a member of the Cross-the-Canal Social Aid and Pleasure Club wearing a white T-shirt with a message printed in large red and blue letters: "water don't stop no foot work." How many of us are recalling the days immediately following Katrina, when thousands of residents evacuated to the highway, camping out on the blistering hot concrete, waiting in vain for assistance? I knew that the sentiment attached to this landmark had a deeper historical precedent than Katrina, because Harold Dejan's funeral in 2002 had ended in an ecstatic celebration under the bridge, but my inquiries would have to wait for this moment of euphoria to pass.

"RE-BIRTH!"

"RE-BIRTH!"

EPISODE 1.4: Developments in the Tremé

In regard to time, Harold Dejan's jazz funeral in 2002 and the annual Tremé Sidewalk Steppers Social Aid and Pleasure Club parade in 2007 surround the events of Katrina, and in regard to place, the processionals are themselves events that reinforce a deep attachment to neighborhoods and communities for many New Orleanians. Parades march through virtually every corner of the city, Uptown and Downtown, by the mansions along St. Charles Avenue, through the city's most stigmatized housing projects, and into neighborhoods still devastated by Katrina's floodwaters.

Both the Dejan funeral and the Steppers second line parade started in a neighborhood with an exceptional reputation and history. Tremé is one of the oldest neighborhoods in New Orleans, located just "back-a-town" (away from the Mississippi River) or "lakeside" (toward Lake Pontchartrain) from the French Quarter. The first use of the land was as a plantation and a public square known in French as Place Congo, and development of the neighborhood began in 1794, when Claude Tremé inherited the plantation and began laying out streets and selling plots of land, many to Creoles of color. Tremé may well have been the first neighborhood of free blacks in the United States, and the area remained a hub of black culture long after the Congo Square dances were stopped in the 1840s and slavery ended in 1865. In the first half of the twentieth century, jazz musicians such as clarinetist Alphonse Picou played in Economy Hall and other sites linked to the emergence of jazz, and in the latter half the Olympia, Dirty Dozen, Rebirth, New Birth, Tremé, and numerous other brass bands got their start marching past the Creole cottages and narrow shotgun houses that line the streets.

Tremé is cultural ground zero for the city's identity as an exceptional place, to the point where the recent television series about post-Katrina New Orleans took its name from the neighborhood. *Treme*, which was created by David Simon and Eric Overmeyer in 2010 as a follow-up to their acclaimed series *The Wire*, portrays the lives of workaday musicians participating in the city's musical traditions. (For instance, the Sidewalk Steppers parade discussed in the previous episode was the setting for the opening scene to season 1 of *Treme*.) Only a portion of the action takes place in the neighborhood, which makes the name choice all the more telling: Tremé is a part of the city that is nonetheless representative of the whole of New Orleans exceptionalism. The incomparable nature of the city is reaffirmed by the show's setting in the immediate aftermath of Katrina, creating a kind of southern Babylon-meets-Atlantis *über*-site unlike any other.[20]

New Orleans is no doubt a singular city. In this chapter I look at its most distinctive cultural tradition, the jazz funeral and the second line parade, through the lens of its most iconic musical ensemble, the brass band, and in particular the most celebrated band at the turn of the twenty-first century, Rebirth. But hovering above culture, in all its glorious idiosyncrasy, is an infrastructure that is not specific to New Orleans but rather representative of urban restructuring throughout the United States. Urban planners and developers have remapped the Tremé, gentrification has displaced many lower-income residents, and aggressive policing has resulted in the arrests of musicians.

The policies and patterns that have marginalized black residents of Tremé long predate Katrina. The construction of the Municipal Auditorium on the former site of Congo Square in 1926 signaled the beginning of a redevelopment scheme that lasted five decades, clearing large swaths of land and displacing residents. In *Tremé: Race and Place in a New Orleans Neighborhood*, the geographer Michael Crutcher notes, "The dismantling of much of Tremé's built landscape and the deterritorialization of its residents succeeded because of policies that refused to acknowledge the neighborhood's poor and increasingly African American residents."[21] Environmental projects rhetorically framed as urban renewal combined with official policies and informal practices of racial discrimination, such as the rejection of the NAACP's attempt to desegregate the auditorium in the late 1930s, to disempower black New Orleanians. In 1964 the city staged a land grab subsidized by the federal government, displacing 122 families in the name of slum clearance, to make way for a proposed cultural center modeled after New York City's Lincoln Center (which itself required the demolition of a predominantly black neighborhood). Seven years later, when construction finally began in the Tremé, more families were displaced to make room for a parking lot. When bulldozers took aim at community landmarks such as the San Jacinto Club and the Caledonia Club, Tremé residents organized a jazz funeral for the "death" of these buildings, with the Olympia Brass Band marching behind the "pallbearers" carrying a coffin with a dummy inside.[22] The dummy was buried, or cut loose, as the saying goes, when the coffin was thrown inside the vacated Caledonia. Soon after, the Theater for the Performing Arts opened as home to the New Orleans City Opera and the New Orleans Ballet; in a masterstroke of historical distortion, it was later renamed the Mahalia Jackson Theater, after the famous gospel singer from New Orleans. When it became clear that the remainder of the "Lincoln Center South" project was not financially viable, the grounds were redesigned as a green space, enclosed by an iron fence to limit access, and named Louis Armstrong Park.

The racialized remapping of the Tremé occurred in the midst of the civil rights movement — including the integration of New Orleans public schools in 1960, the Civil Rights Act of 1964, and the Voting Rights Act of 1965 — when many whites and middle-class blacks were moving to new suburban developments.[23] New Orleans became a majority-black city for the first time in its history; population loss led to urban decay while suburban growth led to increased commuter traffic and demand for highway expansion. The colloquialism *white flight* is appropriate here not only because it was predominantly whites who were leaving the city for the suburbs, but also because their relocation was enabled by government programs such as the Federal Housing Authority, which denied loans to black Americans and restricted development to segregated neighborhoods.[24] The urban planner Robert Moses drafted a commuter plan for downtown New Orleans that called for the construction of a new interstate overpass through the French Quarter, along an industrial shipping zone by the Mississippi River, but a well-organized and well-funded preservation group was able to block the project.[25] Residents of Tremé again paid the price when the tree-lined median of Claiborne Avenue, at the time a thoroughfare and center of social life in the Tremé, was razed to make way for Interstate 10, irreparably altering the landscape and forcing the closure of many black-owned businesses. The urban studies scholar Daniel Samuels interviewed locals who witnessed the long-term effects of the changes and found the decision to construct the highway through their neighborhood "not so much as the impartial product of an engineering decision as . . . the result of a political calculus, in which the decisive factor was the disenfranchised status of the black community."[26] Residents watched commuters to the central business district pass by on twin concrete decks designed to accommodate fifty-four thousand vehicles a day.

Though the landscape of the neighborhood had been disrupted, social and cultural activities that had long defined life in the Tremé remained relatively intact. In 1983, when Philip Frazier, Keith Frazier, and singer and trumpeter Kermit Ruffins founded Rebirth, the Tremé was filled with venues featuring live music. "This place on the corner right here used to be the Caledonia," Keith explained while standing on a street corner one afternoon in 2007. "There used to be another bar over there, where the Tremé Brass Band used to play at, the Petroleum Lounge." In the other direction is a large renovated house. "That two-story building? That was the Tremé Music Hall." Rebirth practiced by marching in the streets; when they began playing professionally they rented a band house that became a favorite hangout for aspiring brass band musicians. "There was music on just about every corner," Keith told me, but all of the bars have closed and no one in Rebirth lives in the Tremé any longer.

Because of the Tremé's central location, its beautiful old houses, and its history as the oldest black neighborhood in New Orleans, property values have been rapidly rising and the neighborhood has been gentrifying since the late 1980s. Newer residents, many of whom were drawn to the area because of its cultural history, founded the Historic Faubourg Tremé Association to "take aim at blight, crime and grime," as their slogan states, within an area newly defined as "Historic Tremé" that includes the blocks between the French Quarter and the interstate while excluding those on the other side of the overpass.[27] Architectural preservation (from "blight"), increased security (against "crime"), and beautification (of "grime") protect the investments of association members, many of whom own multiple properties in the neighborhood. Since 2006 the State of Louisiana Residential Rehabilitation Tax Credit RS47:297:6 has become an added incentive to rebuild historic homes in Tremé. However, the efforts of association members extend far beyond their property lines, as the organization has leveraged influence with the city council and the New Orleans Police Department to enforce laws and enact zoning codes that place limitations on cultural performances.

Derrick Jefferson, a longtime Tremé resident, purchased a dilapidated corner storefront in hopes of opening a nightclub called the Caledonia. However, his application for a permit to serve alcohol was rejected, and his city council member informed him that the neighborhood association board requested power of approval over all permit requests. Derrick told me that he has been harassed by police, ostensibly due to noise complaints for construction: "I been jacked up on a squad car with a paint brush in my hand, just for trying to renovate this building." When I passed by the building in September 2009, Derrick was nowhere to be found, and there was a For Sale sign on the door.

There are other instances of using juridical means to block the performance of live music and the sale of alcoholic beverages, such as when Little People's Place, a neighborhood bar that offered live music and served as a stop for second line parades since the 1960s, was closed in 1998 after neighbors filed a successful lawsuit. The attorney Mary Howell defended against the plaintiffs, including Adolph Bynum, who lived around the corner from Little People's with his wife, Naydja. The couple moved to the neighborhood in the 1980s, first fixing up a neglected house as their residence and then purchasing other homes on the block to renovate into upmarket rental properties. Though relatively new to Tremé, they are native New Orleanians, Adolph having followed in his father Horace's footsteps as a pharmacist and owner of Bynum Pharmacy, which eventually expanded to three locations named Bynum and Sons. Adolph's entrepreneurialism extended to real estate, and since Katrina destroyed the family business he and his wife have directed their energies toward the twenty or so properties they now own and manage in the Tremé.

The Bynums are no strangers to local culture. Because of his long-term commitment to families living in the Desire housing projects, where the first pharmacy opened in 1947, Adolph was twice named king of the annual parade sponsored by the Nine Times Social Aid and Pleasure Club, made up of residents of Desire. When interviewed by club member Corey Woods for the book *Coming Out the Door for the Ninth Ward*, cowritten by members of Nine Times, Adolph described the "camaraderie" he felt at his first parade in 2003 as "a highlight, at that point, in [his] life."[28] Yet, as the lawsuit that led to the closing of Little People's indicates, local culture can also be identified as a cause of blight, crime, and grime. As founders and directors of the neighborhood association, Adolph and Naydja have been complicit with a noise abatement campaign that systematically targeted each of the live music venues in the Tremé, and police have been called upon to disband informal parades and house parties that failed to secure a permit (see episode 1.7).

These developments may have taken place in the most distinctive black neighborhood in New Orleans, but they adhere to nationwide patterns and policies that have picked up where racist governmental policies—such as the regulation of segregated housing or the targeting of disenfranchised communities for highway construction and other capital "improvements"— left off.[29] The Black Studies scholar George Lipsitz argues in his book *How Racism Takes Place*:

> Decades and centuries of segregation have taught well-off communities to hoard amenities and resources, to exclude allegedly undesirable populations, and to seek to maximize their own property values in competition with other communities. These nearly universal strategies for class advantage follow a distinct racial pattern in the United States. They subsidize segregation and produce rewards for whiteness.[30]

While gentrifiers in the Tremé are not exclusively white, and while part of the allure of "renewing" Tremé is its unique racial history, the formation of a neighborhood organization to sway power over local government and enforce permit and zoning laws is a national and even global model for obtaining "prosperity, predictability, and security" while "exacerbating residential inequalities."[31] What distinguishes the case of Tremé is the cultural traditions that are being alternately celebrated and targeted. As the landscape has been dramatically altered in cycles over the course of several centuries, outdoor festival traditions have registered these changes, from slave dances to traditional jazz funerals, proceeding from neighborhood funeral homes to hip-hop–inflected second line parades swarming under the concrete interstate.

On the corner of South Robertson and Villere Streets, one block from the Claiborne Avenue overpass and just down the street from the church where Philip and Keith's mother was the organist, Rebirth played a show at Joe's Cozy Corner every Sunday night throughout the 1990s. The bar was also the home base for the Sidewalk Steppers Social Aid and Pleasure Club and a regular stop for the many parades that passed through the Tremé. On January 18, 2004, when the owner, "Papa Joe" Glasper, tried to forcibly remove a vendor who was illegally selling beer outside the bar, the vendor,

Richard Gullette, was shot and killed. Joe was arrested, and while awaiting sentencing in May 2005 he died of heart failure in jail. When Katrina struck a few months later, the Glasper family evacuated to Houston, where Joe's son "Lil' Joe" also died of a heart attack.

The neighborhood association took advantage of the regrettable circumstances surrounding the shooting at Joe's Cozy Corner to further their mission. Joe's was shut down by the Alcohol Beverage Control Board, purchased by an association member, Gladys Marigny, and turned into a duplex apartment; the exterior was restored to reveal the original signage for Jax Beer and Ruth's Cozy Corner (the predecessor to Joe's), preserved as a mini-exhibition of museumified artifacts to enjoy on a passive stroll through history. The large two-story building across the street, under renovation by the Bynums, is remembered by the Steppers and Rebirth as the Tremé Music Hall, and Harold Dejan would most likely have known it as the home of Alphonse Picou. Just down the block, Gladys Marigny purchased a neighborhood grocery and transformed it into Café Tremé, a coffee shop featuring "a safe clean atmosphere with soft, background music, free Wi-Fi, and a destination that 100% respects and embraces the unique, treasured culture of Tremé."[32] The café conforms to the new Residential Development Overlay, a zoning change proposed by the neighborhood association and enacted by the city council, permitting certain residences to be zoned commercial, as long as they "aren't allowed . . . to house businesses featuring live music or selling alcohol," according to a *Times-Picayune* reporter.[33] In a seemingly inexplicable but actually rather systematic progression of events, Naydja Bynum has sought an exception to the same Residential Development Overlay that she campaigned for in order to rezone one of her residential properties into a restaurant offering alcohol and live music during limited hours.[34]

The heady entanglements of urban development, property rights, and the exaltation of local culture as a historical artifact (such as a preserved building) but not a vital contemporary activity helped me to understand the emotional intensity of the Steppers parade discussed in the previous episode. It was at the site of the former Joe's Cozy Corner, on the sidewalk where the Steppers and Rebirth had grown up socializing with friends, family, and neighbors, that a truncated jazz funeral had memorialized the death of Joe and his son and the community's loss of a social hub. When the parade resumed, it passed the Candlelight Lounge, the last open bar in the Tremé neighborhood. In a study of Joe's Cozy Corner, Rachel Breunlin writes of these bars as "sites where aspects of community life, such as live music and second line parades, are preserved."[35] The loss of venues in the Tremé has altered the lives of parade participants, who call forth memories of people and places that have gone, memorializing them in sound and bodily movement.

After marching by the Candlelight, the Steppers and Rebirth headed directly toward Claiborne Avenue. Of all the landmarks of progressivist development in the Tremé, the overpass is the most salient symbol of dispossession through the jurisdiction of space, and the community's ongoing opposition has even managed to ensnare current Mayor Mitch Landrieu in debates about tearing down the elevated structure. The construction of the overpass and the shuttering of bars in the Tremé exemplify how the built environment has been used as a political technology to assert power. Conversely, the way the concrete structure of the interstate has been integrated into contemporary funerals and parades helps us understand why the combination of instruments and voices careening off the bridge gets second liners hyped.

Surveying the events thus far, the physical and sonic presence of musicians and parade participants under the bridge can be interpreted as a way of staking a claim on contested space. But as Helen Regis's foundational research has shown, the potential for parades to disrupt racial-spatial orderings is always present, regardless of proximity to the bridge or the Tremé neighborhood. Helen locates the collective agency of moving crowds primarily in the corporeal, the visual, and the spatial: black bodies, adorned in band uniforms or printed T-shirts, transform urban space by "taking it to the streets."[36]

Community parades are rarely expressly political, yet they share many characteristics with social movements where crowds assemble in public space for a spectacle of unity. In this way, events peculiar to New Orleans share equivalencies with other people and events in other places. In a study of public spaces in Costa Rica, the anthropologist Setha Low discusses how "architecture contributes to the maintenance of power of one group over another . . . through enclosure and the organization of individuals in space" as well as the counterresponse "of individuals and groups to these architectural forms of social control." The Plaza de la Cultura in San José was designed as a modern space of cultural consumption bordered by businesses, hotels, and theaters but was reappropriated by street performers, singing groups, political speakers, and teenagers as a social gathering space. To recuperate the agency of subjects, Low draws upon other social theorists—Walter Benjamin's invocation of the flâneur, Michel de Certeau's analysis of "walking in the city," and Henri Lefebvre's emphasis on the "social production of space"—to locate individuals "creating and representing public space rather than [merely being] subjected to it."[37]

In New Orleans occupying city streets through black cultural traditions articulates a right to the city. Instead of signs, banners, and speeches that enunciate an explicit political agenda, it is music that mobilizes this social movement; as Helen writes, "The second line takes people in. It incorporates all those who will move to its music, who become a single flowing movement of people unified by the rhythm."[38] Theirs is a politics of pleasure sung and played in a different key, on musical instruments as well as the voice.

"Second lining to me is a boost in my life," said JeNean Sanders of the We Are One Social Aid and Pleasure Club. "When there is a celebration [second line], a memorial [jazz funeral], or even when people want to protest the injustice in their lives, we can come together, clapping our hands and singing, see our friends and family, and get the strength to overcome." For Sanders, the pleasure of parading can be understood only in relation to injustice, as a way of overcoming, and it is music that organizes the experience and gives her a welcome "boost." As she put it, "The brass band brings us together."[39]

The quotes from JeNean Sanders are taken from a legal affidavit filed by the Social Aid and Pleasure Club Task Force, in collaboration with the ACLU, the attorney Mary Howell, and the anthropologist Helen Regis, as part of a 2007 lawsuit against New Orleans Police Department superintendent Warren Riley, New Orleans mayor Ray Nagin, and Louisiana governor Kathleen Blanco. The plaintiffs were seeking an injunction against a 300 percent increase in fees for mandatory police escorts and parade permits, from $1,250 to $3,760. The justification for the increase was that shootings had occurred at two parades in the year following Hurricane Katrina, but Social Aid and Pleasure Club members responded that they were not responsible for the shootings and the violence had occurred away from the parade routes, after the parades had disbanded.[40] Tamara Jackson, president of the VIP Ladies Club and an administrator at the Louisiana Department of Health and Hospitals, organized the Task Force coalition to contest the "unconstitutional fees and bonding requirements" as a "violation of the First and Fourteenth Amendment rights to freedom of speech."[41] The term *speech* is not to be taken literally here, for what forms of expression does JeNean Sanders advocate for protest? "Clapping our hands and singing." What binds participants and their different perspectives to one another? "The brass band brings us together."

The display of exuberance within a racialized power structure upheld by policies of governance—the passage of zoning changes, issuance of permits, abatement of noise, formation of neighborhood organizations, campaign against blight—is a deeply embedded tradition in New Orleans. Parades are a forum for social communication, and the participatory music that mobilizes them is, quite literally, a practice of being heard.[42] That peak moments consistently occur underneath the overpass tells us something about how local knowledge, experience, and memory (of the destruction of a meaningful public space) is embodied by the musicians and second liners (dancing in close proximity and producing sound with instruments and voices). Under the bridge, where the second line was chanting "RE-BIRTH! RE-BIRTH!," the dancing bodies are closest together; the band is playing at its loudest; the built environment provides optimal acoustics; these human, technological, and environmental forces interconnect, and everybody is hyped.

The ways individuals orient themselves to these soundful events does not always conform to preconceptions of racial identity or social location. The Bynums, for instance, are black, and for that matter, so were their city council member and mayor until 2010. Adolph's father, Horace, was a lifetime member of the NAACP, having run the local chapter from 1968 to 1973. Though it would be possible to cast the Bynums as hegemonic agents of social control and to cast musicians and second liners as oppositional agents of dissent, it would take some intellectual acrobatics because their actions do not fit snugly within categories of resistance or accommodation; instead they demonstrate the complexity of struggles over power, the contingencies of subjectivity, and the possibilities and limitations of human agency. Musical sound mediates the relations of these individuals and groups, providing them with a point of orientation. The only entity that sound resists with certainty and consistency is silence.

At the Tremé Sidewalk Steppers parade, Rebirth demonstrated their leadership in keeping a sturdy tradition in tune with the experiences of contemporary black New Orleanians. For traditions to continue to provide coherence and a culturally particular sense of place, they cannot remain static but must march in step with the motion of time and space.[43] As the environment is remapped by planners, residents, and "nature," Rebirth enhances their social mobility within the community in which they were raised by mobilizing tradition: playing faster and louder to correspond to the speed and noise of the cars traveling above on the interstate. They compose and curate a repertoire that represents their experiences, and they make the acoustics of the built environment work to suit their purposes and preferences. In the following episode, the biographies of the Frazier brothers and other members of Rebirth demonstrate how a select group is able to fully tap the cultural capital of the brass band tradition.

EPISODE 1.5: The Bass Brothers

Born in 1909 under Jim Crow, before there was such a thing called jazz, and passing away in 2002 at a time when his youngest disciples were playing hip-hop, Harold Dejan was witness to massive social and cultural change. More, he was an agent of change. It was Dejan's Olympia that marched the brass band tradition into new spaces where a spectrum of audiences came to understand the brass band not only as a form of functional entertainment but also as a form of heritage to be celebrated. The Olympia were invited to perform at the Smithsonian Festival of American Folklife in 1967, they marched onto the field during the halftime show at the 1970 Super Bowl in New Orleans, and they regularly toured Europe, Japan, and America.[44]

The upward mobility of the Olympia was not only a product of their success in circulating beyond neighborhood boundaries.[45] On Sunday afternoons the Olympia continued to play in parades sponsored by Social Aid and Pleasure Clubs from every corner of the city—including the Money Wasters downtown in the Tremé and the Jolly Bunch uptown in the Third Ward—and funerals, parties, and other functions filled their calendar on other days of the week. Over the years they were able to retain their popularity with new generations thanks to the progressive trumpeter Milton Batiste, who had updated the band's sound with rhythm and blues songs from Professor Longhair, Fats Domino, and others. As the first band to wear T-shirts printed with their logo, the Olympia modernized their appearance at community performances while reserving their formal uniforms for funerals and staged concerts.

1.3 *Musician Sitting on Drum.* 2001. 66″ × 60″. © WILLIE BIRCH.

By retuning traditional brass band music to resonate with diverse audiences in varied performance contexts, Harold Dejan, the Duke of Olympians, attained a degree of social mobility. His resplendent jazz funeral attests to his privileged status as a cultural icon who elevated the profile of an entire musical genre. The power accrued by Dejan and his Olympia band as the rising status of the brass band coincided with the civil rights movement carried over to Philip and Keith Frazier with Rebirth when the hopes attached to the movement gave way to the harsh realities that set the stage for the emergence of the "hip-hop generation." Like Dejan, the Fraziers attained prestige first through their entry into a proud tradition and second through their capacity to retune tradition for new audiences. And like Dejan, they raised their status by a process of accumulation: by selectively combining old and new musical practices and by appealing to audiences across boundaries of social and geographic location, they harnessed the cultural capital of the brass band to amass social and economic capital.

In a classic sociological study, Seymour Lipset and Reinhard Bendix defined social mobility as "the process by which individuals move from one stratum of society to another."[46] Lipset and Bendix noted that within the "lower strata," "the chance for potential leaders to develop the skills which will take them up from the ranks may be small, but sooner or later some will break through."[47] For Dejan and the Frazier brothers, overcoming the particular challenges facing black Americans led them to achieve the so-called American dream of transcending obstacles to success. However, their status should not be confused with what W. E. B. Du Bois termed the "talented tenth"—those who represent "the Best of this race," educating themselves in pursuit of the communal goal of "guid[ing] the Mass away from the contamination and death of the Worst"—because black brass band musicians have sought to advance their own social mobility within the free market through their creative labor.[48] This episode measures the far reach and full potential of contemporary New Orleans brass band musicians through a genealogy of the Frazier brothers, while the following episode demonstrates the precariousness of social mobility by tracing the very different trajectories of drummer Derrick Tabb and trombonist Tyrus Chapman.

In the book *Thinking in Jazz: The Infinite Art of Improvisation*, the ethnomusicologist Paul Berliner found that young people became socialized as jazz musicians in a multifaceted process that includes immersion in a community of practitioners, self-disciplined practice, knowledge of standard repertoire and canonic performances, and experience in performing.[49] Philip's and Keith's experiences fit snugly within this pattern. They were introduced to music through their mother, Barbara, who played piano and organ at the Christian Mission Baptist Church in the Tremé. Known to all as "Mama Rebirth," Barbara raised her six children—Philip and Keith Frazier, and Sandra, Nicole, Kerwin, and Robin James—in apartments all over town, including stints in the St. Bernard, Desire, and St. Thomas housing projects, before settling in the Tremé neighborhood.

The brothers' foundation in church music was augmented by formal music education in school, beginning at Joseph Kohn Junior High School in the Upper Ninth Ward, where Philip picked up the trombone and Keith the baritone horn. While an overall majority of brass band musicians have formative musical experience in church, by my estimate the number of professional musicians who played in marching band approaches 100 percent. There is a marching band belt stretching from Florida to Texas where high school bands emulate those of historically black colleges and universities such as Southern, Grambling, and Florida A&M. In New Orleans school marching bands are also integrated within an expansive tradition of street music performance, including jazz funerals, second line parades, Mardi Gras Indian ceremonies, and Mardi Gras parades, and they serve as a feeder system for the brass band tradition. Band directors require students to learn the rudiments of reading and playing music in an ensemble while luring them with arrangements of contemporary popular music, known as "radio tunes," which in Philip and Keith's day meant soul and funk bands that featured horns, such as the Gap Band, Stevie Wonder, and especially Earth, Wind & Fire.

In the late 1970s, when the family moved to Tremé and the brothers attended Joseph S. Clark High School, Philip switched to tuba and Keith settled on bass drum. Philip was eventually named band captain, and he relished the responsibility, practicing his rudiments into the night, sometimes falling asleep curled up with his tuba in bed. "It was calling me," he says of the instrument that would later give him a new nickname ("Tuba Phil") and phone number (504-xxx-TUBA).

Though budget cuts and an increased emphasis on standardized testing in core curriculum subjects have shrunk music education programs, high school bands remain prominent in New Orleans, and on November 6, 2007, I organized a workshop called Brass Band Music across the Generations to introduce high school students to brass band performance practices.[50] The Musicians' Union Hall was packed with young musicians from John McDonogh, Joseph S. Clark, and St. Augustine high schools hoping to follow in Rebirth's footsteps out of the band room and onto the world stage. One girl wearing a band uniform and holding a trumpet asked Rebirth about the faraway places they have been able to travel to, while another wanted to know whether it was possible for a young woman to achieve success in a brass band scene dominated by men.

In school band, students are socialized not only as musicians but also, more generally as young men and women. Band members are positioned within gender hierarchies that equate with specific sections: brass and percussion are predominantly male, while woodwinds are predominantly female. The ways that gender maps on to instruments is common across genres of black music, and all cultures have developed gender norms in domains of musical performance, but in the New Orleans brass band tradition these associations have played out in powerfully limiting ways.[51] While female participation in band is substantial, there have been virtually no professional female brass band musicians, and I know of only one working band, the Pinettes, that consistently features female instrumentalists. Rebirth's initial lineup included clarinetist Cheryl McKay, but since her departure the band has remained entirely male.

In the summer of 1983, when Philip, Keith, Cheryl, and the rest of Rebirth were the same age as the boys and girls attending the Brass Band Music across the Generations workshop, they made their debut at a function in the Sheraton Hotel. Enthused by the positive response, they decided on a whim to walk over to the French Quarter and play for tips. They returned to the Quarter throughout the summer, with trumpeter and singer Kermit Ruffins suggesting new songs to build up their catalogue. To make things as official as they can be for a high school band, Keith used electrical tape to spell out "RE-BIRTH JAZZ BAND" on his drumhead and Philip did the same on the bell of his tuba.

The kids made a splash on the brass band scene and caught the attention of Jerry Brock, who had recently cofounded the community radio station WWOZ. Brock convinced the owner of Arhoolie Records, Chris Strachwitz, to schedule a recording session, setting up during off-hours at the Grease Lounge, a bar in the Tremé that is now the Candlelight. There the band ran through a set of spirituals, modern jazz, and funk that neatly encapsulated their versatility. An original song with the prophetic group chant "Hey don't go nowhere / Rebirth's here to stay" was chosen as the title track to *Here to Stay*. Philip, who was a senior at Clark when the record was released in 1984, remembers strutting through the hallways with his band captain patch on his uniform and his LP under his arm, a big man on campus.

Philip and Keith's immersion in black music began in church and the band room and then spread to the streets of the Tremé. "Parades would come right by our house," remembered Keith, "so we would just stand on the porch and watch the parades pass." By the spring of 1984, when the LP was released and Philip and Kermit were looking ahead to graduation and weighing future options, Rebirth was becoming established on the parade circuit. Philip accepted a band scholarship at Grambling University in northern Louisiana, but returned to New Orleans after just a year, eventually setting up a band house in the Tremé and devoting himself full time to Rebirth.

Philip explained to the audience at Brass Band Music across the Generations that there was no formal system of mentorship into the brass band tradition; instead he and the others in Rebirth observed senior bands and "took from the stuff they was doing." The leadership role that Rebirth was now demonstrating to the young people in the audience (some of whom had already formed bands like the Baby Boyz) belonged to the sturdy Olympia and the rising Dirty Dozen a generation prior. "We were one of the last young bands to play a street parade with the Olympia," said Keith by way of demonstrating his fluency with traditional performance practices, but he was quick to add, "We were more into Dirty Dozen." By the early 1980s the once innovative Olympia had become known primarily as a traditional band, while the Dirty Dozen's new approach was opening up brass band music to new audiences. As the leader of Rebirth, Philip's goal was to extend the Dozen's innovations, reconfiguring the music to be in tune with contemporary audiences just as the Olympia and the Dozen had done before him: "We put all their music in our repertoire and then started writing from where they started at and took it to another level."

Philip was still in school when he first saw the Dozen at a funeral; they grabbed his attention with their matching T-shirts and their fast, funky, angular songs like "Blackbird Special" and "My Feet Can't Fail Me Now," which begin with a tuba riff that then becomes the foundation for the melodic flights of the front line. Riff tunes based on prominent tuba melo-

dies became the template for new brass band repertoire, and Philip cultivated a talent for composing tuba lines on new-school standards such as
"Feel Like Funkin' It Up" (1989) and "Tornado Special" (1992).

Keith worked in tandem with his brother to create densely layered
grooves that propel the music forward. His bass drum patterns are busier
than those of his predecessors, filling up the spaces between the notes of the
tuba melodies. When I asked Keith to compare an early Rebirth recording
of the spiritual "Sweet Bye and Bye" (1989) with a later recording of the R&B
song "Casanova" (2001), he immediately disparaged the earlier example as
"first-grade bass drum work": "The bass drum sounds straight: 1–2–3–4,
1–2–3–4. . . . Just follow[ing] the tuba. There's nothing going on." By contrast, on the more recent recording, he explained, "I play drums as if I were
playing a horn. More intricate, more complicated, . . . [and] a lot quicker."

The bass drum part on "Casanova" is a tresillo pattern: a compact, one-
measure rhythmic cell that repeats with trance-like consistency. The tresillo
has its own diasporic history as a variant of the Afro-Cuban *clave* pattern,
the fundamental unit of organization for much Latin music and an example
of what Jelly Roll Morton famously identified as the "Spanish tinge" that was
a "necessary ingredient" for New Orleans jazz.[52] The tresillo, with its accent
on the first downbeat followed by two lilting, syncopated hits on the up-
beats, recurs throughout the recorded history of New Orleans music, from
Jelly Roll's "New Orleans Blues" (1924) to Professor Longhair's "Mardi Gras
in New Orleans" (1949) and Rebirth's "Casanova" (2001). It thickens the
texture and accelerates the flow of the rhythm, and to my knowledge it was
Keith who integrated it into the brass band tradition.

Keith's innovation was to string together different songs continuously,
retaining the tresillo pattern with variations in accent and adjustments in
tempo. "I just started playing faster. And longer. Faster. And longer. We
would just never stop." Uninterrupted music is another quality associated
with African-derived rhythm, and more broadly with the nonlinear "virtual time" associated with musical events, and in this case is partly derived
from the turntable techniques of DJs who seamlessly sequence songs without pause.[53]

Keith's comments are taken from a workshop I organized at Tulane University in October 2009 meant to demonstrate traditional parade rhythms
and Rebirth's innovations to an audience of music students. After a historical lesson on African hand drumming and the sparse, syncopated bass

drum patterns of early jazz and brass band music, Keith explained how Rebirth thickened the rhythmic texture, raising the profile of the drums and tuba, pushing the back row front and center. "Philip and I, we call ourselves the bass brothers. We're the bottom, the foundation of the band." Though the other positions have rotated over time, the brothers have retained their place in the back. "One of my sayings is, 'If the bass ain't knocking, the band ain't rocking.' . . . Because you need that pulse. . . . That's the thing that's going to make you move."

Translating the energy from the moving street parades to static stage shows is, first and foremost, a matter of getting the bass rocking. Initially this took some adjustment, but decades of touring and playing every stage in New Orleans have taught the band to give specific directions to sound engineers. Philip drops a microphone right down the bell of his horn to make sure everyone can hear the subterranean notes, and Keith aligns his bass drum head directly in front of a microphone. "We're trying to get the rhythm section to push everything," Keith explained at the workshop:

> I tell them, "Look, this is what we want: we want you to put the bass drum in all the monitors, all around, because if [the other band members] can feel the bass—which is very Afrocentric, because it makes you move, makes you dance—they're going to know where they're supposed to be going at." . . . Like when you get in a car, you put your bass in the back and your tweeters in the front. We don't want the front pushing the back, we want the back pushing the front.

Far from the stage and the street, in the perpetually sterile environment of the recording studio, Rebirth gathers all the members in the same space despite the protestations of sound engineers intent on isolating instruments for more control over balance and tone. On a series of recordings for Rounder Records from 1989 to 1994, they honed the live-in-the-studio approach as a way of safeguarding the improvisation, rhythmic flow, and participatory nature of brass band music. For the 1989 recording of their most durable original composition, "Do Whatcha Wanna," the band's initial performance was augmented with tambourines, cowbells, clapping, and vocal whoops and hollers that recontextualize the recording out of the studio and into the streets and intimate spaces of live performance.[54]

If the second line atmosphere of "Do Whatcha Wanna" rooted it in the streets, the lyrics propelled the song forward into the thematic spaces of hip-hop. Kermit's words to the refrain—"Do whatcha wanna / Hang on the corner / Mardi Gras morning"—signal that this is a party song in a new key, expressing the desire to do what you want, when you want (including hanging on the corner instead of attending to more productive endeavors) that resonate with urban black music in the post–civil rights period. Rebirth's success in updating the tradition of New Orleans party songs was evidenced by the popularity of "Do Whatcha Wanna" among listeners of a hip-hop radio station in the late 1980s. In a daily contest in which two songs were played back-to-back and listeners called in to vote for their favorite, "Do Whatcha Wanna" won eight weeks in a row.

After Kermit left in the mid-1990s to start a swing band modeled after Louis Armstrong, Rebirth brought in younger members—including Glen Andrews and Derrick "Kabuki" Shezbie on trumpet, Stafford Agee and Tyrus Chapman on trombone, and Derrick Tabb on snare drum—who further updated their sound. The band parted ways with Rounder Records and recorded two albums, *We Come to Party* in 1997 and *Hot Venom* in 2001, which are essentially hip-hop transposed to horns and marching drums. This is the progressive music that I hear my students at Tulane play in their brass band ensembles and I watch the high school students learn for their pickup bands, because it resonates with styles of popular music that they have been engaging with their entire lives. The innovations attributed to Rebirth and the Dirty Dozen before them are now part of the tradition that younger musicians inherit and will themselves transform (see chapter 3).

I have invited Philip and Keith to collaborate on several public programs because of the degree of attention they pay to their craft and their capacity to articulate precisely how they execute their vision. The bass brothers make an ideal team not only because they work so easily together but also because they are so different. Philip is the consummate bandleader, jovial and conscientious but also exacting, and always representing Rebirth in public appearances, looking clean in his seemingly endless supply of sneakers and baseball hats. Keith is more subdued and less interested in his appearance, inconspicuous in his sensible Nissan Murano, but when approached he modestly reveals a deep knowledge of local culture and his place in it. Whenever we are on campus together he visits the Hogan Jazz Archive and imagines pursuing a graduate degree in music or history to complement his bachelor's degree from Southern University of New Orleans. Neither of the brothers partakes in marijuana or drinks alcohol often, and they are both attentive to their wives and children. They have accrued status by being astute: mobilizing tradition into new territories and delivering it to new audiences, including new generations of black New Orleanians and fans around the globe.

"I remember playing in the French Quarter, putting the box down for tips, and now I'm traveling all over the world," says Philip. "Nothing wrong with hard work. Nothing at all."

EPISODE 1.6: Lives in Motion

If Rebirth has been most successful in mobilizing the brass band across all sorts of social and geographic boundaries, and Philip and Keith are the members who have guided Rebirth's ascent, there is a danger that these exceptional men are evaluated as representative of the average brass band musician. In actuality there is no prototypical example; there are only individuals whose actions and subjectivities distinguish them within the collective tradition. Accessing musicians who move with relative freedom has been far easier for me than those whose movements are, for whatever reason, more restricted, and this creates a tension in my work: the first step in demonstrating the limitations placed on urban black Americans is to present those who have had success in overcoming those limitations. But there are others who were not so fortunate, who have been struck down by violence, who have faced more than their share of hardship, or who were simply unequipped to become a professional musician or navigate through the labyrinth of U.S. structures of power.

There are hundreds of brass band musicians in New Orleans, and among their ranks are many who barely manage to get by. I might not have noticed them, moving like phantoms among the pickup bands, if I didn't recognize their faces or hadn't heard their names, spoken with a shake of the head and an "It's sad, man."

There's the drummer who can outplay all the others but can't keep straight enough to hold down a steady job. For a while he was playing with a famous local jazz musician and then he was gone and the groove went with him, replaced by someone and something more predictable. Occasionally a bandleader will urgently track him down to sub on a gig: "Meet me at the funeral home on Claiborne in fifteen minutes. Bring your black and whites!" His routine, like all our routines, is Hurry up and wait. Hurry up and wait. The trick is how you fill up the hours, days, years of waiting. We marshal our full resources to balance pleasure and productivity, creativity and monotony.

Marijuana use is common among brass band musicians, perhaps even more than the ever-present Crown Royal whiskey, but the crack and the cocaine and the heroin eventually take all but the sturdiest musicians out of the game. They might start out by animating the creative recesses of the mind, but they nearly always wind up wreaking havoc on personal and professional relationships, until there is nothing to schedule and few to communicate with. At this point the job of the bandleader, which requires sobriety and organization to mediate the interactions of employees and clients, is to intercede so as to protect the interests and livelihoods of the other band members.[55] "We fire no one," says Keith of the role he and his brother play as Rebirth's watchdogs. "You fire yourself."

In the mid-1990s Rebirth went through a shift in their lineup, and among the new members were two young, restless innovators. Derrick Tabb would go on to achieve great recognition within and beyond the local brass band scene, while the path for Tyrus Chapman was far more difficult. Their contrasting adulthoods, sprung from a common childhood, form a case study of differing subjectivities among those with shared identities.

Derrick Tabb is widely considered to be the most progressive and skilled snare drummer in a city of many, many snare drummers. At six and a half feet tall, he is an imposing presence, his head always peeping out above the others from his spot in the back, between the Frazier brothers. Onstage he stands upright and still, moving only his arms. When he is given space in a song to execute a press roll on the snare drum, his wrists flail so quickly that the strokes on the drumhead are indistinguishable from one another, each blurring into the next, the sound building in spurts like a revving engine until he reaches out his forearm and ends with a piercing cymbal splash.

Derrick is part of the Andrews clan that includes his half brother Glen David Andrews (trombone) and cousins Troy Michael "Trombone Shorty" Andrews (trumpet and trombone), James "Twelve" Andrews (trumpet), Glen Andrews (trumpet), and Terence Andrews (bass drum), all raised in the Tremé and active on the local jazz and brass band scene. Being born into a musical family and immersed in local culture, Derrick learned from the earliest age that, to quote the musicologist Susan McClary, "actual people usually create the sounds that constitute music."[56] Derrick was playing professionally by the time he was eleven years old, touring Europe and the Caribbean with the Olympia Kids and Young Olympia bands. He would go on to found the High Steppers, MacBirth, and Hot 8 before joining Rebirth in 1998. He accomplished all of this by the time he turned twenty.

As a child Derrick lived with his grandmother Juliette, a neighborhood drug dealer in the Tremé. Juliette lavished him with attention, but the nature of her work also allowed Derrick a lot of freedom to roam. On the one hand, the lack of restrictions on his time and movements allowed him to develop his musicianship at an alarming pace. He darted around the city on his bike with a pair of drumsticks in his back pocket, visiting schools where marching bands were practicing and challenging their best drummers to a battle. On the other hand, his inquisitiveness led to his own experimentations with drugs and alcohol, and at age ten, when a drug dealer approached him to deliver a package, Derrick accepted the money.

These were the kinds of social and musical endeavors that characterized Derrick's daily life when he entered A. J. Bell Junior High School in seventh grade. "I did that music, came to school in nice clothes, but there was always something pulling me towards the troubled life," he recalled of the choices he faced at that period in his life. Juliette had passed away the previous summer and Derrick, who had no inkling of her reputation as a "gangster," spun into a tailspin. "I just wanted to rebel, and everyone was trying to tell me, but I was independent."

One of Derrick's running partners was Tyrus, part of the same class at A. J. Bell in the Tremé and then John McDonogh High School. The youngest of seven, Tyrus came from a relatively stable family; his father was a longshoreman with a steady union job, and his mother spoiled him to keep him off the streets. "She gave me anything I wanted so I didn't have to be outside," remembered Tyrus, including a full deejay setup that he used to accompany local rappers such as Cheeky Blakk and Pimp Daddy while still in junior high. But for both Tyrus and Derrick, the music with the most pull was marching band.

Derrick was already on a path to becoming a professional musician, so he approached his audition for the A. J. Bell band with confidence. But after tryouts, band director Donald Richardson posted the names of those who had made it, and Derrick was shocked to find his name missing from the list. Richardson explained to Derrick that he had no knowledge of reading music or basic drumming techniques and he would have to "relearn" the rudiments to secure a place in the band. "He was strict," remembered Derrick admiringly, and he responded to the challenge by dutifully practicing his strokes, rolls, and paradiddles until the week of the last football game, when Richardson rewarded him with his own fitted uniform.

Donald Richardson taught teamwork and determination, pairing up known enemies so that they would be forced to work out their differences together. If a band member was acting up in class, a teacher merely had to mention the possibility of alerting Richardson and the student would suddenly be on his best behavior. In a broken school system that continually rates among the lowest in the country, a band director can be an agent of change, committed to transforming the lives of students through lessons that resonate with New Orleans's distinctive performance traditions and other forms of black popular culture. For Derrick, the lure of the marching band began to outweigh the lure of the streets. "He saved me," Derrick said of his teacher, who he credits along with others—Demetrius Smith of Olympic Kids, Milton Batiste of Young Olympia, Anthony Lacen of Chosen Few, and Philip Frazier of Rebirth—for fulfilling a mentorship role that he now provides to young people.

Tyrus played trumpet in school band, but unlike Derrick he had little awareness of the related brass band tradition, which his mother had shielded him from in her efforts to keep him off the streets. Tyrus first heard a brass band on a bus trip to a Mardi Gras parade, when the driver, known as Pocketbook, played a cassette tape of Rebirth's *Feel Like Funkin' It Up.* "Man, I'm like, 'Pocketbook, what is that?' Because I had never heard no horns like that. I really didn't have an idea horns could do this. He told me that was Rebirth. I'm like 'Damn, could I have that tape?'" After the parade, Pocketbook gave Tyrus the tape, which he proceeded to dissect until he could play each part for every instrument. By this time Tyrus and Derrick were in high school, both having turned down a scholarship to attend St. Augustine to stay with their friends at John McDonogh. They started their first brass band, MacBirth, which included Greg Veals on trombone (later of Lil' Rascals and Rebirth), Damien Francois on tuba (later with Soul Rebels), and other up-and-comers in the marching band.

Derrick and Tyrus had very different reputations among their peers. Derrick, tall and assertive, was among the first to experiment with alcohol, drugs, and sex. By contrast, Tyrus, short and deferential, was a Goody Two-shoes who wouldn't drink or chase girls. Then something changed, something he describes in retrospect as "turning towards the wrong path," which began when Greg Veals brought a bottle of Mad Dog 20/20 to a parade on the school bus:

> To me, that was like "Cool! Nigger blowing loud, too, full of that what-ever they drinking! Blowing! Let me hit that!" That's when it came about, the curiosity, the false courage, whatever you want to call it. And then I drunk it and I thought I was blowing louder than I normally could blow. I'm playing notes I didn't think I could hit. "Shit, we march tomorrow? Let's do this shit again."

In quick succession, Tyrus was smoking weed and having sex, and by twelfth grade he was bringing a baby daughter to band practice. He earned a reputation as an improviser and innovative composer, fueled in part by the liberating effects intoxication has on inhibition. After stints with MacBirth, the Soul Rebels, the High Steppers, and the Lil' Rascals, Tyrus caught the attention of Philip Frazier, who needed a trumpet player to substitute for Kermit on a seven-week tour of Africa. By the time they returned home, Tyrus had joined the band on trombone, eventually dropping out of school before graduation. Derrick became a full-time member soon after, and together with Glen Andrews, Stafford Agee, Derrick Shezbie, and others just out of high school, the new recruits reinvigorated the Rebirth sound.

The 2001 album *Hot Venom* is a startlingly modern and aggressive record that has Tyrus's hands all over it. It is not his trombone playing so much as his singing and songwriting, two prized qualities in a scene overflowing with instrumentalists who can play hundreds of traditional songs at a moment's notice. But only a handful have extended tradition by composing a song that all the other bands have to learn. "Let Me Do My Thing" is one of those songs, and if the vocal timbre is gospel-soul, the fierceness and assertiveness is pure hip-hop. Tyrus's voice—his singing and his songs—is one reason why *Hot Venom* has achieved legendary status among the young musicians who passed the CD around the hallways in school along with those of local rappers Soulja Slim, Juvenile, and Lil' Wayne.

But whatever creative energy was driving Tyrus to compose songs such as "Let Me Do My Thing" also led him to heroin and other self-destructive activities that would ultimately diminish his creativity. Out on the road with Rebirth, Tyrus might go searching for a fix to avoid getting sick: "I'll take the rental car, go on a hunt. The show for ten [o'clock], I'm way in the next city somewhere with all the instruments." Eventually, to borrow Keith's words, Tyrus fired himself. "I walked away from Rebirth. I couldn't take it no more. . . . I ain't care about nothing but getting high." He was in and out of jail until he was handed a two-year sentence, during which he completed his GED and joined Narcotics Anonymous.

When I first noticed Tyrus in 2007, he had straightened out, and Hot 8's bandleader Bennie Pete had given him a chance. Maybe Tyrus had reallocated his earnings toward clothes, because he looked sharp, clean, in his oversized polo shirt, shiny new sneakers, and baseball hat perched askew on his cornrows. He diligently played through the Hot 8's repertoire and then sprung into action for "Let Me Do My Thing," singing like a changed man. But when the Hot 8 returned from a European tour, Tyrus was out again.

At Rebirth's twenty-fifth anniversary show in 2008, Philip and Keith had arranged for all former band members to make a guest appearance. A parade of acclaimed soloists, "retired" performers, and washouts, in about equal numbers, joined the current lineup. The sound was big yet crisp with the edginess of competitive musicianship, thrilling the crowd pressed up close to the stage at the cavernous Howlin' Wolf club. When Philip sounded out the tuba line to "Let Me Do My Thing," Tyrus appeared on mic, seemingly possessed, raising the level of intensity. Declamations poured out of a mouth full of gold with precise pitch and vocal control:

> *I tried hard to do right, but I keep on doing wrong*
> *Let me do my thing (Let me do my thing!)*
> *You say stop, I say go, I don't know how far to go*
> *Let me do my thing (Let me do my thing!)*

The song ended to a roar from the audience and a round of congratulations from the musicians. With the start of the next song Tyrus made his exit. I went looking for him, but he had left the building, and anyway, every other time I had tried to initiate a conversation he had lowered his gaze and kept on moving, in a hurry. Then in 2010 I saw him on the *Treme* program, playing an unnamed trombonist in a brass band, expertly reading his lines. Bennie told me that Greg Veals, also a recovering addict, was sponsoring Tyrus, and gave me his phone number so I could finally reach out to him.

In the quiet neighborhood where his father retired, we sat at the dinner table in a living room with a big television, matching sectionals, and a framed certificate of appreciation from the longshoremen's union on the wall. "This is the last place on the block for me," noted Tyrus. "Everything else, I done burned that motherfucker." He exuded the calm and worldliness that is a kind of trademark of reformers and twelve-step participants, his words half testimony and half confession: "When you leave, I could go do me one and nobody ain't going to know. I could go get me a bag. Nobody will know. Get me a hotel room—I have money—and just come out when the high go away." But Tyrus has been down that road many times. "I *know* where my ass is going if I use, I'm going to either die or I'm going to prison." So he attends meetings at the Bridge House treatment center or repeats the principles he has learned there: "A day at a time. I'll deal with tomorrow when it get here. Just for today, I know I ain't got to use no dope."

When still with Rebirth, Tyrus co-wrote a song with bandmate Glen Andrews that, for me, sums up the imperative for all brass band musicians: "Roll With It." Tyrus has somehow managed this, and these days he plays in the Hot 8 regularly and with any other band that calls for a sub, including Rebirth. He also holds down a day job at a furniture store because child support requires some financial security. Tyrus's status, as well as his schedule, contrasts with that of his childhood friend Derrick Tabb. While Tyrus received an occasional phone call from his girlfriend and the mother of his children while we met, my conversations with Derrick are forever interrupted by work-related calls and text messages. At the point in their twenties when Tyrus turned toward a path that took him away from Rebirth, Derrick took advantage of the opportunity Rebirth offered for ongoing financial stability and creative expression.

Back at the drum workshop at Tulane, Keith asked Derrick to demonstrate a beat that "every drummer in the city has been trying to learn": the introduction to "Talkin' Loud and Sayin' Nothin'," a 1970 song by James Brown that was wholly reinterpreted by Rebirth. The band had heard the original on the car stereo while driving south on Interstate 5 from Seattle to Portland, with Keith explaining the message of protest while the horn players sketched out the melody. Without any chance to rehearse, the band launched their show in Portland with a close approximation, transposing Brown's original from major to minor, adding a strident trumpet melody and a wordless group chant, and retaining only Brown's lyrical refrain: "You're like a dull knife / That just ain't cuttin' / You're talkin' loud / And sayin' nothin.'"

"It actually came out a lot better than what we expected, but I felt the drumbeat I was playing on it was just boring," remembered Derrick. "So Stafford was like, 'You always whining about what you playing. Do something different!' I said, 'All right, I need to shut him up!'" Derrick practiced until he had devised a new beat that became the song's introduction, working in a dexterous fifteen-stroke roll that he came up with by adapting a rudimentary exercise he had learned from Donald Richardson years earlier. It is now required learning for up-and-coming snare drummers in the tradition.

Derrick's drumming, incubated in the streets of the Tremé and nurtured by Donald Richardson, has provided him with material and immaterial wealth, and recently he has capitalized on his status in order to provide opportunities for young black New Orleanians who could benefit from the type of mentorship Richardson provided him. When I first met Derrick at the Brass Band Music across the Generations workshop, he approached me about a music education program that he was attempting to launch called Roots of Music. He had prepared a thoroughly researched proposal that outlined the social, educational, and economic benefits of marching band and asked for help in securing donations to implement a program for middle school students. Within a year Derrick and his assistant director, Allison Reinhart, were overseeing a daily afterschool music program that offered free instruction, transportation, and food for over a hundred students.

Derrick presides over Roots of Music with unflinching authority, hand-picking and overseeing a small group of devoted instructors who instill discipline through music. Three of Derrick's four children—De'Kea, Lil' Derrick, and Tudda—have played in the band, and naturally Derrick spares them zero leeway in their obligations. When we meet for pitch meetings, Derrick's presence is similarly commanding. He picks me up in his blue Titan pickup truck, dressed clean in "grown folks" hip-hop wear. (His preferred brand is Coogi.) Once the meeting begins, he states his intentions agreeably but firmly, sometimes making a show of silencing his cell phone. His determination has gained him much media attention, and in 2009 he was chosen as a "Hero" by CNN and honored in a gala ceremony with tributes by Nicole Kidman, Louis Gossett Jr., Carrie Underwood, and other celebrities. The recognition stems from Derrick's ability to carry forward the legacy of the mentors that positively intervened in his own life, creating opportunities for social mobility.

I assist Roots of Music through fund-raising and promotion and provide academic tutors through a service learning program at Tulane University, and Derrick offers me introductions and insights into the experiences of New Orleans musicians. In my career as an academic, collaborations such as the public programs I have mentioned would be evaluated as applied anthropology or community service, but the power dynamic of our relationship is more complex.[57] Derrick commands more prestige, has a higher public profile, and earns more money than I. Coming from humbler beginnings—and this from someone who is always eager to chat up his Syrian family's path from Damascus to the textile mills of the Northeast and on to assimilation—he has by every measure accrued more status than I. The basis of our relationship is occupational reciprocity.

If we have been out of touch for a few weeks or more, Derrick and I greet by grasping right hands and leaning into one another with a pat on the back. To get a sense of how ridiculous this must look, Derrick's basketball jersey is about as long as my whole body. Standing with his arm on my shoulder, he jokes that he has bestowed upon me a "ghetto pass," providing me entry into the interconnected networks of brass bands, marching bands, and community organizations. The issues of ethnographic authority and the politics of representation remain relevant—you are, after all, reading my story about Derrick—but there is no question of who is in control when we work together.

Tyrus Chapman's social networks are more circumscribed and his social mobility more limited. I had some difficulty in reaching him, and his appearance on these pages is perhaps in tension with that of the other musicians in this chapter, who have had relative success in accumulating cultural capital. My representation of Tyrus highlights the distance between our social locations, and consequently the problem of ethnographic authority is more acute because our relationship more closely resembles those that fill the anthropological record: privileged white author and marginalized non-white subject (see the conclusion). But it was only by reaching across the distance that separates us that I was able to grasp the complexity of Tyrus's subject position, to understand the depth of experience that lurks beneath "Roll With It" or "Let Me Do My Thing," an inimitable song from a musician unlike any other. Tyrus's agency is in picking up his horn; his subjectivity comes through in his song, and his voice resounds in his singing and in his story. The lesson I take from him is to roll with it, to do my thing in words, to tell his story through my voice.

EPISODE 1.7: When This Life Is Over

In their day, the members of the first black brass bands in New Orleans gained status by dressing in Prussian military uniforms and playing composed marches; a generation later Louis Armstrong relished wearing his uniform and blowing hot jazz as a member of the Tuxedo Brass Band; Dejan's Olympia brought the sounds and aesthetics of soul into the tradition; the Dirty Dozen were faster, funkier, and cooler. Today the cultural capital of the brass band has only increased, and musicians dress in hip-hop gear and play hip-hop–inflected music for enthusiastic audiences who are attuned to contemporary styles and aesthetics.

Derrick Tabb, Keith Frazier, and Philip Frazier represent the possibilities for upward mobility in the brass band tradition, but this has not made them invulnerable to suffering. Band members who are recognized as celebrities while holding sway over large audiences are not immune to being targets of racial profiling and aggressive policing. Loved ones die too young from poor health or interpersonal violence. This is upward mobility in a space with a low ceiling.

Hurricane Katrina had immediate consequences for those in Rebirth: it devastated most of their homes and scattered them and their families out of New Orleans. The road back for some was longer than for others. Derrick had stayed in New Orleans with his wife, Keisha, and children, and when the levees broke he stole a passenger van in order to drive his family to safety in Houston. Keith had planned his evacuation to Dallas, and when he and his wife, Yolanda, realized their home was lost they relocated there permanently. Philip acted quickly to reunite the band for a U.S. tour, and by early 2006 most of the band had resettled in New Orleans.

In the midst of all the tumult of relocation and recovery, Philip and Keith's younger brother, Kerwin James, suffered a stroke and fell into a coma in Houston. The family has a history of heart trouble, and Kerwin had struggled with his weight throughout his short life (his nickname was "Fat"). There was also the stress of Katrina, which factored into the deaths of many evacuees in ways that are ultimately unquantifiable. The combination of stress, heredity, personal behaviors (excessive eating, unhealthy food, drinking, recreational drugs), and structural failings (prohibitive cost and other obstacles to health care, lack of nutritional education, inaccessibility of healthy foods in black neighborhoods) has resulted in a high risk of hypertension among blacks.[58] But no one is prepared to lose a loved one at age thirty-three, and Kerwin's family traveled to Houston often to be by his side and they relayed updates about his condition to one another via cell phone.

Philip runs Rebirth with seemingly invincible enthusiasm—he is a benevolent leader who metes out decisions with a cheerful flash of his gold-capped teeth—but the stress brought on by the cataclysmic succession of events had upset his equilibrium. At a benefit concert for Kerwin at the nightclub Tipitina's in November 2006, Philip began the night dancing onstage with his longtime girlfriend, Linda Porter Tapp, while Kerwin's band New Birth played, but by the time he reappeared onstage with Rebirth he was uncharacteristically distressed. After a few songs he interrupted the typically seamless flow of upbeat music to address the crowd with a raw, emotionally intense speech that began as an elegy to his brother and then shifted to anger over the perilous status of brass band musicians in New Orleans.

"One line . . . from my little brother Kerwin will stay with me until I die." Philip pats his hand over his heart as he starts.

"Can I get everybody's attention?" Unprepared for a break in the action, the crowd makes idle chatter and the musicians busily tune their instruments and check sound levels. "This is so special to me," pleads Philip in an unusually quiet and low-pitched voice.

"When Kerwin was like thirteen years old, he was on a video tape and [someone asked him], 'Why you playing tuba?' Know what my little brother said?" Philip steps away from the mic for an instant, gesturing toward the ground, pausing to control his emotions. "My little brother said this: 'Because my big brother Philip taught me how to play tuba.'"

There is a smattering of applause and shouts, but the crowd is mostly split between respectful silence and discomfort with the outpouring of emotion at this otherwise celebratory event. Philip's voice rises in volume and pitch.

"I don't give a *damn* about what's going on around the world. *My little brother* gave me that much respect to say 'My big brother Philip taught me how to play tuba.' . . .

You know, *my brother's lying in that goddamn bed* with all them wires hooked up to him and shit . . . so right now I got to represent him."

At this point, the tone and content of Philip's speech turns from reflective to sermonizing, as he tries to reconcile his suffering with his status as the founder of the most celebrated brass band of his generation.

"Everybody sees us on TV all the time . . . but y'all know, this shit is about hard struggle. . . . I seen a lot of people lose a life every day.

And I'm representing New Orleans. . . .

Every time a musician travels around the world, all of us get treated like Michael Jackson. . . . [But] every time we come back here local . . . they don't treat us like that. But we love y'all . . . because we love doing what we're doing. So please, show some respect back."

Philip then calls his mother at Kerwin's bedside and puts the phone up to the microphone so she can thank the audience for their support. At the call's end, Philip picks up his tuba, resumes his spot in the back, and launches into a rendition of "A. P. Tureaud," a song with a booming tuba riff that Kerwin composed for his band. The musical tribute continues without interruption for the rest of the concert.

Kerwin remained in a coma for almost a year before passing away on September 26, 2007. On the night after his death, his family and friends returned to the Tremé neighborhood where many of them were raised and led an informal procession through the familiar streets. Musicians call this warm-up for a proper jazz funeral "bringing him down," and their intention is to create a sound powerful enough to communicate with the dead. It certainly caused a stir among a few of those still living. At 8 p.m., in response to a noise complaint, multiple police cars—lights ablaze, sirens drowning out the music—descended on the procession of about a hundred people, and officers arrested Derrick Tabb and trombonist Glen David Andrews as they were playing the traditional spiritual "I'll Fly Away." The charges were Disturbing the Peace and Parading without a Permit.

"They came in a swarm like we had a hundred AK-47s and we only had instruments," explained drummer Ellis Joseph of the Free Agents Brass Band a few days later. Ellis was standing in solidarity alongside members of many other brass bands—including Philip, Keith, and Derrick of Rebirth and Hot 8 bandleader Bennie Pete—in front of a handful of news media at a small protest organized by musicians and community leaders. "They were threatening to use force and all this kind of stuff. Because we're playing instruments? Something that's a part of our culture that builds New Orleans? Our city wouldn't be what it is if they didn't sell it off of us."

The disconnect between the city's reliance on musicians as the foundation of the tourist economy and the treatment of those same musicians by politicians and the police was a recurring theme at the gathering. Addressing the media, the hip-hop artist and accountant Joe Blakk asked, "When the mayor and all the politicians are running for election, what's the first thing they do? Call up Philip Frazier with Rebirth: 'Rebirth, we need y'all.' Where are they when we need them? The poster child for the rebuilding process of New Orleans is the jazz bands and the parades, but they get the most disrespect."[59]

Blakk's questions resonate with and bring clarity to Philip's onstage speech from a year earlier, when his lament for his dying brother led to frustration over the predicament of brass band musicians. Rebirth and select other bands have benefited from their association with New Orleans music, as evidenced by the media present at their press conference, but their enhanced status does not free them from the struggles disproportionately facing black New Orleanians. Further, the causes of these struggles are less overt than in the eras of slavery or Jim Crow. As I discuss in chapter 2, the "disrespect" of living in a city that places local tradition in the center of economic initiatives but continually relegates the bearers of tradition to the margins is at once a legacy of a culture industry that has forever exploited black musicians and a more recent product of the neoliberal service economy. Respect is now determined squarely within the structure of market relations, unfettered by yesterday's segregationist laws.

For the many musicians who are the equivalent of service workers in this marketplace, the lesson from the relative success of Rebirth is that social location is never fixed; it is always mobile. But that also means it is never secure, always requiring reinforcement. To be sure, there are resources to be exploited within the category of blackness, such as the prestige of carrying forward the celebrated legacy of black music, and then there are also the ever-present threats of insecurity, dispossession, and neglect. Lipset and Bendix, whose 1959 book *Social Mobility in Industrial Society* remains a standard text on the topic, nevertheless failed to factor in race as a hindrance to social mobility when they measured "the degree to which given backgrounds determine the level of education, the acquisition of skills, access to people at different levels of social structure, intelligence, and motivation."[60] At the risk of stating the obvious, the uneven experiences of musicians offer a corrective: race can be a hindrance to social mobility.

"When we cry, who hurts for us?" asks Joe Blakk. "Nobody but us."

Following an event-filled week, this sentiment still echoes on the morning of October 6, 2007, when a jazz funeral is held in honor of Kerwin

James. There is nothing extraordinary about a jazz funeral in New Orleans; I would estimate that, on average, there is about one per day, led by one of the twenty or so organized brass bands in the city, hired by the family of the deceased. But when a fellow brass band musician dies, any and all musicians are welcome and even expected to be present, instrument in hand, the only form of reciprocity being the assurance that one day musicians will honor them in turn. When that musician is young, the circumstances ensure a level of emotional intensity matched by the sheer force of dozens of musicians playing at full volume.

The steps of the Christian Mission Baptist Church are lined with horn players, and drummers spill off the sidewalk and onto the street. When Kerwin's silver casket appears at the church door, the snare drummers play a soft roll, the bass drummers tap out a sparse beat, and the horns begin the legato melody of "Just a Closer Walk with Thee" as Kerwin's body is placed in the hearse. After the dirge winds to an end, snare drummer Kerry Hunter, who played alongside Kerwin in New Birth, launches into a fast drumroll, the horns fall in step with the melody of "I'll Fly Away," and in a heartbeat the emotional register of the event shifts dramatically. Some in the second line break out cowbells and tambourines, others yelp, twirl, smile; the excitement borders on the chaotic but is actually highly choreographed. The musicians organize themselves into sections: a dozen trumpets, half a dozen trombones, a handful of tubas and saxophones, and a full battery of percussionists. They fill up the narrow street so the second liners take to the sidewalks or weave in between instrumentalists, parked cars, and the occasional pile of debris outside a flood-damaged house. The sense of collectivity peaks when the horn players take their instruments from their mouths to sing, and we join them in unison: "One great morning, when this life is over . . ."

Glen David Andrews marches past the corner where he was arrested earlier in the week, and it is around this spot that the members of Rebirth band together and burst through the ranks of fellow musicians to launch a renegade version of a song with an unambiguous message. "Who Dat Call the Police?" was originally written by the local rapper Kilo and his lyrics conflate three or four recurring themes in hip-hop: anti-police ranting, misogynist posing, partying, and representing place (in this case, housing projects across New Orleans). The song is one of a dozen or more additions to the stock repertoire of brass bands that demonstrate the affinity of hip-hop and brass band as street musics, and it was Kerwin who added the signature tuba melody that travels up and down the notes of an F-minor chord. It is that riff that propels Gerald Platenburg of the Nine Times to hop onto the roof of a car, shaking his legs, dropping to his knees, bouncing back up in an instant, and raising his arms with his index fingers pointing toward the sky. The emotional register has shifted again without losing its intensity and we all follow Rebirth's lead, moving faster, chanting "Nobody run when the police come!" As we turn onto a wider street, the parade gathers momentum and grows in size as the sound lures more second liners to join in.

When the procession reaches the perimeter of historic Tremé, the boundary marked by the imposing Interstate 10 overpass, Rebirth is now leading the procession with "A. P. Tureaud," a New Birth original. Philip's tuba bounces in the air as he repeats the one-note riff that his brother composed for the song.[61] It is difficult to fathom how a tiny instrumental fragment could be identified with a single musician participating in a vast tradition that stretches back for generations, and for many second liners there may be nothing noteworthy or even identifiably different about "A. P. Tureaud," but from the perspective of the musicians, playing this song at this moment is a purposeful act intended to call forth specific memories and meanings, and their instrumental articulations echo off the concrete structure of the highway and propel the unrestrained and ecstatic dancing under the bridge.

The funeral might have ended on this high note, but Philip instead calls for a final dirge. He begins the tuba part not to a sacred hymn, but to an R&B ballad popular in Rebirth's youth, "It's So Hard to Say Goodbye to Yesterday," originally from the soundtrack to the 1975 movie *Cooley High* and covered by the a cappella group Boyz II Men in 1991. As a listener who previously found little redeeming in this pop confection, I have to reorient myself to accommodate its abundance of meaning for the musicians playing it as a spiritual meant to honor their fallen brother, on archaic instruments that echo off city streets where Louis Armstrong, Harold Dejan, and generations of followers have marched and played.

Each of these musicians accrued status through their affiliation with a cultural legacy that, in turn, has retained its vitality through their innovative strategies to recalibrate tradition. They have done so within an infrastructure that has enriched the cultural capital of the brass band while simultaneously constraining the social mobility of its practitioners through policies of urban planning, acts of aggressive policing, and other systemic problems such as lack of health care, education, housing, and social welfare programs.

Pursuing a career as a brass band musician opens up the possibility of social mobility, but the process is highly selective and the outcome is always provisional.

EPISODE 1.8: Voices and Instruments

At the jazz funeral for Kerwin James and the Tremé Sidewalk Steppers second line parade a polyphony of voices resounded in the public sphere.[62] These cultural traditions offer a lesson in the way that voices and instruments function materially (in the production of sound) and metaphorically (as symbolic icons). The collective singing and the sound of the instruments echoing off the city streets can be heard as a voice suffused with racial, regional, and religious symbolism.

Sacred songs such as "Just a Closer Walk with Thee" and "I'll Fly Away" provide a foundation for the brass band and jazz funeral traditions, which are local manifestations of black religious practices that have deep sonic, vocal, and textual resonance. Throughout the antislavery movement and the subsequent struggle for equal rights into the twentieth century, Frederick Douglass, W. E. B. Du Bois, and others praised the negro spiritual as evidence of black humanity. "I have sometimes thought that the mere hearing of those songs," wrote Douglass in his autobiography, "would do more to impress some minds with the horrible character of slavery, than the readings of whole volumes of philosophy on the subject could do."[63] Du Bois began each chapter of *The Souls of Black Folk* with a quote from a "sorrow song" paired with its melody in musical notation, and he devoted the last chapter to "these weird old songs in which the soul of the black slave spoke to men."[64] Through the resignification of Christian texts on suffering and salvation as commentaries on the black experience, the black voice has been interpreted as an assertion of power going back at least to the broad popularity of the Fisk Jubilee Singers in the late nineteenth century.[65]

Voice has served as a metaphor for identity and subjectivity in many cultures. For example, in the philosopher Gayatri Spivak's essay "Can the Subaltern Speak?" the ability to speak is equated with power and knowledge among subjects in postcolonial India. However, while Douglass and Du Bois understood that the symbolic power of voice is derived from specific materialities of black singing—"wild" for Douglass; "weird" and "sorrowful" for Du Bois[66]—Spivak's invocation of voice is entirely metaphorical. In an essay titled "Vocal Anthropology," Steven Feld, Aaron Fox, Thomas

Porcello, and David Samuels gesture toward symbolic references to voice such as Spivak's: "Phrases like 'giving voice,' 'taking voice,' 'having voice' are now routinely linked to the politics of identity, the production of difference, to the ability of the subaltern to speak, to the ability of indigenous movements to 'talk back' and for class, race, and gender politics to 'back talk' the dominant."[68]

What these and other anthropologists of voice have attempted to make explicit are the connections between material soundings and metaphorical meanings that were implicit, for example, in studies of black singing. The anthropologist Amanda Weidman writes that theories of voice based on readings of static texts decontextualize voice "as a mere vehicle for expression, something that is a *sign* of agency but has no power in itself."[67] In Weidman's research on singers of South Indian classical music, voices and instruments are not subservient to referential content, nor are they mere conduits for expressing agency in some predetermined form, but rather generative forces that themselves enable action. By relocating the voice in the body and situating texts within the complexly layered discourse of human interaction, anthropologists have gestured to the multifaceted power of voice, as Aaron Fox found among regulars at a Texas honky-tonk in his book *Real Country: Music and Language in Working-Class Culture*: "The preeminent semiotic technology of discursive mediation is the sounding, talking, singing, crying, narrating voice—the actual medium of mediation, the principal tool of expression, and the material sign both of the essential self and of all the social relations into which the self enters through voicing."[69]

At Kerwin's funeral, voices resounded in the singing of spirituals during the church service and the communal chant of "I'll Fly Away" during the procession, extending a legacy of spirituals in which black singing is a form of agency. Yet to limit interpretation to the physical voice would be to diminish the overall power of musical sound—both material and metaphorical—at this or any other performance. Where does voice reside in a song stripped of words ("Just a Closer Walk with Thee") or a fully instrumental composition ("A. P. Tureaud")? Sung texts do not constitute a script that is overlaid on an accompanying musical soundtrack; the sound is an integrated whole, a polyphony of voices that is made up of actual voices as well as instruments. There is a particular set of associations that musicians and listeners make with the instruments of the brass band that are as culturally relevant as the sounding, talking, singing, crying, narrating voice in a Texas honky-tonk. If the voice is not only an expressive outlet but also a constructive tool for producing the self and community, then musical instruments also circulate meanings.

Throughout history the "pure" sound of instruments and vocables— musical utterances unanchored to language—have posed a challenge to rational thought. Much ink has been spilled trying to decode the wordless songs of Homer's Sirens or the sounding of the biblical shofar capable of breaking down the walls of Jericho.[70] In the *Symposium*, Plato tells the story of Marsyas, whose wind instrument, the *aulos*, is no match for Apollo's stringed lyre because it "impede[s] the flautist from speaking" and acts as an alluring and dangerous "substitute for the voice," according to Adriana Cavarero.[71] Cavarero notes that the fable of the Pied Piper of Hamelin resurrects this fear of the seductive nature of instrumental music, teaching us that "sound is more powerful than speech" precisely because there is no stable referential content.[72]

Anthropologists of music have mined this fertile territory where language, voice, and instrument meet. Steven Feld's body of research on the Kaluli in a remote rain forest in Bosavi, Papua New Guinea, offers an extended analysis of Kaluli voices (weeping, poetics, and song), environmental sounds (waterfalls and birdcalls), and instruments (percussion) as an integrated sound world in which language is but one layer of semantic content.[73] In Weidman's studies of Karnatic music, virtuosic singing came to be understood as the "natural and authentic sound" of South Indians, and the violin indexed the presence of British colonizers.[74] Regula Qureshi has traced how a particular instrumental sound can become an icon of tradition and locality in North India. The sarangi, a bowed instrument played in Hindustani music, "is endowed with associations of sadness, loss, and mourning," as evidenced in powerful national events such as the memorials of the leading political figures Jawaharlal Nehru, Indira Gandhi, and Rajiv Gandhi.[75] The shared associations and connotations between North Indians and a nonverbal, musical sound leads Qureshi to suggest that "if musical sound has the potential to 'speak' socially as well as individually, then its sounds may turn out to be potent icons of social practice as well as of personal experience. Music becomes as much a political tool as it is a language of feelings."[76]

Legacies of black music also attest to the metaphorical power attributed to instrumental sound. Black Americans practicing Christianity have taken the biblical call to make a joyful noise literally, using Gabriel's trumpet and God's trombones along with heavenly voices to inspire congregants to catch the spirit. ("Lord, how loud should I blow it?" asks Gabriel in the nineteenth-century slave spiritual "In That Great Getting-Up Morning." God responds, "Loud as seven peals of thunder. Wake the living nations.") Drums too have a history in some African and diasporic cultures of serving as a surrogate for speech, with specific pitches and rhythmic patterns transmitting signals across great distances.[77] Someone could rewrite the history of jazz as an assertion of cultural value and self-worth articulated predominantly by instruments.

The sound of the brass band in New Orleans has acquired meaning above and beyond its properties of expression to become an icon of race and place. As demonstrated in studies of other instruments in other places—such as the sarangi in North India and the violin in South India—an instrument's capacity to express is partly due to the powerful associations that accumulate among listeners over time, as indicated by the multiple meanings of the term *instrument*. In the most general sense, an instrument is a tool, or what the *Oxford English Dictionary* defines as "anything that serves or contributes to the accomplishment of a purpose." Musical instruments, specifically, are engineered to produce sound: they are an extension or augmentation of the voice, an example of what the philosopher Donna Haraway calls "prosthetic technologies."[78] The instruments in the brass band become instruments of power because by expressing things ("giving voice") they are also instrumental in accomplishing things; they extend, complement, and even replace the voice.

There is something fundamental happening here that may be in danger of being overlooked: young people respond to their circumstances by picking up an instrument; in so doing, they produce material sound that is imbued with metaphorical powers of expression and liberation in a context where other types of instruments—such as the guns discussed in chapter 4—are tools of violence and suppression.

The capacity of the Rebirth Brass Band to harness musical instruments as instruments of power—to voice their experiences as black men, as New Orleanians, and as cultural ambassadors in ways that move diverse audiences—is the basis of their enhanced status. The dual meaning of mobility as both physical movement and social status roughly correlates with voice as both material sound and symbolic agency. By mixing standards and spirituals with progressive original compositions, infusing tresillo rhythms, fifteen-stroke drumrolls, and hummable tuba riffs into a sturdy musical idiom, and adjusting tempos, volume, and repertoire to maximize audience participation from the backstreet to the main stage at Madison Square Garden, Rebirth mobilizes and voices. Through the collective suffering of Katrina and the personal loss of loved ones, and through the triumphs of presiding over the most renowned weekly gig in a musical city and earning adoration in far-flung lands, Rebirth utilizes their voices to keep everyone moving.

EPISODE 1.9: Life at the Top

On February 11, 2012, Rebirth won a Grammy Award for their album *Rebirth of New Orleans*. The following Tuesday, minutes before the homecoming show at the Maple Leaf, Derrick handed out custom-printed T-shirts proclaiming Rebirth as the first New Orleans brass band to be honored with a Grammy. The band members appeared on a second-floor balcony in their matching shirts to play a victory march for a smiling crowd gathered below in the street, some holding cell phones in the air to capture the moment of glory. A friend of the band could be seen carrying the award through the audience, stopping to pose for pictures and passing it around to those who wanted to touch it.

Since Hurricane Katrina, Keith and his wife have lived in Dallas, where they bought a suburban home and Yolanda works in health care. Keith makes all of Rebirth's tours and comes to New Orleans for long stretches to play gigs, staying with his mother in an apartment she has rented in the Seventh Ward neighborhood since the storm. Rebirth has a substitute at the ready, Derrick's cousin Terence Andrews, a freelance bass drummer who can closely replicate Keith's parts.

Rebirth faced their toughest challenge when Philip suffered a stroke on December 11, 2008. In the hospital Philip's physical therapist suggested that he use the tuba to help his recovery. Initially his fingers were not getting the proper signals from his brain, and Philip had to relearn the fingerings for parts he had written himself, starting with "Feel Like Funkin' It Up." After a month he had regained enough strength to head home to his girlfriend, Linda.

The leader had encouraged his band to keep playing, and they had arranged for Jeffrey Hills as a replacement. But after only a month of home rest, Philip returned to the stage of the Maple Leaf, where he has played virtually every Tuesday night since 1992. At first he could manage his way through only one set, but within a few weeks he was playing on his own until show's end, around 2:30 in the morning. By Easter Sunday, Philip was back on the street, marching for miles in the Pigeon Town Steppers second line parade, the bell of his tuba with the trademark REBIRTH BRASS BAND peeking out above the heads of the club members with just a little less bounce than before.

Derrick Tabb was not on snare drum for the parade, but I noticed him pull up in his pickup truck at one point and linger on the perimeter, perhaps checking out his sub Kerry Hunter and likely seeing how his bandleader was holding up. When commitments to Roots of Music coincide with those of Rebirth, Derrick opts out of gigs. He also admits to an aversion to marching in parades, preferring to have the complete stage setup of cymbals and other percussion instruments at his disposal. And there have been a few vague references to concerns over Philip's health and the physical stress of performing, especially during the grueling four-hour parades. Trombonist Stafford Agee also bows out of most parades, increasingly since he started consulting on the *Treme* show, teaching the lead actor, Wendell Pierce, how to play trombone and recording his parts for the soundtrack. Trombonist Corey Henry joined the funk band Galactic and was replaced by Greg Veals, Keith splits his time with his family in Dallas, and subs have been recruited to fill the various vacancies.

With Rebirth's membership in a state of flux, younger brass bands sensed an opportunity for upward mobility. The Stooges in particular have made an effort to establish themselves as prime contenders, culling a roster of the most ambitious young musicians and drawing steadily increasing crowds to their shows and parades. After building up a weekly gig at the Rock Bottom Lounge, the band moved across town to the Hi-Ho Lounge, which straddles the line between the predominantly white Bywater neighborhood and the largely black Upper Ninth Ward. It quickly became a destination gig for a diverse mix of club members, fans of jazz, brass, and dance music, and a rotating cast of curious others. This is where I see Gerald Platenburg on many a Thursday and also where I take visitors for a night out. The Stooges' popularity has spilled onto the street, where they are in demand virtually every Sunday afternoon for parades, and in the fall of 2010 they won a brass band contest sponsored by the energy drink company Red Bull and were crowned "Street Kings" in an emotionally charged battle with the Soul Rebels, To Be Continued, and Free Agents bands.

Stooges bandleader Walter Ramsey acknowledges his debt to Rebirth

1.4 *Olympia
(Old-Timer with
Saxaphone).* 2002.
60" × 44".
© WILLIE BIRCH.

and credits Tuba Phil as his primary influence on the instrument. When he was a student at Charles E. Gayarre Elementary School in the 1980s, Rebirth came to play in the auditorium: "And they got onstage in front of the student body, and right then and there I was like, 'This is what I want to do.'" Walter's founding of the Stooges while in high school is a testament to Rebirth's influence, but in recent years the youthful drive of his bandmates and the realities of competing for gigs and status instigated a spirited rivalry between the bands. Taunts went out on social networking websites, feuds developed between members, and chilly exchanges were detectable any time the bands were billed on the same show. The tension boiled over at a second line sponsored by the Big 9 Social Aid and Pleasure Club on the Sunday before Christmas 2009. The sluggish parade came to a stop and the Stooges initiated a battle by turning around to face Rebirth, who was marching behind them with another division, and firing off a song at full volume. "Rebirth! Rebirth! Whatcha gonna do? Whatcha gonna do when we come for you?" chanted the Stooges to the tune of "Bad Boys." The Stooges had assembled a much larger band for the parade, complete with two tubas, and this might explain why Rebirth brushed aside the provocation until trumpeters Glen Andrews and Derrick Shezbie dropped their horns and sprinted toward their rivals; fists went flying, police on horseback intervened, and the parade resumed only after the bands were separated by yet another band who had been leading the division up front.

Band battles are a time-honored tradition among musicians playing in the street, where skirmishes are unexceptional and rivalries often play out in boasting songs aimed at one another. ("You don't want to mess with me! Rolling with the RBB!" is answered with "Stooges got Fire!" and all the bands drop in the Mardi Gras Indian chant "Let's Go Get 'Em" when facing off.) But the fervor of this particular clash was clearly intended to signal a changing of the guard. The Stooges were aiming for the top, where Rebirth has resided ever since they informally inherited the "street kings" title from the Dirty Dozen in the mid-1980s, and they detected an opening with the compromised health of Rebirth's bandleader and the shuffling of his membership.

The point of sharing this episode is not to draw attention to any lack of momentum or decline of Rebirth. Try as the Stooges may, the mighty Rebirth has command over a vast network of performance offerings that will remain without equal until Rebirth decides otherwise. Rather, the intensity of the competition serves as an indicator of how high the stakes are for working brass band musicians in New Orleans. From this archaic ensemble of instruments, played acoustically, out in the open, are derived modern careers and identities, alliances and rivalries, money and prestige.

The Stooges' challenge to Rebirth speaks to the senior band's privileged status as purveyors of an iconic tradition in a caustic environment of scant opportunities, as innovative individuals who command respect. They secured their position by strategically approaching musical performance as a form of social action that, in this case, is engineered to get people moving. Brass band music pays dividends when practitioners are capable of mobilizing across social barriers, accumulating economic and other forms of wealth from diverse sources. Rebirth leads by example here, and many others follow. As the song goes, "There ain't no party like a Rebirth party and a Rebirth party don't stop."

A primary source of income is the tourism industry that packages the sounds and images of parades for cultural exhibitions and marketing campaigns. In the following chapter I track the myriad ways that the brass band acts as a resource for musicians, cultural administrators, and other entrepreneurs who utilize local culture to generate earnings. The brass band circulates as a symbol of local distinction, but only a few of the musicians have been as successful as Rebirth in exploiting this potential.

CHAPTER 2

CONSTRAINTS

EPISODE 2.1: Down on the Corner

Passengers landing at the Louis Armstrong International Airport are greeted with a customized mix of local music piped through the public address system and a banner proclaiming "WE'RE JAZZED YOU'RE HERE!" Tourism is the city's largest industry, and it is culture—specifically the holy trinity of food, architecture, and music—that makes New Orleans a desirable destination. In this land of dreams, where the deadly sin of gluttony is always alive and kicking, visitors arrive with the expectation that an authentically New Orleans experience is one of excess—of food and drink, of music and dance—and a massive cultural workforce is ready to meet them.

In the summer of 2010 the New Orleans Convention and Visitors' Bureau (CVB) launched a new advertising campaign intended to lure last-minute vacationers out of their routine spaces of work and home and into an entertainment zone designed for pleasure. Readers of the *Washington Post* were shown an action-filled picture of a brass band parade on Bourbon Street and told "You can do whatcha wanna in NEW ORLEANS" (a reference to Rebirth's song "Do Whatcha Wanna"). In another ad, a smiling young couple festooned with beads stands in the street sipping cocktails out of "go" cups with straws: "Right now in New Orleans, there's a brass band playing on Bourbon and a jazz combo jammin' on the corner."

In actuality, right then in New Orleans, on the evening of June 15 to be exact, "Quality of Life" police officer Roger Jones was ordering the To Be Continued Brass Band to cease and desist their performance at the corner of Bourbon and Canal Streets. Band members faced a court summons if they refused to sign a form acknowledging they had violated Section 30–1456 of a city ordinance, which Jones produced on New Orleans Police Department letterhead adorned with the names of Mayor Mitch Landrieu and Police Chief Ronal Serpas: "It shall be unlawful for any person to perform any street entertainment on the sidewalk of Bourbon Street . . . between the hours of 8:00 pm and 6:00 am."[1] Officer Jones was not confrontational, and he encouraged the musicians to exercise their rights in challenging the ordinance, but he was also clear that he would comply with orders to enforce it.

The critical backlash against the incident was swift and relatively effective. The band, known as TBC, worked with their manager Lisa Palumbo to launch a Facebook page "Don't Stop the Music: Let New Orleans Street Musicians Play!" that added ten thousand members in under a week. Two articles by the investigative journalist Katy Reckdahl, appearing on the front page of the *Times-Picayune*'s Metro section, fanned the flames of controversy. Mayor Landrieu and City Councilwoman Kristin Gisleson Palmer responded to a deluge of complaints with a joint statement calling for cooperation between musicians, residents, and the police. The following year, however, Palmer was again embroiled in controversy as the author of a city noise ordinance that included new limits on live music.

As a city that sells itself on cultural distinction, New Orleans's economic survival is dependent on young musicians to renew culture and to do so in publicly accessible spaces, but the corner where musicians gather slips into a gray zone between competing discourses of marketing, policies of governance, and value chains of the cultural economy. In a video Palumbo posted on Facebook, TBC's Sean Roberts attests to the formative role that playing in the street had on his musical development: "I didn't know how to play trumpet for real until I started playing on this corner." The TBC is the most recent in a long line of bands that got their start playing for tourists' tips in the French Quarter, and some of those musicians—including the founding members of Rebirth—have gone on to successful careers. "This is the birthplace of jazz. It's what we're known for," says Roberts. "For them to just stop it is just wrong."[2]

At a protest organized on the corner where the TBC has played for several years, in a high-traffic area alongside a Foot Locker shoe store, a middle-aged black woman danced and held up a sign reading "KEEP OUR MUSIC CULTURE ALIVE." The TBC was playing a song with the provocative chant "Why you worried about me if I ain't worried about you? / If you don't fuck with me then I won't fuck with you!"[3] Palumbo solicited testimonials from tourists like Melanie Wilson from Southern California: "I just can't tell you how wonderful it was as we were walking down the street to hear this music. It just drew us in. It was what, in my mind, I'd envisioned of New Orleans."[4] Mary Howell, a civil rights attorney whose many years of advocating for citizens' rights provided the basis for a character in the *Treme* television series, was quoted as saying, "To enforce an ordinance like this is counterproductive and silly."[5]

Pressure may have come from Vieux Carré Property Owners, Residents, and Associates, Inc., a nonprofit corporation dedicated to the "preservation, restoration, beautification and general betterment of the Vieux Carré."[6] This powerful association has shepherded the steady transformation of the French Quarter from a predominantly working-class residential neighborhood at the start of the twentieth century to a preservation and entertainment district at the start of the twenty-first, supporting zoning ordinances and legislation (such as the neighborhood's designation as a National Historic Landmark) to control development, enforce architectural regulations, and maintain quality-of-life standards that have raised property values dramatically.[7] In the recent past, this meant working closely with the police and city council in an attempt to rid the neighborhood's central park, Jackson Square, of musicians, tarot card readers, select artists, and the homeless. It took the intervention of a street musician, Anthony "Tuba Fats" Lacen, to successfully negotiate an allowance for musicians to continue to play in the square at designated times and at reduced volume levels, and the pact held after Tuba's death in 2004.

Hot 8 bandleader Bennie Pete shares his instrument and his genial nature with Tuba Fats, but his admiration was soured by the economic limitations imposed on his predecessor. "I used to look up to him, because he's the tuba player. But I always said, 'I ain't going to be like him.' Because I used to

be catching the bus with my horn and I'd see him limping to the bus stop."
Reflecting on a mentor who failed to accumulate economic status commensurate with his social status, Bennie then zoomed out to the larger context of
the local economy. "They don't got no great infrastructure here. They don't
got no Fortune 500 companies here. They sell the city off of music and food,
so why the musicians is hurting like this?" Rather than police musicians in
a district set aside for entertainment, Bennie wondered why the city does
not reward those same musicians. "I feel like Tuba Fats and all them people
who been playing in Jackson Square . . . the city or somebody could sponsor
them [so] they get paid to go play . . .

. . . I don't want to be no old tuba man, limping . . .

. . . I want to make it better for the cats who play tuba behind me . . ."

In chapter 1, the agile Rebirth demonstrated the potential for musicians
to mobilize across great social and geographical distances. The experiences
of Bennie and the members of the TBC laid bare the policies and economic
patterns that effectively constrain the social mobility of brass band musicians. By using the police force and elected officials to limit live music, the
state prohibits musicians from fulfilling the promises made by another arm
of the state, the tourism offices. Breathing new life into an old tradition requires, first and foremost, loosening an asphyxiating chokehold.

The possibilities and predicaments of being a brass band musician are
most apparent in parades staged for tourists, a common occurrence at conferences and conventions. In these performances—variously called "mock"
parades, "hotel gigs," or simply "white gigs"—musicians are hired to play
the familiar repertoire and appear in traditional uniforms. They march
through lobbies and meeting rooms behind a parade marshal adorned with
a sash and an umbrella, demonstrating second line dancing to the uninitiated. These jobs are frequently contracted by a Destination Management
Company that arranges venues, suppliers, and entertainment for meeting
planners, such as Bonnie Boyd and Company's jazz funeral package, "complete with pallbearers, mourners, Styrofoam coffin and 'widow woman.'"[8]
While such companies receive direct financial compensation for exhibiting
local culture, there are myriad other institutions, ranging from the Jazz &
Heritage Festival, to Harrah's Casino and community Social Aid and Pleasure Clubs, that benefit indirectly from their affiliation with the brass band
tradition.

The Bonnie Boyds, the Quality of Life officers, and the limping tuba players are each part of an ensemble of obstacles and opportunities that musicians face and that require expert navigation to overcome and potentially exploit. There are so many vectors intersecting here—including the incorporation of community traditions via heritage industries, the provisional value added to black music via cultural tourism schemes, the disappearance of urban industrial labor via the service economy, and the ongoing marginalization of racial subjects via ostensibly color-blind governance—that focusing on one would downplay their cumulative impact on people's lives. The effect of these forces in shaping the experiences of musicians is not always calculable because there is no longer an overarching policy, such as there was in the days of Jim Crow rule, and so one's position in the new order may appear as the capricious outcome of economic transactions, social interactions, and individual responsibility. Locating success within the labyrinth of penalties and rewards requires mobility both literally (off the streets and onto festival stages, casino floors, and hotel lobbies) and figuratively (across social and political boundaries). As I followed musicians on the move, I learned that the pace of their movement and the distance traveled are not conducive to static reflection or unilinear analysis; instead I adopted mobility as the methodological model used to confront the constituent parts of the unruly ensemble. Situating the experiences of musicians within larger economic and racial structures called for a multisited ethnography, leading me into the real and virtual spaces where the parade tradition is bought and sold.

In the second half of the twentieth century, when New Orleans shifted away from industrial labor and toward service work, cultural tourism became the foundation of the local economy. Tourist dollars now amount to $5 billion per year, presenting a model case study of what the cultural studies scholar George Yúdice calls the "expediency of culture": local culture is identified as an economic resource and recontextualized in new spaces for exhibition and consumption.[9] As the sociologist Kevin Fox Gotham has shown in his book *Authentic New Orleans: Tourism, Culture, and Race in the Big Easy*, the culture of this particular city provides income for culture workers, curators, and brokers who profit directly from the production of heritage, and a host of others (property owners, retail operators, college professors) who benefit indirectly.[10]

A productive comparison could be made with blues music in Chicago, where the sociologist David Grazian found tourists and other spectators participating in a "symbolic economy of authenticity." Whether in modest blues bars in North Side neighborhoods or upscale blues-themed nightclubs in the downtown district or the stages of the Chicago Blues Festival, musicians recycle standards for a revolving cast of spectators.[11] If, as Grazian argues, the significance of a song such as "Sweet Home Chicago" is enhanced by musicians' awareness of its status as a "crowd-pleaser," then the same is true for the spiritual-turned-slogan "When the Saints Go Marching In" in the nightclubs, festivals, convention centers, and sports arenas of New Orleans. The rootedness and durability of these songs and musical styles is due in part to their ubiquitous presence in musical exhibitions that take place in "urban entertainment destinations." Areas such as the French Quarter and the Chicago Loop have been rezoned for consumer convenience and security in order to compete in the global tourist market.[12]

Within the pantheon of local culture that marks New Orleans as an exceptional space of festivity, the brass band parade holds a particular distinction as both practice and symbol. The jazz funeral, in celebrating life at the moment of death, has become a kind of stand-in for the identity of the entire city, akin to other ritual events that fill the anthropological record, such as the Balinese cockfight famously interpreted by Clifford Geertz or Victor Turner's theorization of Ndembu rites of passage as amalgams or compressions of total social structures.[13] But while Geertz and Turner understood ritual as self-contained and relatively autonomous, the brass band parade, like the Chicago blues, has accumulated cultural capital from multiple points, with community parades in the backstreets at one end of the spectrum and fully curated exhibitions manicured for tourist-consumers at the other:

> EXAMPLE 1: A bumper sticker sold in the trinket shops along Bourbon Street proclaims, "New Orleans: We Put the 'Fun' in Funeral."

> EXAMPLE 2: Inside the fairgrounds of the New Orleans Jazz & Heritage Festival, brass bands appear onstage one minute and parade through the fairgrounds the next, initiating festival-goers into a local community tradition even as many musicians complain that their pay is not adequate for the specialized service they provide.

> EXAMPLE 3: The examples are not confined to touristic consumerism: Habitat for Humanity is building a "Musicians' Village" intended to pro-

vide "housing and a music center for Katrina-displaced, low-income musicians," but musicians have been consistently rejected for failure to verify their income due to their reliance on informal cash economies. Rebirth's trumpeter Glen Andrews was turned down even though he was pictured playing his trumpet next to Habitat's online donation form. The majority of homes have gone to nonmusicians.[14]

EXAMPLE 4: Nor can the examples be deconstructed and critiqued from a safe distance. At our wedding in 2000, Alex and I hired the New Birth Brass Band to lead a parade through the French Quarter. How should our negotiations to secure an economical rate be situated within infrastructural patterns of racial marginalization? While I have consistently arranged gigs for brass bands, and I have always done so under the condition that they are paid equitably, this has not released me from the bonds of a provider-consumer relationship.

The participatory nature of the second line parade creates a space of pleasure that is eminently compatible with spaces manicured for consumption; they are open to anyone willing and able to pay the price of admission. The commodification of culture as a representational medium has been a recurring theme in anthropological and cultural studies. Dick Hebdige identifies this shift as the incorporation of the subcultural by the dominant culture.[15] For Barbara Kirschenblatt-Gimblett, the move is one from actuality to virtuality, from the performance of tradition ("music that is part and parcel of a way of life") to the production of heritage (music "singled out for preservation, protection, enshrinement, and revival").[16] And Helen Regis's research situates second line parades specifically within a long history of racial exploitation, referring to the practice of staging parades as a "minstrel-like appropriation of a black cultural tradition by the city's elites and the tourism industry."[17] While the primary question surrounding this work on cultural exhibition relates to changes in *meaning* from the perspective of various actors, I take as a given that meaning is situational and focus instead on agency. Musicians are culture workers who destabilize categories — subcultural and dominant, tradition and heritage, emancipated and appropriated — in their everyday attempts to stitch together a living.

In their book *Ethnicity, Inc.*, Jean Comaroff and John Comaroff shift the anthropological emphasis from structures of meaning to structures of power, with particular attention to economic flows. They argue that social identities have become increasingly entwined with the circulation of cultural products and spectacles: "Ethnicity is *both* commodified, made into the basis of *value-added* corporate collectivity, and claimed as the basis of shared emotion, shared lifestyle, shared imaginings for the future."[18] They make reference to Pierre Bourdieu's notion of cultural capital, the symbolic value of affiliating with a particular culture, and suggest that it has become inseparable from economic capital:

> Being founded from the first on a misleading antinomy between the symbolic and the substantive, the immaterial and the material, [the distinction between cultural and economic capital] can no longer be sustained when the two species of capital merge so overtly: when culture is objectified by those who inhabit it, thence to be deployed as a brute economic asset, a commodity with the intrinsic capacity to compound wealth of its own accord.[19]

Scholars of Latin America have been at the vanguard of studying culture as a monetary resource for practitioners and investors. Building on Néstor García Canclini's research into the utility of ritual as folkloric performance and traditional crafts as cultural commodities, Yúdice's *The Expediency of Culture: Uses of Culture in the Global Era* offers a series of case studies on how institutions, entrepreneurs, and artists have capitalized on the resourcefulness of culture.[20] In a study of cultural agencies and nongovernmental organizations in Colombia, the ethnomusicologist Ana María Ochoa notes that bureaucrats have become increasingly attentive to "the way that culture forms an instrument for the mobilization of symbolic, social, economic, and political practices."[21]

These case studies of national and ethnic identity in Latin America, along with those assembled in *Ethnicity, Inc.*, generally correspond to my research on racial identity in New Orleans. But the legacy of black music as a cultural form that is both commodified and claimed as the basis of identity reaches back much further. Brass band music is not an example of the "creeping commodification of . . . cultural products and practices" because music does not exist in a prior state;[22] music is always already commodified. A contrasting example from the New Orleans cultural tourism industry will clarify.

Gerald Platenburg is a member of the Nine Times Social Aid and Pleasure Club and an executive chef at the Bourbon Orleans Hotel restaurant. The annual Nine Times parade generates money for clothes designers, food vendors, bar owners, police officers, and others who rely on parades for income, but the members themselves do not earn money for their parades. Rather they mount parades at great expense, and Gerald is able to pay his share by catering to the expectations of hotel guests seeking Creole cuisine. His customers are the target audience for staged parades, but Gerald's options for tapping into this lucrative service work are very limited: only a handful of parade marshals are able to hire themselves out. Gerald and the other members of Nine Times are unique in that they authored a book that gave them visibility and even money, but in general club members are not self-commodified to anywhere near the degree of musicians who regularly provide services to customers. Consequently Gerald's "work" is integral to the cultural economy, but his "play" is incidental.

Musicians meanwhile get paid for all their endeavors. They are service workers who maneuver unencumbered through community traditions and exhibitions of heritage, navigating different social networks and spheres of capital as they play for their work. Once we acknowledge the extent of cultural commodification, the question, following the Comaroffs, is "who benefits, who suffers, and in what proportions?" Unsurprisingly, patterns of imbalance persist: "Difference, patently, may produce profit in a wide variety of ways. But those who embody its essence are often too marginalized by it to be able to control its potential market value."[23] Here again, in the case at hand, the double edge of opportunities and impediments is not new but rather defines the legacy of black musical production. "The history of black music has been a continuous replay of the uncontested and lucrative expropriation of black cultural forms," writes Norman Kelley in *R&B (Rhythm and Business): The Political Economy of Black Music*.[24] Economic patterns initiated in the days of minstrelsy have been dynamically reshaped while remaining tenaciously lopsided; the precarity of insecure and flexible labor that is so often linked to the rise of the neoliberal state has been a state of perpetuity for black musicians.

This is not to suggest that the recent effects of neoliberalism, particularly the proliferation of low-wage service work, have not had a measurable effect in New Orleans. The economic gap between black and white New Orleanians dominated public discourse following Hurricane Katrina, when countless images of those most vulnerable to devastation were beamed to every corner of the globe, "exposing" masses of urban black poor and underscoring, to quote the author and activist Mike Davis, "the devastating consequences of federal neglect of majority black and Latino big cities and their vital infrastructures."[25] Blacks were twice as likely as whites to have suffered storm damage, and their rate of return to New Orleans has been hampered by an inaccessibility to public housing and an increase in the cost of living, including a 46 percent rise in rent.[26]

The experiences of black Americans during and after Hurricane Katrina do not, however, represent a radical break with the past. Instead they are consistent with a history of crisis: the collapse of Reconstruction, the implementation of Jim Crow, and the failure of civil rights legislation to ensure equal opportunities. Before Katrina, New Orleans was the sixth poorest metropolitan region in the United States; 35 percent of black New Orleanians lived below the poverty line, and the median income of black households was 47 percent lower than whites.[27] Katrina was a colossal disaster that, for many New Orleanians, can be situated within a history of crisis, a "state of emergency" that Walter Benjamin found was "not the exception but the rule."[28]

Patterns of vulnerability that were determined long before Katrina create a thorny predicament for brass band musicians. On the one hand, their racial and geographic identities make their professional identities possible because the cultural capital of New Orleans music creates jobs. On the other hand, these jobs do not provide a reliable way out of poverty because their earning power is equivalent to others in the service industry. A report from the local musicians' nonprofit Sweet Home New Orleans revealed that 80 percent of New Orleans musicians have returned since Katrina, but they face fewer performance opportunities and lower fees because audiences are smaller. While cultural policy has changed to accommodate the shift to a tourism economy based in local culture, patterns of marginalization have remained intact. The brass band musician is given the chance to achieve social mobility, but following procedure is anything but a guarantor of wealth.

In a place where the local economy is increasingly dependent on local culture, the stability of the city's infrastructure rests on the backs of culture workers. Without the work of musicians, the CVB and the New Orleans Police Department would face drastic budget shortfalls; the properties owned by the members of the Vieux Carré neighborhood association would be devalued; my wedding would have been comparatively silent and dull, and more critically, my own work would evaporate, along with all the benefits I reap from it.

Though many of the musicians I write about are able to maintain a viable career, many others identify with the majority of black New Orleanians as the working poor. They may be better positioned for career opportunities than their peers pursuing other lines of work, but their livelihoods are characterized by insecurity. This is the view of the cultural economy from the bottom looking up.

EPISODE 2.2: Where Culture Means Business

In a 1918 *Times-Picayune* editorial entitled "Jass and Jassism," an anonymous author contrasted "truly great music," which can be heard in the "great assembly hall of melody," with jazz and other black musical forms, which he located "down in the basement" in "a kind of servants' hall of rhythm." There was nothing exceptional about the essay—jazz was the latest genre of black music to be perceived as a threat to highbrow culture across Europe and America—except that it marks the first recognition among the white elite in New Orleans of their city's relation to jazz: "It has been widely suggested that this particular form of musical vice had its birth in this city— that it came, in fact, from doubtful surroundings in our slums." How do the author and fellow members of "polite society" assess their affiliation with jazz? "We do not recognize the honor of parenthood."[29]

In 1958 another editorial about jazz ran in the same newspaper. By this time, the belief that New Orleans was the birthplace of jazz was widespread, and the music critic Sim Myers questioned why city leaders had yet to exploit this "honor of parenthood": "With jazz so much in demand and with most of the world willing to accept that it originated [here], it seems a shame that this city should let its thunder be stolen." With successful jazz festivals launched in Newport and Tanglewood, Myers asked, "Why could not such an event be a vital part of the New Orleans scene?" He concluded, "As a city noted for capitalizing on its various assets, it seems that in this respect New Orleans is letting a whale of an opportunity slip by."[30]

It was not as though members of the New Orleans elite were oblivious to jazz and brass band as forms of local music. From jazz's beginnings, black bands entertained whites on riverboat excursions and at levee camps along Lake Pontchartrain, such as Milneburg, West End, and Spanish Fort. Subscription dances at Tulane University featured jazz bands for five decades before the first black student was admitted in 1963, and black brass bands had long been hired by white Mardi Gras Krewes to march in their parades. Black bands operated within elite social spheres as thoroughly ordinary forms of entertainment.

It would require an infrastructural shift in the city's economy to convert clients into curators and alert them to the investment potential of local black culture. In the postwar period, New Orleans began moving away from an industrial economy based in the oil and shipping industries and toward a tourist economy based in local cultural traditions. The culture industry became largely synonymous with the tourism industry as hotels, restaurants, convention centers, nightclubs, and other venues sought to incorporate live music into promotional strategies designed to meet visitors' expectations of an authentically New Orleans experience. Institutions such as Preservation Hall, New Orleans Jazz & Heritage Festival, and Tulane University's Hogan Archive of New Orleans Jazz were established to preserve and promote what has been variously termed "traditional," "authentic," or "indigenous" music. Regardless of how government administrators and economic entrepreneurs have continued to assess the musical value of local jazz, brass band, rhythm and blues, and other black forms, they most certainly came to recognize the honor of parenthood.

In December 2004 Lieutenant Governor Mitch Landrieu convened the first of many Cultural Economy Initiative summit meetings to announce that the Louisiana Department of Culture, Recreation and Tourism (CRT) had received a grant from the National Endowment of the Arts (NEA) to launch a statewide study. "For too long we have separated art and culture from what the business community calls economic development," said Landrieu in his opening remarks. "Our citizens are finally recognizing that we are underutilizing our natural assets and raw talents and we are limiting our own potential to create more jobs and growth."[31] The research would be undertaken by Mt. Auburn Associates, a consulting firm that had recently completed a report on the development potential of the World Trade Center site in the aftermath of September 11. With the NEA funds, CRT contracted Mt. Auburn to "quantify the economic importance of arts and cultural activities" in the state of Louisiana.[32] The result, *Louisiana: Where Culture Means Business*, serves as the centerpiece for my own study, relocating me off the streets and into the spaces of governance and finance where policies and economic initiatives are generated.

Landrieu unveiled the study at the next summit meeting, and after a day of PowerPoint presentations and panel discussions the Tremé Brass Band escorted attendees to a nearby restaurant with a second line parade. There was talk of a storm brewing in the Gulf. The date was Friday, August 25, 2005. When Hurricane Katrina struck three days later, cultural economy initiatives would have to be put on hold. Or so it first appeared.

Within weeks Landrieu had assembled a new document entitled "Louisiana Rebirth: Restoring the Soul of America," which based the state's recovery on a simple premise: "Louisiana has an economic asset that other states can only dream of: a multifaceted, deeply rooted, authentic, and unique culture. The outpouring of support for Louisiana following the devastation wrought by Katrina is evidence of the strong association and affection that people all over the world have for Louisiana's unique culture."[33] With the lives and livelihoods of Louisianans at stake, now, more than ever, government and economic leaders were relying on local culture to save the day.

The fact that Katrina expedited rather than delayed the monetization of heritage in Louisiana is no surprise; after the state's long history of cultural incorporation, who would question the resourcefulness of creative labor in the post-Katrina economy? Certainly not Landrieu, who succeeded Ray Nagin as mayor in 2010 and continues to push cultural economy initiatives with what I find to be a genuine belief that the market is ideally democratic and universally beneficial. My research on the ground indicates that all but the most entrepreneurial musicians hold out their cups to collect a trickle of finances, but to start we can all agree that there is no longer a need to demonstrate the expediency of local culture. The more pertinent issue is this: For whom is expediency constituted?

Louisiana: Where Culture Means Business spells out what is common knowledge to those working in the service and entertainment sectors: tourism is one of the state's largest industries—catering to 25 million visitors a year, generating $635 million in tax revenues, and providing employment to 116,000 workers—and cultural tourism is the foundation of the industry because Louisiana's unique assets give the state a competitive advantage over other sites.[34] New Orleans is the most visited destination in the state, and tourism accounts for 35 percent of the city's annual operating budget. The city boasts its own Convention and Visitors' Bureau and a sprawling convention center, a powerful hotel and restaurant industry, the central entertainment corridor of Bourbon Street, and a cultural calendar filled with annual events ranging from Mardi Gras to the Decadence Festival and the Sugar Bowl.[35] If cultural production is the fuel that powers the economy, and cultural policy is the ever-expanding system of roads and highways that direct traffic, tourism is the vehicle that transports consumers and places them in contact with cultural products and producers.

The performance studies scholar Joseph Roach refers to New Orleans as "the only inhabited city that exists simultaneously as a national historical park,"[36] and tourism professionals cultivate this image through slogans such as "The Big Easy," "The Great Southern Babylon," and "The City That Care Forgot." In a promotional video produced by the CVB entitled *The Business of Pleasure*, viewers watch conference attendees exit the convention center and enter an exceptional space of leisure where social norms are abandoned in the pursuit of food, drink, and dance. Creating a tourist destination requires the exhibition of cultural artifacts, and in New Orleans displays are more likely encountered in nightclubs and restaurants and out in the streets than in a museum.[37]

Within the cultural sector of the tourism industry, the category of entertainment is dominated by live musical performance, made evident by the number of music festivals scheduled throughout the year—including the Jazz & Heritage Festival, Essence Festival, French Quarter Festival, Voodoo Festival, and Satchmo Summerfest—all of which rely on the staging of local musical talent to a degree that would not be possible with, say, the Newport jazz and folk festivals or the Milwaukee Summerfest. As the popular music scholar Connie Atkinson writes in a study of music and tourism, "No city's image has been constituted and evoked through its music more often than that of New Orleans."[38] We know, for instance, that visitors to New Orleans are two to three times more likely to attend a cultural event and participate in nightlife and dancing than in other destinations.[39] However, music's value as an economic resource is ultimately immeasurable because it is difficult to gauge how the expectation of hearing live music influences visitors' decisions to attend a conference, a business meeting, or a sporting event in New Orleans. Directly or indirectly, the city's association with live music invites visitors and spurs the economy.

The juncture of the tourism and culture industries uncovers a dimension of the artist's role in society that receives little scholarly attention: a musical performance, in addition to being a creative endeavor, is also a service provided by a worker (musician) to a client (curator), both of whom are catering to a customer base (the audience). This art world is driven by economics as much as creativity and is facilitated by negotiation as much as collaboration. To use the language of the Mt. Auburn report, it is a place where a musician joins the ranks of the "cultural workforce" and is tasked with the responsibility of originating "cultural products."[40]

The central issue, then, becomes one of *labor*, creative labor as a means of turning a knowledge strength into cash. Surprisingly, perhaps, to anyone clinging to the notion that art should ideally remain autonomous from politics and economics, there seems to be broad agreement among musicians, curators, and others in the cultural sector about the role of artists as workers. As an example, one of the Social Aid and Pleasure Clubs that I have studied has very explicit guidelines about the professional pursuits of their membership, including careers in music. The Black Men of Labor was established in 1993 to honor those who literally built the city in which they live, and the club's mission statement leaves no room for ambiguity about the role of musicians as laborers. In addition to celebrating the "men and women who worked as longshoremen, domestics, waiters, cooks, fruit and produce peddlers, sack-sewers, ditch-diggers, seamstresses, street cleaners, tailors, [and] merchant seamen," the document lists "Louis Armstrong, Danny Barker . . . The Olympia Brass Band, the Onward, the Excelsior, Tuxedo, Eureka Brass Band, Doc Paulin Brass Band, E. Gibson Brass Band, Reliance Brass Band, George Williams Brass Band, Cal Blunt Brass Band, [and] Royal Brass Band" among those "whose work, toil, and sacrifices made who we are, possible." This statement is printed on stationery that features an illustrated graphic of various "tools" along the margins: a telephone, a stethoscope, an electric drill, a wrench, an electric razor, and a trumpet (see episode 3.3).[41]

Research by the anthropologist Nick Spitzer uncovered a long history of local musicians balancing earnings from day jobs with nighttime work as performers, beginning before the emergence of jazz with the likes of Johnny St. Cyr, who was a plasterer before and after he played banjo with Louis Armstrong, and trombonist Edward "Kid" Ory, who was a bricklayer and marble cutter.[42] But the premise of the Black Men of Labor club points to another relationship: that of music *as* labor. When I spoke with a founding member, Benny Jones, who also leads the Tremé Brass Band, he equated musicians' work with other jobs more conventionally understood as labor.

> **BENNY:** If you want to join the club you have to have a job. Like the longshoremen, the postmen, the carpenters, and the bricklayers, and the guys [who] work on the pillar and wagon — the guys been doing all the work around this city — they have their own skill, or their own trade.
>
> **MATT:** And do you count musicians in that?
>
> **BENNY:** Well, we count musicians, exactly. Everybody have their own skill, with their own business. It's a labor, and that's why we count them in.

Throughout the 1970s and into the 1980s, Benny spent his nights and weekends playing bass drum with the Dirty Dozen Brass Band while driving a truck for Fisk Electric on weekdays. Like many musicians, he is comfortable with functionalist definitions of art that position the musician as a skilled laborer, and he draws parallels to jobs in the building arts and other trades. Of course, in the early twenty-first century the availability of skilled craft jobs has diminished and the largest sector in New Orleans is the service economy.[43] What emerges from the discourse of working musicians such as Benny Jones, and is presented as common sense in *Where Culture Means Business*, is how brass band musicians are situated within the cultural economy as service workers. The level of training and proficiency required for this work means that musicians are classed as skilled workers, equivalent to the kitchen position of a station chef rather than a busboy. But while integral to providing competent service, musicians are ultimately interchangeable with other cultural producers, and, as we shall see, this drives market competition among bands vying for clients whose musical choices may be driven more by budget considerations than aesthetic preferences.[44]

What level of compensation corresponds to the capabilities of musicians as self-commodified laborers? In New Orleans, as in many other locales, the cultural capital of being a local artist is greater than the economic capital most earn for creating art. Dr. Johann Bultman put it to me this way: "Tourists come to New Orleans because of music and food, and that's why we had such a great convention business . . . but many, many times the musician is the last to be paid, paid as an afterthought, and isn't appreciated as part of our cultural economy." Johann and his wife, Bethany, founded the New Orleans Musicians' Clinic to provide health care for musicians who, like the vast majority of service workers, are uninsured.

In the past, the Union of New Orleans Musicians may have been reasonably effective in standardizing pay rates, but membership in Local 174–196 has dwindled drastically over the years, and at this point very few brass bands belong to the union. Further complicating issues of reciprocity are intellectual property laws that protect the use of sounds and images in marketing schemes. A member of the Tremé Brass Band related that his picture graced the cover of the maps issued to tourists by the CVB, but he was never paid for the rights to reproduce his image or even notified that he was being depicted. He learned about the map only when he passed by a tourist information center and saw himself, dressed in band uniform and playing his trumpet, staring back at him. Tamara Jackson, director of the Social Aid and Pleasure Club Task Force, says that musicians and club members represent community, but this representational power is exploited by the culture industry with minimal reciprocity: "Just about any commercial you see, you're going to see a band and a gentleman with a sash and a umbrella. That's what is represented here. That is us. . . . Even [the] Bell South [advertisement] has a second line. You got [the] Lamarque Ford [advertisement], he's singing with a band. . . . We are marketed all over. . . . And they're not appreciating what we bring to this city." These comments by musicians and others invested in local culture bear out an observation by the ethnomusicologist Martin Stokes: "People are often highly conscious of how things are being represented to them, or how they themselves are being represented to others."[45]

In conducting interviews with culture workers for their report, the Mt. Auburn researchers determined that black musicians in New Orleans felt the "most exploited" of all artists in the state.[46] In a subsection under the heading "The African-American and Creole Communities Feel That They Do Not Capture the Economic Benefit of Their Considerable Contribution to Louisiana's Wealth," the authors noted a "profound distrust" among "African Americans and Creoles whose African-based culture is at the root of so much of Louisiana's culture" because "their work is being used to make profits for others."[47] It is in this section, about black music performance in the state's largest city, where Mt. Auburn locates a gap between the discourse of state and industry and the experiences of culture workers: "What is striking . . . is the disproportionate amount of wealth generated by culture relative to what finds its way back to the originators of that culture."[48] The problem, musicians and Mt. Auburn researchers agree, is that *culture* begins with culture workers who originate content, but *cultural economics* ends with these same workers, who are the last to receive any financial return. There is no cultural economy without their labor, but the bulk of the finances they generate accumulates elsewhere.

However valiant the efforts of the researchers to identify this economic gap, in their recommendations for rectifying the problem they continue to devalue the originators of culture. This manifests in some striking analogies, including one that is clearly meant to resonate with those familiar with another of Louisiana's largest economic sectors, the petrochemical industry: "Louisiana is now realizing that, in culture, it may have a new source of largely untapped economic energy. But if culture—abundant, renewable, and clean—is Louisiana's metaphorical new oil then it requires the industrial equivalent of the skilled workers, refineries, pipelines, and business entities to bring it to the global marketplace."[49] Later, the culture-as-utility analogy is extended through a four-step value chain of the cultural economy:

> STEP 1, ORIGINATION: is the natural resource, the raw material on which the economic sector is based. In cultural terms, it is the creative people, the writers, musicians, designers, chefs, and artists who generate and interpret literature, music, design, cuisine, and visual arts. . . . Louisiana has an abundance of cultural "oil," but much of it remains untapped and economically dormant. . . .

> STEP 2, PRODUCTION: In the oil and gas industry, production refers to the refineries that process oil into marketable products, . . . [requiring] a skilled workforce, a population of entrepreneurs and businesses, research and development capability, and finance needed to transform creative output into marketable goods and services. . . .

> STEP 3, DISTRIBUTION: Once oil has been extracted and refined, it needs an infrastructure of pipelines and fueling stations to get it to the consumer market. . . . In the case of culture, an effective distribution system requires branding, marketing, and the development of cultural import and export markets. . . .

STEP 4, SUPPORT SYSTEM: In the case of the oil and gas industry, the general support environment includes the government policies applied to the industry and the associations and networks that are involved in advocating for the industry. In the case of culture, social attitudes, trust and confidence, and networks are critical components of this support system.[50]

What does this metaphor of extraction tell us about how culture workers (Step 1, and to a lesser extent, Step 2) are assessed relative to cultural enterprises (Steps 2, 3, and 4)? Cultural labor is objectified, compared to oil, the extraction of which has decimated the natural environment, making culture workers more vulnerable to disaster. The oil analogy is meant to appeal to business investors and politicians who might not otherwise evaluate culture as a resource, but this only underscores the principal motive behind the plan: it is intended, above all, to spur investment, to bring a profitable return, with less regard to those on whose labor the plan is based. The work of culture workers is interchangeable; they are ultimately expendable, as long as their labor generates profit.

In Louisiana culture means business. Culture is recognized by all as an expedient resource, but the musicians and others who lay the foundation for the cultural economy are rarely given a seat at the table and are far more likely to be directed to the back of the bread line. The oil analogy is certainly apt here. Oil is extracted for profit with little regard to the consequences for workers and citizens whose lives and livelihoods are placed in jeopardy or the ecosystems that need to be nurtured to ensure survival and growth. As Louisianans learned from the BP Deepwater Horizon oil spill in 2010, the burdens of cutting costs and maximizing extraction are shared by all while the benefits accumulate at the top of the value chain. In taking on financial risk, entrepreneurs earn the right to curtail profit sharing and control levels of sustainability, thus making many more vulnerable to other types of risk.

The services that musicians offer are instrumental to the economy, but the expediency of culture is different for cultural originators than for cultural enterprises. When tracking historical developments in New Orleans since World War II, it appears that cultural policies were adapted to accommodate black culture as an asset, while patterns of marginalization remained relatively intact, creating a predicament for many musicians.

2.2 *Dancing Nasty (Uncle Lionel Doing the Bambara).* 2002. 72¾″ × 36″.
© WILLIE BIRCH.

2.3 *The Last Mile of the Way (Mock Funeral).* 2001. 71½″ × 60¼″. © WILLIE BIRCH.

EPISODE 2.3: Bennie's Dilemma

When the Hot 8 Brass Band comes marching down the street, the first thing you see is Bennie Pete's tuba above the heads of the other musicians and the second liners who surround them. Band members come and go in the Hot 8, but Bennie's tuba is a constant; the only time he was without his instrument for more than a few days was when he evacuated for Katrina. As soon as he was allowed to return, Bennie drove back to his flood-ravaged house and looked through the debris until he found it: "My horn was out in the yard, stuck in the ground. I just pulled it out. Pop! I went and got some of that purple stuff—the degreaser from the auto place—and I put it all over there and I wiped it down. And I went to the car wash and got the heavy-duty hose and I just sprayed it down because I needed a horn."

When I ask Bennie about his earliest days as a musician, his stories dart back and forth between good times and tough times. He smiles as he recounts how his mother saved up enough money to buy him the biggest drumsticks she could find so they wouldn't break when he tapped out rhythms on the sidewalk. He gets all worked up when he remembers opening up a textbook he was assigned in school and finding his uncle's name written on the inside cover. "How could they be teaching us from this old book?" he asks, exasperated. At Alcee Fortier High School, some of Bennie's classmates had given up on education and were busy selling drugs. They teased Bennie for wearing worn-out sneakers and for paying attention in class. "People be telling you, 'What you going to go to school for? . . . Get real man.'" It didn't occur to Bennie that being a musician was a potential occupation until a neighbor asked him to play a jazz funeral. "I made twenty dollars. I was so happy."

After graduation from Fortier in 1994, Bennie and some friends from the school band formed the Loony Tunes Brass Band, which was renamed the Hot 8 under the leadership of snare drummer Derrick Tabb and trombonist Jerome Jones, and the name stuck when Derrick departed to join Rebirth and Bennie assumed leadership. The Hot 8 kept Bennie busy with funerals, second line parades, house parties, club dates, and hotel gigs, but the work was not profitable enough on its own. Part of becoming socialized as a brass band musician in New Orleans is learning to navigate the maze of lucrative opportunities and exploitative traps. Even the high-profile gigs, like playing a sold-out show with the Neville Brothers where promoters charged $50 a ticket, only netted the band $500, about $60 per musician. Another time was when Bennie got a call to play at the Superdome.

When the New Orleans Saints football franchise hosts a home game, they arrange for a brass band to parade through the upper balconies of the Superdome. Musicians are hired to fulfill a very specific role for the fans. In a phone interview in 2006, the entertainment director for the Saints explained to me that musicians are instructed to play the standard brass band repertoire for short periods during breaks in the action: "'Bourbon Street Parade,' you know 'South Rampart Street Parade,' things that are associated with New Orleans, things that people can clap their hands with and enjoy for the few seconds that it's played." Not a game passes without the band playing the Saints theme song, "When the Saints Go Marching In," which the administrator told me was chosen "because it was upbeat. It was symbolic of New Orleans." Like any other time a brass band musician is called upon to perform, at Saints games they provide a pleasurable, participatory, and distinctly New Orleans experience for their fans.

When a contractor for the Saints called Bennie to hire the Hot 8, the terms were as follows: the fee was $900, but the contractor himself, who was a musician, assumed the role of leader and charged $200, leaving $700 for the other six musicians to split, or $116 each for a four-hour game. While the rate of $29 per hour may seem reasonable, a friend who sells concessions at Saints games told me that he earns at least $200 per game, or $50 per hour. Musicians do not clock in a full work week, so the amount they receive for intermittent performances must cover the costs of preparation, practice, transportation, and meals. While there is no set pricing structure, rates typically start at $50 per musician, or $350 to $400 total, for a half-hour appearance and can reach $3,000 for a four-hour second line parade. So the Hot 8 could have earned two to three times the rate offered them by the Saints' contractor, but there were no parades booked for the Sunday of the Saints game, and this put Bennie in a predicament.

"[The contractor] got me a few gigs, but at the other hand he hurting me, man." An imaginary conversation ran through Bennie's head—"You done worked your way up to get into a position to hire people and do all this, and you raping us"—but he could not speak his mind without burning a bridge that may ultimately lead to opportunity. "The Hot 8 [wasn't] known yet.

[The Saints were] playing San Francisco, they playing Seattle, they playing all these people out of town. 'Maybe I can get some business cards to some of these people and get a gig out there . . .'

. . . I need the opportunity, so what I'm going to do? . . .

. . . 'All right, I'll take it' . . .

. . . And that's how they playing you."

Bennie's dilemma illustrates how trickle-down economics appears from the bottom up:

STEP 1: Industry (The Saints), in conjunction with the state (owner of the Superdome), determines that the presence of a brass band creates a greater sense of place and increases crowd participation.

STEP 2: A contract is negotiated with a third party, which delegates responsibility to a contractor, who takes advantage of his intermediate position in the value chain to "tax" freelancers.

STEP 3: The remainder, when divided up among the individual musicians, is incommensurate with the amount of labor called for, but this current reality must be balanced against the next step.

STEP 4: There exists, always, the possibility of future reward, offered by the "exposure" of performing for a large, relatively wealthy audience. Perhaps a new convert, seated in the luxury box seats, will cultivate the Hot 8's potential in a way that is mutually beneficial for all parties.

The activities in the Superdome, then, exemplify both the pitfalls and the payoffs for black workers who rely upon their performing bodies to earn a living. While the athletes on the field receive exorbitant sums for utilizing their bodies for sport, the musicians in the stands provide pleasurable music that is undervalued and overtaxed by institutional administrators. This scenario, with minor adjustments to fit the context, is a kind of master narrative of the political economy of New Orleans brass band music, if not black music generally.

"That's how they playing you . . .

. . . But what I'm going to do? . . .

. . . 'All right, I'll take it.'"

Despite being recognized as the leader of an up-and-coming brass band, a notch below the kingpins in Rebirth and the Dirty Dozen, Bennie needed a day job for steady income. In 2005, when the Hot 8 was recording their debut album, *Rock with the Hot 8*, Bennie was working with trombonist Jerome Jones at Loyola University, where they installed carpet. Snare drummer Dinerral Shavers worked in the shipyards along the Mississippi River. Trombonist Keith Anderson played music for tips in the French Quarter. Trumpeter Terrell Batiste squeaked by, living with his family in the Lafitte housing projects. This was how the members of the Hot 8 were living when Hurricane Katrina struck. Despite destroying their homes and forcing them from their hometown, the disaster gave the Hot 8 and other bands an opportunity to expand their audience and capitalize on the increased attention given to cultural icons in Katrina's wake.

Bennie evacuated after playing at a bar on Saturday night, but Dinerral, Terrell, trumpeter Al Huntley, and bass drummer Harry Cook had stayed behind. When the levees failed and the city filled with water, some were able to walk or swim to safety; others had to climb to their rooftops and wait for helicopters to rescue them. They communicated with each other via text messages and made arrangements to regroup in Baton Rouge a few days after the flood. Hot 8's manager Lee Arnold and the musicologist Baty Landis, who had formed the musicians' aid foundation Save Our Brass, arranged to borrow some instruments for the Hot 8. Bennie suggested that they drive over to the River Center, where evacuees from the storm were being sheltered. "So we went and there was a lot of people who come to our weekly gig and follow us all the time. So they crying and stuff. We happy. They happy to hear the music." There were also throngs of journalists there to capture the impromptu performance, and, for a moment, the images of suffering that barraged television viewers were interrupted by footage of men and women, young and old, euphorically dancing and singing to the sound of a brass band, "bringing a bit of home to those who don't have any," as CNN's reporter Rusty Dornin observed. The way Bennie remembers it:

> Here was a scene where they was showing the evacuees, and then they had the military walking with guns, they had these people looking for their loved ones and people crying, and all the sudden they had this band show up and everybody just dropped everything and they was jamming, shaking their legs, jumping up and down. And all the sudden these people who was evacuees, they turned into just like party people. They had done put all their worries and troubles behind.

The music provided local evacuees and global television audiences with evidence that, as Dornin ended her report, "the spirit of New Orleans lives on, one note at a time."[51] With the spotlight on New Orleans, media outlets and relief agencies, politicians and promoters found the brass band an expedient symbol of everything distinctive about New Orleans. Rebirth opened a benefit concert at Madison Square Garden by performing a jazz funeral through the aisles of the arena. For another benefit concert at Jazz at Lincoln Center, New Orleanian Wynton Marsalis composed a new song, "Ain't No," which was based on second line parade rhythms and featured a choreographed second line dance. And in his first presidential address after the flood, George W. Bush spoke to the nation from Jackson Square, concluding his speech with a metaphoric description of a New Orleans brass band performing in a jazz funeral:

> In this place, there's a custom for the funerals of jazz musicians. The funeral procession parades slowly through the streets, followed by a band playing a mournful dirge as it moves to the cemetery. Once the casket has been laid in place, the band breaks into a joyful "second line"—symbolizing the triumph of the spirit over death. Tonight the Gulf Coast is still coming through the dirge—yet we will live to see the second line.[52]

The president's closing remarks demonstrate the utility of culture in attracting television viewers or boosting dismal political ratings, and as the recovery progressed the president continued to find New Orleans music a bottomless resource. He invited jazz trumpeters Irvin Mayfield and Kermit Ruffins to perform at the White House, and he presented a National Endowment for the Arts Heritage Fellowship to the Tremé Brass Band and a National Medal of Arts to the Preservation Hall Jazz Band. On the first anniversary of Katrina, Bush was back in New Orleans, posing for photographs with the New Birth Brass Band in front of the Habitat for Humanity Musicians' Village.

The spotlight shone on the Hot 8 too, and Bennie's phone started ringing off the hook from promoters hoping to latch on to a piece of New Orleans. In New York, when Bennie learned that Spike Lee would be filming the Hot 8 for the documentary *When the Levees Broke*, he took his banged-up tuba to a repair shop and had it fixed. Eventually he came home, moved into an apartment in suburban Kenner, and shuffled the membership of his band in order to take advantage of increased opportunities on the road.

As I write, Bennie and the other members of the Hot 8 have achieved a degree of celebrity and financial stability. In spring of 2011 Lauryn Hill hired the Hot 8 as the opening act on her nationwide tour and then invited the band to be her horn section during her show. That same year the band was featured in the TV series *Treme*, which has had a positive impact, financially and otherwise, on the Hot 8 and many other local musicians. The home-grown identity of the Hot 8 has helped them earn international acclaim as purveyors of a funky hip-hop–brass-band sound that is quintessentially New Orleans. Bennie still hands out his cell phone number for weddings, parties, parades, and local nightclub gigs, but other inquiries are now fielded by a management company in the Northeast. Though their good fortunes could evaporate at any moment, the members of the Hot 8 currently can no longer be classified as the working poor. Their recent upward mobility speaks to the fluidity of class positions, demonstrating how people "cut across rigid class categories," as the anthropologist John L. Jackson found among blacks in Harlem.[53]

The livelihoods of brass band musicians run the gamut from working class to middle class, with most concentrated at the lower end of the spectrum, a pattern that describes the class structure of black New Orleans as a whole. What is so revealing about the experiences of musicians is that they stake their professions on a peculiar knowledge strength, based in a racial identity and a geographic location, that offers substantial reward to a few while offering many more only the chance to get by.

EPISODE 2.4: The Business of Culture

Whether playing in community-based parades or convention center lobbies, musicians operate in systems of exchange that offer little security. Economic mobility requires expert navigation of sprawling patron networks in order to secure economic capital commensurate with the cultural capital of the brass band tradition.

Three institutions are presented here in a scan of the sites, venues, and client relationships that brass band musicians engage with on a daily basis. The annual New Orleans Jazz & Heritage Festival has provided local musicians with the opportunity to present their music to tens of thousands of spectators, even as their fees amount to a fraction of those of the national acts performing alongside them. Back in the streets, community parades have their own economies, within which musicians negotiate with parading organizations for fair pay. The intensity of these intraracial and intracommunal debates complicates any attempt to cast the financial struggles of musicians in terms of dominant versus dominated or state and industry versus grassroots and community. This is made more evident in the final case study of Harrah's Casino, an economic giant that appears to provide adequate pay and acceptable working conditions to the brass band musicians who perform for gamblers each night. There is no formula for determining whether a transactional relationship will be executed fairly and profitably. Very often the needs of musicians are secondary to those of others, and they must assess each transaction and strategize to protect their welfare.

Every spring the New Orleans Jazz & Heritage Festival draws a quarter of a million visitors to New Orleans and creates an economic impact of over $300 million, more than Mardi Gras or any other annual event.[54] Produced and marketed by Festival Productions Incorporated (FPI), Jazz Fest takes place at the New Orleans Fair Grounds racetrack in the Gentilly neighborhood over the course of seven days, and its multiple stages feature the biggest names in jazz, blues, rock, and world music, paired with local music, cuisine, and crafts that fit under the umbrella of "heritage."

The city's first jazz festival was a small and, by all accounts, unsuccessful venture launched by the New Orleans Jazz Club (NOJC) in 1949; it took the intervention of political and economic leaders from outside the organization to realize its full economic potential. In the mid-1960s Harry England, president of Greater New Orleans Tourist and Convention, Olaf Lambert, general manager of the Royal Orleans Hotel, developer Lester Kabacoff, and hotel association president Seymour Weiss convinced Mayor Victor Schiro of the merits of a jazz festival.[55] In December 1964 Schiro invited NOJC members and other prominent businessmen to a meeting to discuss how a jazz festival "might achieve the importance of the Sugar Bowl in this historic city which is 'The Birthplace of Jazz'": "Based on the success of such events elsewhere, we truly believe that the annual Festival would produce a substantial profit."[56]

The International Jazz Festival was launched with a parade on June 27, 1965, featuring the most prominent brass band of the time, the Olympia. The festival, however, was not a financial success, in part because few other local artists were invited to participate. In 1968 the NOJC sought out civic and industry support to expand their festival, arranging for the Olympia to march into the city council chambers, where council president Maurice "Moon" Landrieu (future mayor and father of Mayor Mitch Landrieu and Senator Mary Landrieu) welcomed the interruption, announcing, "A jazz Festival in May will bring visitors to us in a season that now has no other special celebration to attract tourists."[57]

Ultimately the International Jazz Festival was replaced by the New Orleans Jazz & Heritage Festival, which, as the name indicates, placed more of a premium on local culture. Newport Jazz Festival's director George Wein was brought in to produce the festival, and Wein hired two Tulane students, Quint Davis and Alison Miner, to curate local talent. Jazz Fest kicked off in earnest in 1970 with a second line parade through the French Quarter, and the festival gradually became successful based on a winning formula of combining internationally popular artists with local music and cuisine. At any given moment, fest-goers must choose between brass band, traditional and modern jazz, gospel, blues, Cajun, and zydeco music, while savoring jambalaya, crawfish pies, po-boy sandwiches, or boudin sausage. In their article "Producing the Folk at the New Orleans Jazz & Heritage Festival," Helen Regis and Shana Walton write that the ideology of Jazz Fest "spring[s] from a desire to create authentic representations of beloved traditions."[58] From the standpoint of the spectator with enough resources to purchase entry, Jazz Fest is extraordinarily successful at curating representations of authentic culture and presenting them as beloved traditions.

When we attempt to experience the festival from the perspective of a local artist, however, the festival grounds appear as a space filled with contradiction. Onstage, musicians are given the opportunity to recruit a large, enthusiastic audience and respond by tapping their creative artistry. Meanwhile, offstage and behind the scenes, many local musicians feel that FPI takes them for granted, assesses them as interchangeable with other local acts, and treats them as incidental to the national and international stars who perform on the big stages, negotiate premium fees, and stay in luxury hotels offsite. "While Jazz Fest ideology and marketed authenticity remain rooted in folk reverence," write Regis and Walton, "festival practices often result in folk marginalization, as producers are enmeshed in the larger process of cultural commodification of music and arts in the global market-place."[59] Much like the rhetorical gap between the claims and the actions of the Louisiana Department of Culture, Recreation and Tourism, the institution of Jazz Fest finds local culture a plentiful, renewable, and profitable resource, but many originators of culture believe that the profits do not cycle back to them in a balanced way.

The 2006 festival was widely perceived as a triumphant act of recovery for a devastated city. Held only eight months after Katrina, the return of Jazz Fest at its scheduled time and in its regular venue was a sign of cultural and economic reconstitution. The *Times-Picayune* ran daily front-page headlines about the festival, and national news crews televised the crowds streaming through the gates. At a particularly powerful moment, when Bruce Springsteen finished performing "We Shall Overcome" and other folk songs with a resonant message for Katrina survivors, the festival director Quint Davis took the stage and summed up the collective outpouring of emotion: "Witness the healing power of music."

Local musicians, a large percentage of whom remained displaced from New Orleans, were also optimistic about the festival and grateful for the return of an event that represents the apex of their calendar each year. Virtually all musicians, even those who do not perform onsite, benefit from the large crowds who fill the clubs, bars, and restaurants after the festival closes at sundown. Staying in Houston, Dallas, or Atlanta during the last week of April and first week of May was not an option for New Orleans musicians. But with 80 percent of the city having suffered flood damage and the rebuilding process still in its infancy, finding a place to stay was a challenge. There was never any question that national and international artists, whose travel and housing costs are factored into their contracts, would be accommodated, but what about local artists, whose return to the city would be integral to the success of the first post-Katrina Jazz Fest?

This question was on Bennie Pete's mind when a music director for Jazz Fest contacted him. "Right after the storm he called me up and said, 'Could you do Jazz Fest?'" Bennie began to discuss the fee, but there was no room for negotiation. "He going to *tell* me what they going to pay me. 'The gig pay $1,700.' To do Jazz Fest!" This was the same fee as the year before, but Bennie relented. "I say, 'All right, but we going to need housing because we still displaced and none of us live in New Orleans.' Know what they told me? They said, 'Well, we can't get y'all housing and we understand if y'all can't make it this year.'" Bennie called other local bands, and everyone he spoke with had had the same experience. "No brass band musician, no other local musician gets any housing to perform, and they didn't get top dollar either. . . . [Meanwhile] they flying Rod Stewart in, Bruce Springsteen, and they limo-driving them to the stage, and here Jazz Fest supposed to have been started locally, just with the local talent."

The Hot 8 did overcome these obstacles: they returned to New Orleans, made the effort to find accommodations, and performed a powerful set. They also benefited indirectly by playing a series of lucrative gigs at night, where they were the focus of national media attention, and they released an album, *Live at the 2006 Jazz Fest*. Thus the band's financial gain was more than the small festival fee. The question, for Bennie and others, is whether the level of compensation, respect, and institutional support is adequate considering the representational power that brass bands and other local musics bestow on Jazz Fest.

This gap runs deep and wide for those who are contracted to parade through the festival grounds. Every day of the festival two Social Aid and Pleasure Clubs, dressed in full costume, parade with a brass band that is scheduled to perform onstage the same day. Club members and musicians sign contracts, are paid, and enter the site through the performers' entrance, and many relish their role in providing access to New Orleans culture. They are performers, yet, as Regis and Walton observe, "the festival structure also tells them implicitly that they are *second rate performers* in a festival that books national and international stars." Prior to parading, they gather in "parade central" unprotected from the sun, without changing rooms or refreshments. Though they are ambassadors of New Orleans-ness, club members are paid less than $50 each. "The festival gives them access to the world at the same time that it keeps them in their place."[60] This valuation of Social Aid and Pleasure Club members is equally applicable to the brass band musicians who follow the clubs through the Fair Grounds and other local artists who make Jazz Fest a singular event.

In 2007 discussion among brass band musicians was particularly animated because Rebirth's bandleader Philip Frazier was depicted in one of two official posters that the festival offers each year. The silk-screen print by a local artist, Terrance Osborne, is a faithful reproduction of a photograph of Philip playing his tuba, with the band's name spelled out in black tape on the round bell of the instrument. Alterations were made to make reference to the festival: "New Orleans Jazz & Heritage Festival" is written on the bell, and "Congo Square 2007" appears below the bell, replacing the logo for Conn, the instrument manufacturer.

Considering the added recognition the poster would bring to Rebirth, I was surprised when I spoke to Philip's brother Keith a few weeks before Jazz Fest and he told me that the band remained undecided about whether they were going to perform at the festival. Though Jazz Fest had invested much in this image—both because of the notoriety of the brass band (especially the tuba) and because the name Rebirth has taken on new meaning after Katrina—they had not increased their investment in Rebirth the band. Their fee was the same as the year before and lower than what they receive at any other major festival. Keith explained:

> We make more money at the Maple Leaf [bar] than we do at Jazz Fest. . . . Something is not right about that. You have all these outside acts coming in, like [rapper] Ludacris, they want to pay him like $75,000 for an hour show, whereas they pay Rebirth $3,000. . . . So when they sent us our contract we told them, "We can't go for it." And instead of them saying, "Okay, you guys don't want that, what is it that you want?" Or "Let us try to meet you halfway." They're like, "No, we can't pay you."
>
> We was like, "Why not? People coming to see New Orleans culture, not Ludacris. . . ."
>
> We was like, "We know who we are. Do you know who we are?"

Keith's question to Jazz Fest administrators who assess local talent differently than national talent—"Do you know who we are?"—has been voiced by musicians since the inaugural festival. In a document entitled "Budget Check Point Re: Talent for Jazz Fest '69" at the Hogan Jazz Archive, the fee for local musicians amounts to union scale or slightly more, while national acts were able to negotiate and receive exponentially higher fees. So while the entire Onward Brass Band received $475.20 for their onstage performance, Sarah Vaughan received a total of $7,500 for two appearances. Musicians sounded off about the pay discrepancy then and again in 1999, when a local rhythm and blues singer, Ernie K-Doe, refused to perform at the festival unless his fee was increased (and it was the following year).

This act of refusal, of withholding cultural capital as a tactic for increasing economic capital, was also successful for Rebirth in 2007. The band neglected to submit a signed contract, and when a music director of Jazz Fest called to inquire, he was informed that all contract negotiations would now be handled by Rebirth's booking agent in New York. The music director protested that he had always dealt directly with the band, but Rebirth persisted, and ultimately the call between the Jazz Fest office and Rebirth's agent took place and a higher fee was agreed upon. Rebirth performed as scheduled, and the crowd of about fifteen thousand, cheering on the band at the Congo Square stage, was unaware of the backstage maneuvering.

The protestations voiced by Rebirth, K-Doe, the Hot 8, and other local musicians relate to the problem of utility and scale: If local culture makes Jazz Fest unique, how should originators of these cultural practices be compensated? The artist-administrator relationship, like so many others, is characterized by ambivalence: local musicians recognize Jazz Fest's power of promotion, and FPI capitalizes on this power by offering artists the lowest fees they will accept. ("They going to *tell* me what they going to pay.") A few artists, in turn, have harnessed the power of local music in promoting Jazz Fest, forcing Jazz Fest to acknowledge "who they are."

The New Orleans Jazz & Heritage Festival has provided tangible benefits to performers above and beyond their festival fees. The Jazz & Heritage Foundation, which is a nonprofit entity separate from FPI, also provides for musicians' welfare in the form of community enrichment grants, a summer music school, a fund that aids Social Aid and Pleasure Clubs, and a community radio station, WWOZ-FM. Jazz Fest is an asset to local culture, just as local culture is an asset to Jazz Fest. It is nevertheless a social fact that many performers feel their relationship with festival organizers is inherently imbalanced.

The negotiations between culture workers and cultural enterprises evaluated throughout this chapter have demonstrated that these relationships are often lopsided and nearly always contested. But what about transactions and interactions between peers? What of the internal dynamics between brass band musicians and other, predominantly black and working-class New Orleanians who hire them for birthday parties, wedding receptions, jazz funerals, and second line parades? These are the bread-and-butter jobs that keep musicians such as Bennie Pete plugged in to sprawling social networks, and Bennie says that some of his most gratifying gigs are neighborhood parties where a collection is made for the band. After the Hot 8 plays in the house, the yard, or out on the street, the host might say, "'Here's y'all money for performing. That's my rent money. That's my light bill money. But I only [turn] fifty one time and I'm going to jam.' . . . They go to that extreme just to have a good time for their birthday or whatever the occasion may be."

After Katrina, with a reduced black population and a higher cost of living for those who returned, these more informal performances diminished noticeably. Local musicians had more opportunities to travel elsewhere, playing for larger audiences and higher fees, while they slipped into deeper struggles at home. This was the case for the Hot 8, as the band attempted to build a committed audience at home while rising in prominence elsewhere. Trombonist Jerome Jones said, "Financially, of course we struggling. . . . We struggling because brass bands get hired by its own people. And that is poor people. . . . And if the poor is more poor, our financial situation is [more] poor. . . . [They're] in a situation where they can't come to a club we at, or they can't hire us for a birthday party, and that's where our gigs come from."

Social Aid and Pleasure Clubs are a primary source of income for brass band musicians, who get hired not only for the annual parades but also for the dances, dinners, and other fund-raising functions the clubs hold throughout the year. "This culture here has always been held up by the people at the bottom," said Fred Johnson of the Black Men of Labor club:

> The people who make the least money are the people who keep the street culture alive, because in their day-to-day hustle and bustle, this is one of the ways they get to reward themselves. So they're making a small amount of money, they figure out how to make this money work to take care of their daily expenses, and they put a little bit aside so that, when it's time to parade, that's their enjoyment.

The club members, brass band musicians, and other participants in second line culture form an interdependent relationship based on mutual reciprocity. Their interactions are the basis of a surprisingly expansive cash economy that includes hairdressers and clothing designers who outfit club members, clothing shops that print individualized T-shirts for second liners, bar owners who host stops on the parade route, and vendors who sell food and beverages. Ideally beneficial to all, the second line economy is, like any formal or informal economy, not free from market competition, imbalanced transactions, and self-interested strategizing. Brass band musicians, who uniformly attest to the significance of parading traditions, are entangled in relationships that can become antagonistic when conversations turn to monetary exchange. "We want that part of the culture to go on, but we have to get paid properly," said Keith Frazier. "You're working four hours. That's the hardest work you're ever going to do in your life. We even tell them, 'We're not asking for the world, we just asking for a pay increase.'"

Brass bands are large bands. It takes eight to ten musicians to create a formidable sound and keep a parade moving for four hours. Parading organizations and other contractors sometimes ask bandleaders to reduce the size of their bands to lower costs, but this strategy can backfire when the ensemble's sound does not meet audience expectations. "I could go out there with six members just to try to make money," said Bennie Pete, "but I'll hurt myself because we need more instruments for the instrumentation to play certain songs. Plus if I just have one trumpet, one trombone, one sax, and one tuba, one snare, one bass, then nobody has any help."

Clubs with close social ties to top bands such as the Hot 8 and Rebirth make a concerted effort to pay them their full asking price, up to $3,000, but others offer as little as $850 and hire lesser-known bands if an agreement cannot be reached. These negotiations are complicated by the role of nonprofit organizations that make contributions to Social Aid and Pleasure Clubs to ensure that they are able to parade each year. The Norman Dixon, Sr. Fund, a branch of the Jazz & Heritage Foundation, pays a portion of the city permit fee for most parades, and Renew Our Music, the musicians' welfare foundation of Preservation Hall, paid a set amount to hire a brass band for several years after the flood. However, these payments are made directly to the police and parading organizations and are kept separate from negotiations between clubs and bands.

Driving around with Soul Rebels Brass Band leader Lumar LeBlanc one day in 2006, I asked why I had not seen the Soul Rebels perform in a second line parade. "We kind of retired from the streets years ago because it's not worth it," he told me. If a brass band is essential to a second line parade—"the life of the party," as Lumar puts it—why can't more clubs place a financial premium on their labor? "They say, 'Man, we got to get our hats, suits, nice shoes, feathers, and banners, and then we'll get the band last.' And I'll be like, 'But we're the most important part.' I don't care how good you look, if you don't have that band out there marching, people are not going to walk with you because that's just people walking with no music."

The Hot 8 has also spoken up about their contested relations with Social Aid and Pleasure Clubs, dedicating a track on their first album to "fake-ass clubs" who threaten to hire other bands for less money. In a spoken-word rap, trumpeter Al Huntley intones:

You pay more for your [out]fit than you pay the band
But the parade ain't shit without the Hot 8 man
Some of you fake-ass clubs saying we done bad
'Cause now we demand a couple more grand . . .
This is spiritual—we been doing this for ages
How the fuck you think my people made it through slavery?

Occasionally the shared challenges that musicians face will lead to conversations about creating a formal coalition of bands, a sort of union with a set pricing structure. The Hot 8's manager, Lee Arnold, made it a rule to never undercut another brass band's bid on a contract; in other words, when first contacted about a job, he asks if other bands have already submitted a bid, and if so, he will match it. "If Soul Rebels say $950, Hot 8's price will not go below that. Then it's just a choice: them or us." The problem, according to Lee, is that "someone breaks it and then it's all over." Another band agrees to a lower rate, and the potential for a united front remains unfulfilled.

We have, then, the ultimate example of the predicament of the New Orleans brass band musician, caught up not only in entanglements with the state, large institutions, and community organizations, but with fellow musicians. In the case of grassroots second line economies, musicians achieve a degree of recognition and admiration that they often find lacking in other performance contexts, but their pay can be a source of frustration. This is complicated by the income levels of those hiring them as well as the support of fellowship institutions. The contested nature of these interactions indicates how brass band musicians must evaluate every exchange to determine an appropriate strategy for survival, based on their immediate needs and the long-term ramifications of their decisions.

Trying to map out the playing field, or obstacle course, where musicians play is what brought me to Harrah's Casino, one of the largest employers in the city, located on the perimeter of the French Quarter. Harrah's employs dozens of musicians to perform in its restaurants, bars, theaters, and hotel as part of an effort to entertain customers and keep them on the premises and gambling. On the casino floor, amid the beeps and clangs of the slot machines, the clicking of the roulette wheel, and the applause of the crowds gathered around the blackjack table, gamblers also hear the sound of a traditional New Orleans brass band parading by. It is not an uncommon sight to see people leave their seats and strut behind the band, accompanied by parade marshals with their sashes and umbrellas and even a token Mardi Gras Indian tapping a tambourine.

The decision to stage a second line parade six nights a week was made after Katrina, when casino officials determined that representations of local culture suited a shift in their clientele. Casino revenue had remained about equal to pre-storm numbers, but the average gambler was now more likely to be a local, flush with money from insurance payouts or government assistance, than a tourist out for a night on the town. This, combined with the fact that Harrah's new entertainment coordinator was a native New Orleanian, led to the decision to curate a parade as a form of nightly entertainment.

On the evening of October 22, 2006, I enter Harrah's with a sense of trepidation, partly because casinos make me uneasy and partly because, as a card-carrying anthropologist, the casino environment represents the farthest reaches from what I imagine to be the authentic and the real. If all parade exhibitions, on some level, are a minstrelization of community-based parades, then witnessing a cherished tradition performed within a space set aside solely for monetary exchange can only conjure images of slave auctions and slumlords in my mind.

"They want to pimp you and prostitute you," Harrah's bandleader and clarinetist Joseph Torregano tells me during a break at Starbucks. His words echo through my head for the rest of the night, as I follow the band around the casino floor. But Joseph was not referring to Harrah's. He was talking about the high school band he directs, and the small fees they receive to play functions such as Mardi Gras parades and balls. About Harrah's, Joseph can only gush: a regular job, four nights a week, with limited hours, long breaks between sets, and a reasonable fee of approximately $200 per night per musician. "We're fortunate in this job here," he says. "You'd be surprised at how many people are trying to get in this band or keep saying, 'Look, if y'all have openings give me a call.'"

2.4 *The Leader (Michael White).* 2004. 41″ × 60″. © WILLIE BIRCH.

I look around. There is Jeffrey Hills, the first-call tuba player for the Tremé and New Birth brass bands. Shamarr Allen, formerly of Rebirth and Hot 8, is on trumpet, and so is Kenneth Terry of Tremé and New Birth. The parade marshals are Wardell Carter and Wayne Gaspard, regulars on the parade and funeral circuit. Monk Boudreaux, the renowned Mardi Gras Indian chief of the Golden Eagles tribe, wears a modest Indian suit. Then there is Joseph, veteran music teacher and one of the few remaining clarinetists schooled in the brass band tradition.

Does the performance environment for this all-star cast reward creativity? Not likely. Is this the career these musicians aspired to when they began performing? Again, probably not. But in comparative terms, the musicians at Harrah's are recognized for their creative labor and compensated accordingly. Seen in the most positive light, the Harrah's example is diametrically opposed to the example of a low-paying second line parade: the performances at the casino are not creatively challenging or community-oriented, but they are also not physically grueling or financially insubstantial. This, of course, does not begin to compensate for other employee practices that Harrah's maintains in New Orleans; unlike their Las Vegas location, for instance, casino workers in New Orleans do not belong to a union and have no collective bargaining rights.[61] Yet in a capitalist reality, good capital, profitable capital, can aid workers and offer them tangible rewards. It can even enable musicians to perform within their communities for lower fees. Here, in the space where currency buys currency, the "purest" form of capitalism, musicians have found a way to earn their share of capital.

New Orleans brass band musicians navigate social networks, enter into spheres of capital, and cross societal boundaries with relative ease as they attempt to earn a living. Their social location is more flexible than that of many other service workers in New Orleans, but they face the same obstacles to capital accumulation. They seek out opportunities for financial reciprocity and stability such as the Harrah's Casino job, but they question whether the money that trickles down to them is commensurate with the money generated by their very presence, and market competition causes friction, even in negotiations with peers.

The example of second line economies complicates any assumption that exploitation can be equated solely with racial difference, or that black music is inherently an expression of resistance to disenfranchisement by white "colonizers" or the "mainstream."[62] In terms of local infrastructure, for example, a powerful black middle class is a commanding presence in city government offices that an independent advisor assessed as "the most corrupt . . . [he had] ever seen in this country."[63] This racial reality, along with the knowledge that select black musicians have profited greatly by perpetuating brass band music, offer evidence that the pursuit of capital is universal even as it often accumulates in pools of white privilege. In the following chapter, friction among black New Orleanians is pursued in more depth in regard not to economics but to musical practices. The prestige attributed to the brass band has raised the stakes for musicians, but there is disagreement over how tradition should be carried forward.

CHAPTER 3

PROGRESSIONS

EPISODE 3.1: You Don't Want to Go to War

When I returned to New Orleans about a year after Hurricane Katrina, the brass band scene was in a state of relative disarray and a new band was picking up the lower-profile gigs that Rebirth, the Hot 8, and other, more established bands could not take. The appropriately named Free Agents started cropping up at parades, funerals, house parties, and anywhere else their bandleader and bass drummer Ellis Joseph could get them booked. At the outset, they were a roving band of trollers fishing for scraps, but their persistence gradually earned them recognition, solidified by the success of a song that managed to distill the experiences of local audiences in a precise time and place known as "post-Katrina New Orleans."[1]

"Made It through That Water" is a composition that, in many ways, fits snugly into the standard repertoire of the New Orleans brass band. Its rhythmic continuity, collective improvisation, textural density, and group singing are all musical characteristics that have defined the brass band tradition since the emergence of jazz. And then, in other ways, the song represents a break in its musical, thematic, aesthetic, and contextual alliances with hip-hop.[2]

"Made It through That Water" begins with a compact phrase, or "riff," on the tuba that then repeats throughout the entire song, in

3.1 *Second Line Parade (Females in White)*. 2004. 69³⁄₄″ × 60¹⁄₄″. © WILLIE BIRCH.

the pattern of funk bass lines that were then sampled, sequenced, or imitated in hip-hop. After group chants and instrumental melodies that draw upon the spiritual "Wade in the Water," we hear another striking extension of tradition: a solo vocalist rapping over the drums and horns:

> *Please Mr. Officer, don't shoot*
> *'Cause I ain't in a rage, I was stuck up on that roof*
> *They trying to make an excuse but they running from the truth*
> *We know they blew them levees, man, but we ain't got no proof*
>
> *Whatever they do I can't turn my back*
> *I was born right here, so right here's where I'm at*
> *Send them troops home, little daddy's in Iraq*
> *And tell FEMA we going to need more than ten stacks*

Solo singing in brass band music dates back only a single generation, and it was not until the 1990s that rapping was introduced to the tradition. The lyrics to "Made It through That Water" and other new-school standards depict experiences more explicitly and articulate perspectives more subjectively than do the universalist texts of spirituals and palatable themes of popular standards (such as "Bourbon Street Parade" or "I Ate Up the Apple Tree") that made up the stock repertoire until the 1980s. Tradition has been mobilized in a reciprocal dialogue with new generations of listeners who engage with brass band music not only in street parades but also in spaces where musicians and audiences are relatively stationary.

Soon after returning to New Orleans, late on a Sunday night in fall 2006, I drive along A. P. Tureaud Avenue in the Seventh Ward neighborhood, past the shotgun houses still caked in dirt left by Katrina's floodwaters to the Duck Off Lounge, where the barren cityscape is disrupted by a cluster of parked cars and a line of people waiting to enter. After being frisked by security guards and passing though a freshly painted corridor with signs that warn "No Drugs Inside—Strictly Enforced" and "No One Under 21 Allowed," I arrive in a long rectangular room filled to capacity, the air thick with smoke. The clientele is entirely young and black, dressed in their nightclub finest, drinking and dancing to the latest hip-hop hits spun by DJ Money Fresh. I watch as a young man carrying a trombone case makes his way through the crowd and stations himself in front of the deejay booth. By 1:00 a.m. an entire band has gathered against the mirrored wall, none of the musicians over the age of thirty.

"Free Agents in the building every fucking Sunday," announces Money Fresh. "Free Agents in the building, you heard me?"

With that handoff, the processed hip-hop recordings give way to a centuries-old acoustic ensemble. Yet the Free Agents repurpose the horns and the drums by making the music played on them compatible with a young audience dancing to hip-hop, like breathing new life into an old, washed-out building brought back from the edge of collapse. Riff tunes, played fast, loud, and aggressively, are augmented by vocals articulating themes straight out of the hip-hop handbook, such as representing place ("You know, and I know, there ain't no city like the N.O.!") and graphic descriptions of sex ("Pop goes the pussy, make the pussy go pop!"). The Free Agents mobilize the brass band tradition in a hip-hop way.

Separating the band from the crowd is a row of three guards wearing navy blue shirts that read "Duck Off—Security" in yellow letters. They stand imposingly with their arms crossed, the slides of the trombones darting over their heads. Some members of the crowd continue to dance, making minor adjustments to their steps, while others continue to socialize without attending to the change in the music. Distinctions between musical genres and performance contexts are blurred to the point where someone unfamiliar with the brass band tradition would have trouble identifying the Free Agents as a group of tradition-bearers. And yet what strikes me the most about the musical and spatial recontextualization—the interruption of a seamless mix of hip-hop records by young men playing live music on comparatively ancient instruments—is how thoroughly routine it is to everyone around me. At the Duck Off, the sounds and the sentiments heard on Money Fresh's records are congruent with that of the Free Agents Brass Band.

The night's culminating song, "Made It through That Water," condenses the contemporary state of New Orleans brass band music into a compact tour de force, a lesson in music, history, and ethnographic experience. Collective improvisations, polyrhythmic grooves, and call-and-response chants based on a spiritual believed to provide escaping slaves with instructions to avoid capture are remixed by and for new generations of black Americans troubled by new waters. No one bats an eye when the live music ends to a smattering of applause, DJ Money Fresh resumes his hip-hop mix, and the Free Agents make their way to the door with their instruments high in the air so as not to disrupt the tightly packed crowd.

"Made It through That Water" is an abundantly clear example of musicians retrofitting brass band music to resonate with contemporary audiences, but the other material played by the Free Agents at the Duck Off is equally revealing. Two songs, "Rockin' on Your Stinkin' Ass" and "Pop That Pussy," were borrowed from Rebirth's 2001 record *Hot Venom*, which arrived during a transitional period for the band, when the recent additions Glen Andrews, Tyrus Chapman, and Derrick Tabb energized Rebirth's sound. Hip-hop permeates all of *Hot Venom*, in the raunchy lyrics of "Casanova," the self-righteous individualism of "Let Me Do My Thing," and especially on the track "You Don't Want to Go to War," which features Soulja Slim rapping over Rebirth's horns and drums. Slim was one of the first New Orleanians associated with gangsta rap, with its stark depictions of poverty, violence, misogyny, drugs, and the pursuit of money.[3] Slim's battles with drug addiction led to multiple incarcerations, and he cultivated the contemporary gangsta persona of the "soulja" from the start of his short career, appearing in 1998 on the cover of his first album, *Give It 2 Em Raw*, wearing military fatigues and gold caps on his teeth. The lyrics to "You Don't Want to Go to War" epitomize the moment when confrontational boasts and unflinching threats of violence became the stock-in-trade of the hip-hop emcee.

After the horns play a series of melodies and solos, the track pares down to the marching drums and a menacing tuba riff, clearing the way for Slim to juxtapose images of militarism and dancing, weapons and instruments: "Y'all don't want to go to war, we got heat / Sounds off like horns, make you move your feet." He then warns his neighbors to keep violence away from the parades that make stops at the bars near the Magnolia housing projects: "Catch them round Kemp's, bring them round Mo's Tavern / The Rebirth is my people, you don't know what's happening." The song ends by celebrating music and dance as an antidote to violence: "We don't want to see nobody get hurt today / All we really want to see is footwork today." Slim's (mixed) messages capture the tension between intraracial brotherhood and violence: you don't want to go to war because we don't want to see anybody get hurt today, and you don't want to go to war because we got heat.

Embedded in several decades of recordings (such as Rebirth's *Hot Venom*) and live performances (such as the Free Agents' appearance at the Duck Off) is a history of contemporary hip-hop's integration into a centuries-old tradition. For the vast majority of brass band musicians who entered the tradition after the efflorescence of hip-hop, classified as members of the "hip-hop generation," tradition must be flexible in order to remain relevant to them. My interactions with Derrick Tabb are instructive here. Derrick's recordings with Rebirth can be heard daily on community radio station WWOZ-FM ("New Orleans's Jazz and Heritage Station"), yet every time Derrick gives me a ride in his pickup, the radio dial is set to Q93-FM ("Your Hip-Hop and R&B Station"). Derrick is a tradition-bearer, a performer of music that stretches back over a century, and he is conversant in traditional brass band music and all the other forms heard on WWOZ (old-school rhythm and blues, jazz, and funk). He also learned to compose with drum machines and keyboards, and with Rebirth he plays hip-hop beats on his snare drum and collaborates with local rappers like Soulja Slim and Cheeky Black. Hip-hop and brass band do not occupy separate domains of his life.

This sense of inclusiveness, however, is not shared by all. There are musicians and others invested in local culture who believe that the dialogue between hip-hop and local musical forms is eroding established performance practices and misrepresenting tradition. In 2003, for example, DJ Davis Rogan was fired from WWOZ for what the station referred to as "tardiness, erratic and sometimes disruptive behavior and *non-adherence to the music that should be played on the New Orleans Music Show.*" Rogan received his dismissal letter one week after he played a song by local rappers UNLV on his weekly program, *New Orleans Music Show*. The station's program director defended the decision in the local newspaper *Gambit*: "Rap is not part of the format. . . . That's not 'oz. . . . There are some avid listeners, and whenever we've played rap, they call and say, 'That's not why we're tuning into 'oz, and that's not why we support WWOZ.'"[4]

The dismissal underscores the intensity of debates about hip-hop's relation to New Orleans music, which was referenced in the *Treme* television program with a fictionalized version of Davis playing a starring role. WWOZ's slogans—"New Orleans's Jazz and Heritage Station" and "Guardians of the Groove"—suggest that certain heritage grooves should be guarded against other grooves that may contaminate or eradicate them. However, the mission statement on WWOZ's website is more expansive and inclusive: "WWOZ broadcasts all of the forms of music that have developed, and are developing in the confluence of African, Latin, European, and American culture that makes New Orleans one of the most unique cities in the United

States."[5] Certainly hip-hop, rap, and contemporary R&B have developed in the confluence of African, Latin, European, and American culture, so what is it about these forms that necessitates their exclusion from the domain of tradition and heritage?

Tradition is a site of contestation and debate as to which practices are deemed traditional or regarded as a threat to tradition and according to whom. In the constellation of New Orleans music, broadly synonymous with black American music harkening back to slave dances in Congo Square, debates about tradition reach peak intensity over the contemporary practices of brass bands, particularly in the second line parades and jazz funerals that were integral to the emergence of what is now called *traditional* jazz, reenacted in such venues as *Preservation* Hall. An ongoing dialogue with hip-hop has reconfigured the musical, thematic, aesthetic, and contextual parameters of the brass band, redirecting the ways processions are mobilized on the street and inciting a backlash from musicians and others, especially older black New Orleanians who have been classified as members of the civil rights generation.

Clarinetist and scholar Dr. Michael White has written extensively on tradition in New Orleans brass band and jazz music and has recorded numerous albums that demonstrate his fluency with tradition. In his essay "The New Orleans Brass Band: A Cultural Tradition," he writes in the past tense and refers specifically to the period 1900 to 1978 when discussing these traditions as "truly a unique and exciting spectacle." After this time, the funeral changed irreparably, leading White to lament, "The once reverent and respectful jazz funeral has become a pale shadow of its original character."[6]

As an example of how the "alternative lifestyles of younger generations" are partially to blame for "increasing signs of decline" in brass band music, White interprets the lyrics of Rebirth's most popular song, "Do Whatcha Wanna," as "sum[ming] up the philosophy and spirit of a new generation: 'Do whatcha wanna, hang on the corner.'"[7] By way of contrast, White's Liberty Brass Band adheres to traditional dress, and his original compositions extend tradition while retaining the self-discipline and restraint that characterized traditional New Orleans jazz. The title track to his 2004 album *Dancing in the Sky*, for example, is a spiritual written in the style of the Baptist church parades White once played on Sunday mornings: "I could never forget the beauty and dignity of those events and the graceful strut and conviction on the faces of the marching club members."[8] While "Do Whatcha

Wanna" is a fast-paced riff tune, "Dancing in the Sky" moves through a familiar series of chord changes at a gentle strut, with lyrics that link the local jazz funeral tradition to the wider tradition of Negro spirituals via an uplifting redemption narrative about an "eternal second line." Like "Do Whatcha Wanna," "Dancing in the Sky" inventively adds to the stock repertoire, but in a way that extends a legacy of respectability and perseverance that culminated in the civil rights movement rather than calling its current suitability into question.

Consider, then, the differing proximity of White and the members of Rebirth to the experiences of Soulja Slim. In the 2004 documentary *Straight from the Projects: Rappers That Live the Lyrics*, Slim joins fellow rapper C-Murder on a tour of the Magnolia housing projects where Slim was raised by his mother, Linda Porter Tapp. We see them swaggering through the project grounds, greeted like the celebrities they are, until the camera freezes and zooms in on a young man carrying a gun or smoking a blunt, at which point the graphic "RIP" appears on the screen above a name ("Porch Boy Joe," "Doe Doe Tough Guy") and then the words "was killed by gunfire." These shots are interspersed with extended clips from C-Murder's and Slim's videos, such as their collaboration "I Don't Give a What," in which the duo play factory workers who ultimately enact revenge on a crooked boss typecast as an overweight cigar-toting white man.

After filming in 2003, C-Murder was arrested for the murder of a sixteen-year-old fan in a nightclub shootout, and Soulja Slim was shot and killed on the front lawn of the house he had purchased for his mother. Linda shares the house with her boyfriend, Philip Frazier, whom she called upon to lead a raucous jazz funeral that included "You Don't Want to Go to War" and some of Slim's own rap songs arranged for brass band. Linda is also the president of the Lady Buckjumpers Social Aid and Pleasure Club, which parades by the Magnolia every year to the contemporary stylings of Rebirth, playing riff tunes at a fast pace, singing songs that resonate with the experiences of the hip-hop generation, and wearing sneakers, baggy jeans, oversized T-shirts, and baseball caps.

The jazz funeral for Soulja Slim and the second line parades organized by his mother exemplify what traditionalists assess as increasing signs of decline. Yet just as *Straight from the Projects* and "You Don't Want to Go to War" extol what gangsta rappers of the period called the "thug life," they also document a historical moment distinct from the era of civil rights that preceded it. For example, the Calliope housing projects where C-Murder came up with his brothers Master P and Silkk the Shocker is remembered by previous generations as a secure, orderly environment. Art Neville, who grew up there with his own musical brothers in the 1940s and 1950s, says, "Today the Calliope housing projects look like a concentration camp, but back then, when the Neville family moved in, we looked at it like better living. . . . I mean, that shit was clean."[9] Decades later, social welfare programs were drastically downsized, leaving housing projects neglected, and a governmental "War on Drugs" targeting the urban poor led to a fivefold increase in incarceration rates for black Americans.[10] Despite the legal gains of the civil rights movement, racialized social control has not diminished but was retrofitted into what the legal scholar Michele Alexander terms the "new Jim Crow," a "caste system" that is no longer sanctioned by law but instead "lurks invisibly within the maze of rationalizations we have developed for persistent racial inequality."[11]

In the canonical works of hip-hop studies, such as Tricia Rose's *Black Noise* and Jeff Chang's *Can't Stop, Won't Stop*, hip-hop is recognized as the central site where these changes were chronicled and the spectrum of responses to them enumerated. In that sense, White's definition of jazz at its emergence near the start of the twentieth century as "a new style that synthesized several musical influences and expressed in music the spirit and emotion of the collective black . . . experience" is compatible with Rose's claim that "life on the margins of postindustrial urban America is inscribed in hip-hop style, sound, lyrics, and thematics."[12] This argument can be made in both cultural terms, with hip-hop as the most recent configuration of what Amiri Baraka famously called the "changing same" of black music, and social terms, as with Todd Boyd's claim in *The New H.N.I.C.: The Death of Civil Rights and the Reign of Hip Hop* that "hip-hop is the place where much of this generational anxiety is being worked out."[13]

Significantly, White recognizes that tradition has also been a productive site for negotiating change in New Orleans. "Jazz," he writes, "has always mirrored contemporary reality," and musical changes can be attributed to social transformations in the public sphere:

> Many of the cultural trends and problems that characterize contemporary urban life in America have affected brass bands. The fast-paced transitory nature of today's world, and an endless number of instantly gratifying options in the "age of the self," are hardly conducive to the team

mindset, self-discipline, and artistic sensibilities necessary for collectively improvised creation essential to playing traditional New Orleans jazz.[14]

Though White understands tradition as flexible and accommodating, he remains distraught over changes that he assesses as detrimental, a view that he shares with many others of his generation. Episode 3.3 profiles members of the Black Men of Labor Social Aid and Pleasure Club, an explicitly traditionalist organization committed to retaining certain ways of dancing, marching, and playing brass band music at parades and funerals. I then present a contrasting case study of the city's most innovative outfit in extending the dialogue between brass band and hip-hop, the Soul Rebels Brass Band. While only a few years separate the founders of these institutions, they coincide with shifting social, political, and racial configurations in the post–civil rights period, including the emergence of an uproariously divisive cultural form, hip-hop.

I am not suggesting that there is a fixed generation gap, with hip-hop as a stable line of demarcation; as I discuss in the following episode, the founders of the Dirty Dozen, who are all technically members of the civil rights generation, experimented with tradition more than any other group in the 1970s and 1980s. One of the founders, drummer Benny Jones, later helped to form two explicitly traditionalist groups, the Tremé Brass Band and the Black Men of Labor. There are also younger progressives, such as Philip Frazier and other members of Rebirth, who are recruited to play traditional music in Black Men of Labor's annual parade. And musical categories are just as porous as the generational categories they are linked to; brass band music classified as traditional has nevertheless gone through an endless process of revision through dialogue with jazz, rhythm and blues, soul, and funk, while the genre of hip-hop subsumes everything from political rap to party rap, gangsta to grassroots, Compton to cookie-cutter suburbs.

Rather than a case of a uniform musical style reinforcing a given generational identity, in the brass band tradition musicians have selectively and subjectively drawn upon a repertoire of musical, thematic, and aesthetic practices to align tradition with their experience. The internal dynamics in this collective of musicians give us a sense of the heterogeneity contained within categories. They also tell us something about how music is central to the politics of representing race in New Orleans at the beginning of the twenty-first century.

EPISODE 3.2: A Renaissance

Danny Barker came up through the tradition in the first decades of the twentieth century, indoctrinated into brass bands and jazz through his grandfather Isidore Barbarin, leader of the Onward Brass Band. Barker was a cosmopolitan musician, a traveler who was based in New York for much of his life and played in the swing bands of Cab Calloway, Lucky Millinder, and Benny Carter. Beyond his performance career, Barker was a researcher and author, conducting oral histories of his bandmates, studying the history of jazz, and publishing books and essays about New Orleans music.[15] After moving back to New Orleans in 1965, he continued performing and researching New Orleans music. He could be found playing in the French Quarter, sipping a beer at the Caldonia Club, or conducting tours at the New Orleans Jazz Museum, where he assumed the position of assistant curator in 1972.

During this time, Barker also single-handedly changed the course of local music by founding the Fairview Baptist Church Christian Marching Band, with teenagers who were taught to perform music and present themselves as traditionalists. Repertoire, performance practices, and dress were intended to replicate the brass bands Barker remembered from his youth. By providing a training ground for musicians, the Fairview band, and the later Hurricane Brass Band, sparked a revival that has been called a "brass band renaissance." The musicians who launched professional careers out of the Fairview band have followed two divergent, though not unrelated paths: those who were intent on sustaining traditional practices and those who were keen on pushing the boundaries of the brass band format.

The first path was laid down by traditionalists who carried the torch for Barker, including clarinetists Michael White and Joseph Torregano, trumpeter Gregg Stafford, and drummer Benny Jones. In addition to playing traditional jazz, these musicians maintain the Liberty Brass Band (led by White) and Young Tuxedo Brass Band (led by Gregg), which perform at venues such as Preservation Hall and Jazz Fest. Their views on tradition are discussed in the following episode through the activities of the Black Men of Labor Social Aid and Pleasure Club.

The other path is identifiable by the spirit of experimentalism that has guided the brass band renaissance since the late 1970s and early 1980s and is universally attributed to one group, the Dirty Dozen Brass Band. Like

Michael White, Gregg Stafford, and other traditionalists, several founding members of the Dirty Dozen—Gregory Davis, Charles Joseph, Kirk Joseph, and Kevin Harris—got their start in Danny Barker's Fairview and Hurricane bands in the early 1970s. But though they were schooled in traditional brass band music, after joining forces with Roger Lewis, Ephram Townes, Benny Jones, and others in 1977, the Dozen came to represent a break with tradition. Gregg says, "Somewhere around the early 1980s, when the new music came onto the street, new ways of dancing came onto the street, new approaches to second lining, and what should be done in terms of what you wear and what you're supposed to wear, if you were a brass band. All those traditions have been broken."

In terms of strictly musical practices, the Dirty Dozen modified rhythms, tempos, structural forms, and other characteristics by integrating contemporary styles of black popular music—especially funk, rhythm and blues, and modern jazz—into the brass band. The Dozen wrote new compositions that featured more singing and covered a wider thematic range than the spirituals and popular songs of previous generations. As far as visual aesthetics, the Dozen gave up traditional uniforms and dressed in everyday clothes in all performance settings, including funerals and parades. And they followed in the footsteps of the Olympia by expanding the venues for brass band performance to include neighborhood barrooms, concert halls, and international festivals.

Many of the Dirty Dozen's transformations of tradition are detectable on their debut recording, a 45 rpm record released in 1981. One side features their signature composition, "My Feet Can't Fail Me Now," the title borrowed from a lyric in Funkadelic's "One Nation under a Groove" (1978). Like much funk music of the period, "Feet Can't Fail Me Now" is a riff tune that prominently features the rhythm section. As the musicologist Anne Danielsen has written of funk, the emphasis on linear song forms is displaced in favor of repetitive grooves, built up from one or two bar phrases that become the "basic units" of a song.[16] In "Feet Can't Fail Me Now" and other new-school brass band standards, the tuba plays a compact, virtuosic riff that repeats for the entire song. It was Kirk Joseph, along with Anthony "Tuba Fats" Lacen, who set this new standard of cyclical tuba melodies, supplanting the tuba's previous role of providing the harmonic foundation by outlining the changing chord progressions. The tempo of "Feet Can't Fail Me Now" is suitable for dancing at nightclubs but too fast for marching in a parade, an indication that the musicians were heading beyond the contexts associated with the brass band tradition and into intimate neighborhood bars such as Daryl's, downtown in the Seventh Ward neighborhood, and the Glass House, uptown in Central City. Ultimately the success of "Feet Can't Fail Me Now" and other innovative songs would catapult the Dozen onto concert stages far removed from the community contexts where the brass band was initially cultivated.

The Dozen's intentions in mobilizing the brass band tradition were evident on the follow-up 45, "Blackbird Special." While the tuba repeats a syncopated riff and the horns play a series of fast bebop phrases, we hear a whimsical conversation between a naïve listener and a hip musician:

> **NEW INITIATE:** Is this Dixieland? No. This is not Dixieland music. This is not the music I heard at Preservation Hall. What is it?
>
> **HIPSTER:** Well, it's a new version of Dixieland. It's a little bit more up to date.
>
> **NEW INITIATE:** What you mean a little bit more up to date?
>
> **HIPSTER:** It's funk. It's New Orleans funk. That's what it is. You like it?
>
> **NEW INITIATE:** I really like it. I really like it. It feels good.

The Dirty Dozen casts their funky innovations in opposition to traditional jazz, or Dixieland music, which even the uninitiated listener would recognize and associate with Preservation Hall. The new listener recognizes that the music is related to more familiar sounds but is disoriented by those musical elements that do not register as traditional. The mere presence of a spoken-word dialogue signals a change, as the conversation was overdubbed in the recording studio and would not have been audible in the context of a street procession. The use of solo voices to express an explicit message, which would become a defining feature of the brass band renaissance, had little precedent in the traditional repertoire, which is primarily instrumental with occasional refrains of group singing.

Touring Europe, Japan, and elsewhere, the Dirty Dozen caught the ears of modern jazz enthusiasts with their complex arrangements, inventive solos, and precise intonation, none of which was associated with traditional brass band performance. These changes laid the groundwork for the proliferation of New Orleans–style brass bands in faraway places, such as Mama Digdown in Madison, Wisconsin, Jack Brass Band in Minneapolis, Black Bottom in Osaka, Japan, and Opus 2 in Lille, France. In 1984 the

3.2 *Three Musicians for Tom Dent.* 2001. 52″ × 48½″. © WILLIE BIRCH.

Dirty Dozen released the first of many records on a national label. The first song on *My Feet Can't Fail Me Now* was "Blackbird Special," newly recorded *sans* vocal, which was no longer necessary. Proclaiming the newness of the sound to audiences would have been redundant because the evidence was everywhere else in the music.

In the late 1980s, when the Dozen were at their height of international recognition, they handed off their parade bookings and weekly gig at the Glass House Bar to their immediate successors in the Rebirth Brass Band. The Soul Rebels Brass Band formed soon after and gradually earned a reputation as the most progressive band among the ranks of the renaissance. Simultaneously another institution was founded, the Black Men of Labor, as a backlash against experimentations with tradition. This Social Aid and Pleasure Club, along with the musicians associated with their traditionalist reforms, operates in tension with the progressives, and their contrasting musical practices and ideologies have caused friction in the contemporary brass band scene.

EPISODE 3.3: Tradition on Parade

Within hours of Danny Barker's death at age eighty-five on March 13, 1994, his wife, Blue Lu Barker, notified friends and family that her husband did not want to be buried with a jazz funeral. "He had gotten to a point where he was so upset with what he had seen on the streets," trumpeter Gregg Stafford, one of Barker's disciples, explained to me in 2006. "Taking the coffin out of the hearse, raising it up in the air, pouring wine on top, beer on top." Though he respected Barker's wishes, it was inconceivable to Gregg that his musical mentor would not receive a jazz funeral. At a meeting at Barker's house, Gregg stood up and addressed Barker's family and others who had gathered to pay their respects:

> I said, "Look, Danny Barker came back to New Orleans and instilled in me and several other musicians . . . the importance of maintaining the brass band tradition. [He] told us how to play the songs, taught us what songs to play, and taught us about how to present ourselves. So, here is the man that was responsible for bridging the gap and perhaps saving the brass band tradition, and not giving him an honorable jazz funeral?" I said, "No, we got to do something."

The key to ensuring a "respectful funeral with dignity," said Gregg, was to assert control over every aspect of the music: "The music on the street dictates the mood and the atmosphere of *what goes on* in the street." The next to stand was Fred Johnson, a community organizer who offered to complement Gregg's musical offering with an appropriate visual display. "I said, 'Miss Lu, I will be responsible for bringing six to ten men who are dressed in funeral clothes to marshal the funeral.'"

By all accounts, Danny Barker's funeral was a stunning display of traditional music and culture. "It was probably the most powerfullest experience I had in terms of a brass band funeral because the music was just awesome," remembered Fred. The band Gregg assembled kept those in the second line moving slowly and somberly with dirge after dirge, while Fred and other members of the Tambourine and Fan marching club walked deliberately behind the hearse, gracefully clearing a path in the large crowd. The musicians and marchers maintained an orderly parade all the way to its exultant end.

Gregg's leadership role in the Barker funeral was a milestone in a successful career as a trumpeter, which began under Barker's tutelage in the

3.3 *Steppin'*. 2002. 81″ × 72″. © WILLIE BIRCH.

early 1970s and flourished in Michael White's Original Liberty band and his own Young Tuxedo band, allowing him to retire from his day job as an elementary school teacher. Gregg owns his own home in the Central City neighborhood, and when I visited him there in 2006 he made a point of showing me a photo album with pictures of Barker's funeral. Dozens of musicians were turned out in black suits with matching band caps and polished shoes, marching in closed formation in precise order. Gregg smiled as he turned the pages. "Look at that. That's the way a jazz funeral is supposed to look. This is dignity."

As the most iconic and sacred local tradition, the jazz funeral is at the center of debates over how tradition is furthered. Historically, slow dirges were performed all the way to the gravesite, and only after burial did the band begin playing up-tempo songs. "Now today, they don't even play dirges most of the time," observed Gregg. "As soon as they put the body in the hearse, they going up the street playing 'Glory, Glory, lay my burden down.' Up-tempo. All the way." Changes in repertoire and tempo have altered the transition from dirges to up-tempo music, the most essential and celebrated aspect of the funeral ritual. "It's all right if you throw a party together, or you decide everybody just want to have a jam session and march around the block and get down a minute, that's cool," Fred told me. "But if you're going to bury somebody, the African tradition is, you bury people with a richness of behavior and a richness all of what you can put into that." In Fred's estimation, that richness is impoverished by changes in musical repertoire, including the substitution of contemplative sacred songs with cheerful secular repertoire.

In addition to musical choices, the way musicians dress for a funeral has also caused friction. Joseph Torregano, who has balanced a career as a professional musician and a public school teacher for thirty-five years, remembered his mentor Percy Humphrey inspecting the younger musicians at funerals. "Percy would look at you over the top of his glasses and check you out: Was your shirt white and pressed? Were your shoes tied? Were your pants neatly creased?" Even when bands began wearing T-shirts to parades in the 1970s, they continued to dress in uniform for a jazz funeral. "Now people come any kind of way: short pants, T-shirts, sandals, tennis shoes," said Gregg. "That's not the tradition that I came through when musicians were respected. Musicians are respected today, but there was something about the integrity that they had for the music as well as for the way they appeared and presented themselves."

Dress is a critical signifier of identity and status, and for black Americans, presenting positive images has been one way of "collapsing status distinctions between themselves and their oppressors," writes the historian Robin Kelley. "Seeing oneself and others 'dressed up' was enormously important in terms of constructing a collective identity based on something other than wage work, presenting a public challenge to the dominant stereotypes of the black body, and reinforcing a sense of dignity that was perpetually being assaulted."[17] For Joseph and Gregg, a group of musicians turned out in their "black and whites," performing in public displays of black culture, is a celebratory form of self-representation that diminishes in significance when musicians wear everyday clothes.

Aesthetic alterations are most evident in contemporary jazz funerals that memorialize young men and women. Helen Regis described a jazz funeral for Darnell "D-Boy" Andrews, who died of a gunshot wound in 1995 at age seventeen. In the procession, a crowd of thousands cheered as D-Boy's father poured beer on his son's coffin, and the mother then danced on the coffin to the up-tempo music of the Rebirth Brass Band, all of whom were dressed in street clothes. As Helen observes, the traditionalists perceive funerals such as D-Boy's as a damaging caricature of a proud tradition: "The fundamental message promulgated by social and pleasure clubs—the respectability of blackness—is best illustrated in the funerals for those who lived to become upstanding elders in the community. D-Boy's funeral is produced in tension with those parades that commemorate lives of dignity and defiance."[18] This tension arises from conflicting ideologies, which have their basis in different musical, thematic, visual, and contextual approaches to local performance traditions.

The role of expressive culture in representing race has been a recurring theme in black studies, reaching critical mass in the writings of Henry Louis Gates Jr., Michele Wallace, bell hooks, and other black cultural critics in the 1980s and 1990s. Gates writes that intraracial disagreement over the "burden of representation," or the "responsibilities of the Negro artist," is "one of the oldest debates in the history of African American letters."[19] For those denied full participation in political, economic, and social spheres, culture becomes a powerful forum for the marginalized to "speak." Isaac Julien and Kobena Mercer pinpoint the dilemma as one of "representation as a practice of delegation": each cultural artifact or event is "burdened with an inordinate pressure to be 'representative,' and to act, as a delegate does, as a statement that 'speaks' for the black communities as a whole."[20] Once the power to represent is delegated to an artist, he or she is expected to present "positive images" of blackness, the logic being, as Wallace writes, that "the first job of Afro-American mass culture . . . should be to 'uplift the race,' or to salvage the denigrated image of blacks in the white American imagination."[21]

Because of the public nature of parading and the value placed on local culture, black musicians and club members are considered racial delegates, and some believe that this role carries specific responsibilities. After the success of Danny Barker's funeral, Gregg, Fred, and drummer Benny Jones decided to form their own Social Aid and Pleasure Club with the specific mission of perpetuating second line traditions in an orthodox manner. Fred told the others, "We need to put a parade together and put the kind of music on the street that *we* grew up in, that *we* accustomed to." The Black Men of Labor emerged over lunch the following Monday and the club took to the streets for the first time over Labor Day weekend in 1994.

After marching in the Black Men of Labor parade in 2006 and experiencing the power of a controlled yet exuberant procession, I was compelled to reach out to Fred and Gregg, initially for a radio segment I produced for the community station wwoz. In an interview at his office in the Central Business District, where he works as an outreach specialist with the Neighborhood Development Foundation, Fred spoke with great pride about his participation in local black cultural traditions, first as a "spy boy" in the Mardi Gras Indian tribe the Yellow Pocahontas, led by chief Alison "Tootie" Montana, and later as a founder of both the Tambourine and Fan marching club and Black Men of Labor.

Fred urged me to recognize the full spectrum of black musics and black identities and not, as he put it, "misread the uniform of this culture." He lamented that the shootings at second line parades "allowed business people, politicians, lawmakers" to "lump us all together . . . as a bunch of weed-smoking, Heineken-drinking, pistol-toting, shoot-'em-up bang-bang." With membership in Black Men of Labor restricted to working men, and with the founders having come of age in the immediate aftermath of the civil rights movement, the premise of the club is based on specific class and generational identities.

Todd Boyd has identified three principal "phases" of black identity since the civil rights era. The initial phase was dominated by "race men" and women who sought uplift through integration and assimilation. Bill Cosby exemplifies this figure in the way that he has countered negative stereotypes with celebratory representations of assimilated, upper-class black Americans. The "New Black Aesthetic" encompasses those who came of age after the gains of civil rights and see "individual power and access to the means of representation as significant goals."[22] In drawing upon the black nationalism of Malcolm X, Spike Lee has presented anti-assimilationist symbols of blackness in the movies *Do the Right Thing* and *Malcolm X*. Finally, Boyd suggests that the representative figures of the hip-hop generation are rappers such as 2Pac and Notorious B.I.G. who produced unflinching depictions of urban experience.

Boyd's categories, while reductive, are useful for situating intergenerational dialogues about music. Because of its prominence across all strata of the public sphere, black music has historically been called upon to represent black people. Cornel West writes, "Since black musicians play such an important role in African American life, they have a special mission and responsibility: to present beautiful music which both sustains and motivates black people and provides visions of what black people should aspire to."[23] Nominating black musicians as delegates and calling upon them to produce "beautiful music" — the sonic correlate to "positive images" — is indicative of a particular subject position, based as much on generation as on class and social status. As a black intellectual and spokesperson for the generation that organized and mobilized the civil rights movement, West valorizes the collaboration and virtuosity necessary for jazz and the unifying messages of spirituals and soul music for fostering a sense of black pride, while his generational counterparts in Black Men of Labor find all of these qualities and more in traditional brass band music.

The Black Men of Labor parade is distinct from those organized by other contemporary Social Aid and Pleasure Clubs because the music, dress, and dance are carefully monitored to adhere to an ideological program that stresses respectability. This program is outlined in a broadsheet titled "A Message to the Citizens of New Orleans," distributed at a press conference held in the moments before the club's first official parade after Katrina, on September 3, 2006. There had been two shootings at parades since the flood, and Fred, addressing a small group of reporters, wanted everyone to know that violence is antithetical to the values of parading and would not be tolerated. Fred and other Black Men of Labor members were prominently featured in Spike Lee's documentary film *When the Levees Broke*, and with the gaze of the media trained on the second line parade and ears attuned to the sound of the brass band, Fred stressed that spates of violence should not lead spectators to associate venerable traditions with "foolishness."

For Fred, violence is linked to the performance of contemporary brass band music, in which younger musicians channel the twenty-first-century sounds and aesthetics of hip-hop through the nineteenth-century ensemble of the brass band: "As a result of the wrong music getting played, then you have the wrong people showing up for the wrong music. That's my theory." Fred appealed to other organizations and musicians to cultivate traditional brass band performance:

> Some people like moderate music. Some people like not so moderate music. We ain't against nobody. Everybody do their thing. But our thing is, we want to do what makes New Orleans special. Everybody around the world knows that New Orleans is special [but] sometimes, most cases, it seems like we the only ones who don't know. . . . People come here looking for the music of Louis Armstrong, Buddy Bolden, and the Olympia Brass Band . . . because that is what made New Orleans famous.

Fred's argument hinges on an understanding of local black culture as exceptional ("what makes New Orleans special"), and this enhanced status makes brass band music a powerful representational medium ("people come here looking" for traditional music). But there are conflicting approaches to harnessing this power, particularly across generational lines ("our thing" versus those "who don't know") as they relate to musical genres ("moderate music" versus "not so moderate music"). Brass band and parading traditions are spaces for the articulation of black identity, and within these contexts music and dance can project positive or negative images of blackness.

The name of their organization also suggests that their parades represent a particularly *male* black subjectivity. Fred portrayed Black Men of Labor as "a group of men who work and do all the things that a man's supposed to do in terms of taking care of his responsibilities." The words he uses to describe traditional practices—dignity, beauty, respect, integrity—articulate a concern over music that may be antithetical to those values.

At the second line parade organized by Black Men of Labor, which kicks off the parade season each Labor Day weekend, those values are put on display in the street. Before a note is sounded, astute bystanders observe something unique about the parade: the musicians gathered on the sidewalk outside Sweet Lorraine's bar in the Seventh Ward neighborhood are wearing white band caps, white button-down shirts, black dress pants, and black lace-up shoes. While many of these musicians can be seen wearing uniforms at other events, especially parades staged for the tourist market, this is the only day of the year when musicians turn out in their black-and-whites for a community second line parade. Club members also differentiate themselves by their appearance; unlike the Sidewalk Steppers, Lady Buckjumpers, and other clubs that march in flashy tailored suits, Black Men of Labor has their outfits designed with West African cloth in distinctive color schemes and patterns.[24] The appearance of the members and the musicians underscores the deep roots of the second line parade as a black performance tradition.

Musical direction is delegated to Benny Jones, who typically organizes two bands, asking all of the musicians to sign a contract specifying uniform dress and musical repertoire. In deference to the Eureka, the Tuxedo, and other bands that stopped parading decades ago, the foundational repertoire of the Black Men of Labor parade is black spirituals and hymns. While sacred music is part of all contemporary second line parades, it is most frequently heard when the parade goes by the house of a member who recently passed away. At Black Men of Labor, on the other hand, second liners hear "What a Friend We Have in Jesus," "Over in Gloryland," and "Down by the Riverside" throughout the parade. The abundance of sacred music reinforces an unbroken lineage of black spirituality, from African religious ritual to distinctly black American forms of Christianity.

When the club members begin dancing single file out of Sweet Lorraine's, the band plays the spiritual "Lord, Lord, Lord." Heading down St. Claude Avenue and into the Tremé neighborhood, the repertoire becomes progressively more modern. We hear the 1950s popular standard "John Casimir's Whoopin' Blues," then Professor Longhair's 1953 rhythm and blues song "Mardi Gras in New Orleans." The repertoire re-creates that of the Fairview band in the late 1960s and early 1970s.

The musicians perform at slower tempos for Black Men of Labor than other parades. "Lil' Liza Jane," for instance, is played at the same tempo as the Hurricane Brass Band recorded it under Danny Barker's supervision in 1975. This is far slower than the Dirty Dozen played the song on their record *My Feet Can't Fail Me Now* in 1984 and is more conducive to the orderly marching and dancing that conforms to Black Men of Labor's ideological emphasis on respectability. Benny Jones had earlier explained to me, "We don't want to be running on the street. We want to take our time." His theories are put to action here as musicians perform at a leisurely tempo that constrains the movement of the first and second liners, actually shortening the overall distance they travel as compared to other parades. The bass drummers play sparse rhythmic patterns rather than the tresillo and other busy, propulsive beats that Keith Frazier developed with Rebirth. And unlike the Sidewalk Steppers parade (discussed in episode 1.3), the songs at the Black Men of Labor parade are not sequenced continuously but are broken up by pauses so the club members and musicians can moderate the pacing.

The members of the Black Men of Labor Social Aid and Pleasure Club, along with musicians such as White and Torregano, have retained aspects of brass band music and have used the public nature of parading to organize displays of black respectability. By contrast, younger musicians, even those already in their forties, grew up in the post–civil rights period as members of what has been called the hip-hop generation, and they have recalibrated tradition to articulate their own experiences and subject positions.

EPISODE 3.4: Music by Any Means Necessary

The Soul Rebels' 2005 record *Rebelution* begins with a military-style press roll on the snare drum and a slurred note from the tuba—*whirrrr!*—before abruptly shifting to a drum machine loop with synthesizer and electric guitar mixed in. "Don't be alarmed. The game has changed," raps bandleader and snare drummer Lumar LeBlanc. "We about making music by any means necessary."[25]

Like most brass bands, the Soul Rebels started out as a group of young men trying to find their place in a sturdy tradition. "We went on the streets and literally learned the music like a passed-down folk tale from the actual people," Lumar told me in 2006. "But once we learned it, Soul Rebels, we had to incorporate that other element." Since forming in the late 1980s, membership has fluctuated, but Lumar has kept the Soul Rebels at the vanguard, extending the dialogue between musical styles as far as possible without threatening their place in the brass band tradition. While all of Rebirth's songs can be performed on the parade route, the Soul Rebels arrange certain songs specifically to be reproduced on record and the concert stage, including instruments and rapping that would not be audible in the streets. For a time they even dropped the "brass band" moniker from their name. "Who says that [Lumar] has to play the snare drum or that there has to be a trombone on [every] tune?" trombonist Winston Turner asked in 2009. "Because at the end of the day, it's still music."

If the musicians discussed in the previous episode are the guardians who have worked the hardest to retain key characteristics of brass band music and parading, the Soul Rebels are the restless innovators who have done the most to revise traditional practices. *Tradition* and *progress* are the terms invoked to demarcate these positions; when Gregg Stafford says "The sacred things and the history of the music and the culture [have been] taken to *another level*," he is expressing concern over the changes brought to bear on tradition. These efforts to maintain traditional practices exemplify what the anthropologist Richard Bauman calls "inertial culture," or tradition "guided by precedent and convention and construed as replicating, in some essential sense, what has been done before."[26] By contrast, Lumar equates innovation with progress: "[Soul Rebels] hadn't started full-fledged with the funk. . . . We really hadn't *progressed* to playing in that style yet." The Soul Rebels endorse what the anthropologist Greg Urban calls "accelerative culture," "an attempt to overcome entropic forces of deceleration, an attempt to impart a positive accelerative force to culture."[27] All of the bands profiled in this book have modeled their experimentations on the Dirty Dozen, and it has been the Soul Rebels that have mobilized tradition furthest from the traditionalist ideal.

In the late 1980s, when the Dozen was at their height of international recognition, Lumar was surveying the local music scene and assessing where he might fit in. He had been a section leader in the famed St. Augustine High School marching band and earned a scholarship to Texas Southern University. After returning to New Orleans, he joined a group of young men also weighing career options as musicians. The Young Olympians served as a training ground for the Olympia Brass Band, mentored by trumpeter Milton Batiste, who arranged for them to perform in jazz funerals, second line parades, and other functions. Lumar recalls that, during rehearsals, the Young Olympians began augmenting traditional repertoire with contemporary music: "We might sneak in 'In the Storm' by Earth, Wind & Fire, [or] Rick James's 'Give It to Me Baby.' . . . We were trying to think of a way we could do it without disrespecting the tradition." Batiste, who himself had updated the Olympia's sound with rhythm and blues in the 1960s, was initially unfazed by the Young Olympians' explorations.

Tensions rose, however, in the early 1990s, when the Young Olympians began composing new material that owed a clear debt to funk, hip-hop, and rap. Especially problematic was the added emphasis on the rhythm section and the vocals. Lumar and bass drummer Derrick Moss were intent on reproducing the highly synchronized and unvarying rhythms of drum machines. Tuba player Damien Francois might repeat an ostinato figure without interruption for an entire song, constructing an arrangement around a single riff in the style of popular funk and hip-hop songs. When Lumar added the speech-like vocalizations of rap over these sounds, the cumulative changes drew the ire of their mentors in the Olympia.

The temporary solution involved a degree of schizophrenia. "Eventually, we felt like, if we want to do this full time with the funk, we going to have to be two different bands, and that's where the Soul Rebels mentality came through," said Lumar. "We were traditionally Young Olympia, and we were funk-, hip-hop–wise, Soul Rebels." Encouraged by the audience response at Soul Rebels performances, the group eventually ended their association with the Olympia band.

The Soul Rebels' debut album from 1994, *Let Your Mind Be Free*, was groundbreaking in part because the band was looking to hip-hop for thematic as well as musical direction. "Through the Eyes of a Vibe" channeled the contemporary sound of "D.A.I.S.Y. age" hip-hop associated with groups such as De La Soul and Tribe Called Quest. At points throughout, such as on the Caribbean-inflected "Culture in the Ghetto," trumpeter Tannon Williams affected the "accent" of Jamaican dancehall, popularized in the United States by Shabba Ranks and others. "Culture in the Ghetto" and especially the album's title track also took a cue from political rap, which was having its heyday in the early 1990s, with lyrics that confronted racial inequality and oppression. "Soul Rebels early on was kind of militant," said Lumar, who models the operation of the group on a business organization and refers to himself as its "president." In addition to black political leaders — "you know, Jesse, Al Sharpton, Farrakhan, all that kind of stuff" — the band drew inspiration from rappers:

> Black-on-black crime was at an all-time high in New Orleans. . . . Some people said it was due to the negativism in music, with some of the rap music, the portrayal of blacks being cold-blooded killers. We wanted to change that stereotype. . . . At that time Public Enemy was strong and we were kind of trying to be like that. Like a Public Enemy–style group, but with brass band.

The song "Let Your Mind Be Free" became a new prototype for contemporary brass band music, assimilating many of the innovations linked to the brass band renaissance while becoming a standard that every band is required to know. Like most brass band songs added to the repertoire since the 1970s, the song starts with a tuba riff, but we also hear a spoken introduction that is notable both for its categorical allusion to rap and the directness with which the words deal with race, poverty, and violence. Saxophonist Byron "Flea" Bernard, who would soon leave to play with Rebirth, begins:

> *This is an original by the Soul Rebels Brass Band called "Let Your Mind Be Free."*
> *When we speak of let your mind be free, first we talk about racial discrimination.*
> *Black, white, red, brown, yellow, it doesn't matter what color you are.*
> *Because we're all of the same Lord, and we bleed the same color blood. Red.*

The monologue continues by calling out to "brothers and sisters" throughout the world, from "South Africa, Bosnia, Haiti" to New Orleans's housing projects, "the St. Thomas, the Magnolia, the Calliope," with a plea: "Stop the killing. Stop the killing. Stop the killing." After an extended instrumental section built around a Calypso horn line, the band starts a unison group chant, the form of singing most common in the brass band tradition, but the theme of racial unity and uplift distinguishes the song from its predecessors:

> *Free your mind with education*
> *Help to build a better nation*
> *Stop killing for recreation*
> *Let your mind be free*

We then hear a montage of conventional and innovative musical moments: a solo singer croons in a contemporary R&B style over the chant; the saxophonist takes a solo; the horns replay their instrumental melody and then modulate to a new key for a *montuno*-like break; over the polyrhythms and shouts of his bandmates, trumpeter Tannon Williams raps in a dancehall style. "Let Your Mind Be Free" culminates with the horns playing the iconic riff from the brass band standard "Joe Avery's Blues," as if reminding local listeners that this is indeed a brass band.

There is much happening in this song, and throughout the entire record *Let Your Mind Be Free*, that signals a revised approach to brass band performance. The thematic connections to hip-hop, relatively unexplored until that point, would become a defining feature of new-school brass band standards. Lumar explained that there is also a lot of nuanced detail in the structure of "Let Your Mind Be Free" that is not typical of brass band arrangements: "We wanted to construct it different. A lot of brass band songs are purely instrumental. A lot of brass band songs don't really have a definite introduction, head, bridge, ending, whatever. So we wanted to make the song—how can I say it?—a little commercially adaptable, to have it where a regular person could hear it on the radio and kind of follow it."

For Lumar and the other members of the Soul Rebels, making "Let Your Mind Be Free" more commercially adaptable meant combining characteristics from other forms of popular music (rapping, crooning, and writing an arrangement that moves in linear fashion through multiple sections) with those associated with the brass band tradition (prominent tuba part, instrumental sections, and group chants). Not surprisingly, the response was mixed. At an interview with Lumar, Winston, and Derrick Moss at Jazz Fest in 2009, Lumar told me that initially "people didn't like it because it was different," and many traditionalists maintained this stance especially after the song "took off like wildfire" at parades, onstage, and ultimately as one of the most recognizable recordings in the brass band tradition. As relatively young men, the Soul Rebels, as their name suggests, were defiant. "We'd always come onstage with a little chip on our shoulder, like 'I got to prove to people that we belong here.'"

In a further provocation, the band focused their energies on recording and performing onstage, effectively bowing out of the parading tradition. "We're not street musicians," Derrick explained at Jazz Fest. "All of us are college trained, we read and write music, and that's a difference that you hear." Lumar and Derrick brought in new members, including Winston and, later, trumpeter Marcus Hubbard, to refine their approach. The band's second record from 1998, *No More Parades*, left no room for ambiguity about their intervention within the brass band tradition. Aesthetically the band was wearing camouflage fatigues in their press photos. Musically they were integrating hip-hop into the tradition. And contextually they were taking the music in new directions, as Lumar and Marcus explained to me:

MARCUS: The thing with *No More Parades*, it wasn't like just saying, "We don't want to mess with that tradition." It was basically like, "We're ready for mainstream."

LUMAR: We're tired of just being, "Okay, let's do this second line." We want to actually be like Snoop Dog, Beyoncé, whoever, Justin Timberlake. We want to be on the main stage too and we're capable of doing it. . . .

MARCUS: Instead of just parades and all the basic stuff that brass bands do. . . .

LUMAR: In no way would I ever disrespect the element of the parade. That's a powerful idiom in itself that needs to be carried on. But don't be mad at a band if they want to evolve from the street to the stage. Maybe that's what [the title] should have been, "Soul Rebels: From the Street to the Stage."

It was during this period when I first encountered the Soul Rebels at Joe's Cozy Corner (described in the introduction). A youthful black audience danced to the uplifting original "Brighter Day," with Lumar trading verses with Winston and original member Mervin "Kid Merv" Campbell, which they recorded the following year for *No More Parades*. By the time the record came out, I was producing the *American Routes* radio program from our studios in the French Quarter, and on occasion I would select a handful of brass band CDs to audition for the show. *No More Parades* stood out. "Makin' Statements (No More Parades)" was a boasting rap, an explicit send-up to traditionalists and a provocation to those "fake ass niggas" who were the Soul Rebels' contemporaries. Then there were party raps like "Rebel Rock" that, as a general rule, would not have appealed to the program's core audience of middle-aged white listeners, and there were even misogynist songs like "Shut Up Ho!!!" that would have required censorship to conform to public radio policy. In the 1990s the very progressiveness that kept the music a living, breathing tradition was potentially threatening to an older, whiter national audience.

For the audience at Joe's, this was the music of the moment; Rebirth had just released their aggressive *We Come to Party* and would follow suit with their own full-fledged hip-hop–brass-band album *Hot Venom*. The changes to the brass band tradition were concurrent with the proliferation of hip-hop throughout New Orleans and especially the emergence of a local style called bounce. Bounce had an instantly recognizable beat based on two drum machine rhythms—the "Triggerman" and the "Brown" beat—which were sampled and resampled for use in virtually every bounce song, such as Juvenile's "Back That Thang Up" (2000), and even make an appearance in the Soul Rebels' recording of "Makin' Statements." Bounce's local identity was also due, in part, to a sustained dialogue with brass band music, including samples of familiar songs such as Rebirth's "Feel Like Funkin' It Up" in Da Sha Ra's "Bootin' Up" or their "Tornado Special" in 2 Blakk's "Second Line Jump," both from 1995.

As Lumar observed, the game had changed. Though the Soul Rebels continued to perform the occasional parade or funeral, they steadily moved away from these contexts that define the brass band tradition and into spaces that allow for the presentation of a hip-hop sound and aesthetic. At their weekly Thursday-night performances at Le Bon Temps Roulé bar in the Uptown district, where Tulane students dance alongside older regulars from the neighborhood, the Soul Rebels construct a new type of musical experience. The musicians shift seamlessly from "throwback" songs like the Jackson 5's "I Want You Back" to the most recent pop and hip-hop, such as a dancehall song by the Jamaican rapper Shaggy and Gnarls Barkley's "Crazy," mixed in with their own compositions.

The Rebels' uncompromising approach is most evident on the 2005 album *Rebelution*, built up slowly and painstakingly after a long hiatus from recording. In the high-tech Ultrasonic Studios the band collaborated with the producer Bill Summers, the percussionist for the Headhunters and Los Hombres Calientes, with the intent of creating a new kind of brass band record. Unlike on every other recording that I am aware of, the musicians did not play live together in the studio but rather stacked tracks using methods of overdubbing, sequencing, and automated mixing borrowed from pop and hip-hop production. On a song like "Groove Train," Marcus and Winston would program a drum beat at their home studio, bring the ProTools audio tracks to Ultrasonic to add horns, drums, and vocals from guests Coppertop and Rhasheed, then return home to layer synthesizers and vocal harmonies over top, before finally returning the completed tracks to Summers and engineer Steve Reynolds for mixing. "Groove Train" is a smooth R&B bedroom jam made recognizable as brass band music only when the brassy buzz of the tuba pokes through the mix or Lumar adds a cymbal crash to accent Marcus's whispering falsetto melodies.

The Soul Rebels have brought a new set of priorities to the brass band tradition by constructing songs that are intentionally produced for recordings and amplified performances. The pace of marching in the streets is not a factor when choosing tempos. Spoken-word raps float over horn lines played at full volume with the knowledge that they can be reproduced live with the aid of amplification. And then there are recorded arrangements featuring electronic or other instruments that are not portable and cannot be incorporated into the traditional contexts in which brass bands perform.

As they have been doing since changing their name from the Young Olympians to the Soul Rebels, the band inspired controversy with *Rebelution*. The record company asked them to make an acoustic version of the album, later released as *Urban Legend*, "the completely organic brass bookend to their album, *Rebelution*, recorded in one overdub-free take," according to the liner notes.[28] Their next record, from 2009, *No Place Like Home*, was recorded live in front of an audience, and the liner notes made clear that the band was stung by the critical response to their mobilization of tradition:

> The group concentrated on making *Rebelution* a project that showcased the many talents and musical interests of the members. It was not brass band music, not New Orleans music, not Jazz, but simply compositions and melodies that represented a piece of each individual member of the band. However, our ability to arrange, sing, direct, recite poetry, write lyrics, program complex rhythm sequences, and bring in other artists to complement Da Rebel sound went unnoticed. The Soul Rebels believed they embarked on a new frontier musically; but while some saw it as a masterpiece, others felt it was "over produced."[29]

At the Jazz Fest interview, Winston gestured toward the festival grounds and spoke candidly: "At this festival right here, there's a main stage, but you're not going to see any of us on it." Derrick added:

> We [used to] go to Europe every summer and they would have us playing at the front gate, standing up outside for people to come in while they go in to the real show. And that really got to us. And that's when we decided . . . we're going to put this on the main stage. And in order to do that, you've got to cut ties with the streets. Because everywhere you go, they look at you as a street band, and it took us ten years of proving that we're not just a street band.

The contrast here between the Soul Rebels and the members of the Black Men of Labor Social Aid and Pleasure Club is striking. Members of the civil rights generation who have positioned themselves as delegates of local culture draw upon established traditions of jazz, spirituals, and parading to project positive images and sounds of blackness. For some in the hip-hop generation, serving as a delegate of tradition is burdensome, and they have drawn upon hip-hop to depict a far broader and more controversial spectrum of themes. Yet, following Michael White, brass band music "has always mirrored contemporary reality": those in Black Men of Labor are members of a generation united by the successful campaigns of activists fighting for civil rights legislation, and they embody particular notions of blackness that were espoused in the movement, while the Soul Rebels came of age in the subsequent era of unfulfilled promises, part of what hip-hop scholars and critics such as Bakari Kitwana, Tricia Rose, and Todd Boyd refer to as the "hip-hop generation." In his book *The Hip-Hop Generation*, Kitwana argues that by the end of the twentieth century "rap artists became the dominant public voice" and helped create "a new medium through which to share a national culture."[30] While music was central to articulating the aspirations of the civil rights movement, with the hip-hop generation, Rose notes, "we have arrived at a landmark moment in modern culture when a solid segment (if not a majority) of an entire generation of African American youth understands itself as defined primarily by a musical, cultural form."[31] Reflecting on these generational differences, Todd Boyd writes, "With hip hop being so vocal, so visible, so empowered through the success that the culture has had, this becomes the dominant mode of address and the primary way in which we can possibly start to make sense of how Blackness functions in the present."[32]

The Soul Rebels have carved out their own niche in the brass band tradition with relative success, playing in venues in America and Europe where they feature their own compositions and arrangements without regard to the precedent of tradition. They have faced their share of struggle in recent years—Lumar and Marcus relocated to Houston after Katrina and commute to gigs; tuba player Damien Francois was replaced by Edward Lee; and Winston left the band in 2010 and started his own project, the Brass-A-Holics—but they continue to march forward at their own pace. As Lumar put it, "You know, New Orleans is the birthplace of jazz, and that music has put New Orleans on the map, but there are also other colors to the spectrum, and Soul Rebels is just another piece in that spectrum."

EPISODE 3.5: Productive Friction

The 2003 recording of "Knock with Me—Rock with Me" by the short-lived Lil' Rascals Brass Band starts with a thickly textured call-and-response melody between the upper and lower brass in standard fashion. But then, in an instant, vocalist Glen David Andrews enters with a full-throated shout and commands the song for its duration of seven and a half minutes. Over a tuba and drum track, played not on electronics but on acoustic instruments that were cutting-edge technologies over a hundred years ago, Andrews runs through a litany of hip-hop themes: competition with rivals ("Rebirth tried to get me! Rascals roll with me!"), representing place ("Tenth Ward tried to get me! Sixth Ward roll with me!"), violent retribution ("Who that shot D-Boy? Gotta get him, gotta get him!"), dance instruction ("Dip, baby, dip! Slide then move your hips!"), and drug peddling ("Gimme a dime! I only got eighths!"), all interspersed with a refrain that matches Andrews's hopeful plea with a group chant of reconciliation:

> *Wipe your weary eyes, Mama don't cry (Mama don't cry!)*
> *Living in the Sixth [Ward], baby, do or die (Mama don't cry!)*
> *Drugs and prostitution, people will die (Mama don't cry!)*
> *They say they're certain there's no cure for AIDS, but that's a lie (Mama don't cry!)*
>
> *Ten years from now, where will I be? (Mama don't cry!)*
> *Will I shine like a star, bright as the eyes can see? (Mama don't cry!)*
> *Will I be kicking the breeze, hanging on St. Philip Street? (Mama don't cry!)*
> *All I can ask the Sixth, is come on and roll with me! (Mama don't cry!)*[33]

Glen David Andrews was only twenty-two when he recorded "Knock with Me—Rock with Me," but his lyrics condense the many events he had already experienced in that short amount of time. His cousin Darnell "D-Boy" Andrews, whose jazz funeral was described in episode 3.3, was murdered the year before, at the age of seventeen. Another relative, Rascals drummer Eldridge "Eldo" Andrews, was killed the year before that. Glen David struggled off and on with addiction, which came to a head after Katrina while living in a FEMA trailer. At the same time, his appearance at the 2007 March Against Violence (described in episode 4.6) and his arrest for disturbing the peace later that year (described in episode 1.7) provided him with a public forum to speak with great force about the significance of local culture and the threats to musicians who move it forward. "Knock with Me—Rock with Me," the author and educator Kalamu ya Salaam writes, "is all about that ugly beauty. Just calling it like it is. . . . [It] isn't a black tie and evening dress thing. It's strictly a paper plate and plastic spoon, 'come as you are' affair."[34]

No less powerful than this progressive experiment is the traditional music that fills the streets of centuries-old Downtown neighborhoods during the Black Men of Labor parade on Labor Day weekend. To see dozens of musicians decked out in their "black and whites," to feel the sheer force of a band of that magnitude playing standards, setting the pace for dancers to strut their moves at a leisurely tempo, is a resplendent event to be a part of. The pride of the club members in organizing a respectable display ripples out in concentric circles to the second liners, who make up the largest and most diverse crowd of the parade season.

Can one tradition accommodate the progressive mobilizations of "Knock with Me—Rock with Me" as well as the relative inertia on display at the Black Men of Labor parade? Just ask Glen David Andrews, who plays the Black Men of Labor parade most years and plays his characteristic mix of jazz, gospel, R&B, and hip-hop most nights. As with the members of the Soul Rebels, Rebirth, Hot 8, and other bands raised in the hip-hop generation, Glen David has reconfigured tradition to be in tune with experience. At the risk of being crude or reductionist, it appears to me that the members of the Black Men of Labor Social Aid and Pleasure Club and traditionalist musicians such as Michael White have also approached tradition as a means of fortifying their subject positions, which happen to be aligned more closely with civil rights–era values of respectability and religiosity.

On the other side of the earth from New Orleans, in Indonesia, the anthropologist Anna Tsing studied the "sticky engagements" between disparate groups from far-flung locales that are brought into connection through the global economy. In her book *Friction: An Ethnography of Global Connection*, Tsing argues that "heterogeneous and unequal encounters can lead to new arrangements of culture and power," which she terms "friction."[35] Back in New Orleans, there are points of friction between musicians who identify as the same race, inhabit the same city, and participate in the same performance traditions. Friction, according to Tsing, not only slows things down but also sets things in motion; friction can be productive as well as destructive. In New Orleans a diverse set of practitioners bring their perspectives to tradition and through their arguments and alliances ensure that tradition remains a relevant space.

We can measure the productivity of the tradition-progress debates through the activities of people and organizations to socialize musicians into the brass band tradition. Michael White, for instance, organized a series of workshops with the Hot 8 in order to help them become more fluent in traditional repertoire and performance practices. Though the Hot 8 continue to appeal to younger audiences attuned to hip-hop, their collaborations with White helped them reach fans of traditional music in Europe and elsewhere.

Members of Black Men of Labor worked in collaboration with the National Park Service to launch a program called Music for All Ages. A brass band made up of teenagers practices every Saturday morning under the guidance of Benny Jones and others from the Tremé Brass Band. At the 2007 Black Men of Labor parade, the students played alongside their mentors, looking and sounding like a modern-day Fairview band. Black Men of Labor also marches with these young musicians at funerals when the family of the deceased has arranged for an explicitly traditional jazz funeral.

Youth brass bands also continue to develop more informally, such as the Baby Boyz, formed by members of the McDonough 35 High School marching band. As with Rebirth before them, the Baby Boyz played for tips in the French Quarter and worked their way up to club gigs, parties, and occasional second line parades. Like their predecessors, they dress in the style of the moment, which is no longer the baggy fit of the hip-hop generation but skinny jeans and "skater" clothes. The Baby Boyz play older repertoire such as "I'll Fly Away" and "When the Saints Go Marching In" together with the music of Dirty Dozen, Rebirth, and other progressives. They draw upon the full spectrum of brass band tradition to carry it forward. They have been trained to recognize distinctions between traditional and progressive music, but they experience these differences from the perspective of young men who were born long after the effects of the brass band renaissance had been incorporated into the tradition.

When I asked one of the young musicians about the song he had just finished playing, he replied, "That's an old traditional tune played by the Rebirth Brass Band called 'Tornado.'"

CHAPTER 4

VOICES

EPISODE 4.1: Structural Violence, Interpersonal Violence, and Musical Articulation

In December 1996 Jacob Johnson was twenty-one years old and already an experienced trumpeter. He started the Loony Tunes Brass Band with his classmates at Alcee Fortier High School and stayed on after they graduated, changed members, and took on a new name, the Hot 8. Jacob supplemented his income by cutting hair on the stoop of his apartment building in the Calliope housing projects, where he had grown up. In the cold months he attended to his clients inside, and around midnight on a Sunday in December he was giving his neighbor a haircut when two men entered the apartment. The men tied up Jacob, his client Mentrel Bartholomew, and Mentrel's brother Dameion Russ with duct tape, then shot each of them behind the ear with a single bullet. Miraculously Russ survived the incident, and his testimony was enough to convict the shooter Lester Duplessis, nineteen, of double homicide.

Jacob was the first of four members of the Hot 8 to die, all four in their early twenties, and three of four killed by gunfire. For the young men continuing in their absence, the process of grieving includes summoning the strength to play a jazz funeral. "We all know that we have to play for somebody's funeral," trombonist Jerome

Jones told me in the days after another band member, Dinerral Shavers, was murdered in December 2006. Jerome gestured to his bandleader Bennie Pete: "He might have to play for mine. I might have to play for his. That's given. Somebody's got to play for somebody's unless we all some kind of way go together." And so it was that on December 14, 1996, Jerome, Bennie, Dinerral, and the others picked up their instruments and began playing dirges, just as they had many times before and would keep on doing, this time for their friend and bandmate.

More than any other area of my research, the response of musicians to the loss of their peers has challenged my ability to explain, to string together a narrative in support of a thesis, because there always remains a surplus of potential meanings no matter how much I try to circumscribe the data. A tragically routine chain of events—murder, private mourning, and public ritual—vibrates with an intensity that spills out of the nooks and crannies of a single life to intersect with critical debates about the black experience in contemporary urban America. There is the submerged infrastructure that unevenly governs our lives, creating racialized patterns of health care, housing, education, commerce, and criminal justice, which materialize as debilitating types of structural violence. There is the interpersonal, intra-racial, physical violence occurring within this infrastructure that continues to shock despite its ceaselessness. There is the role of a black American cultural tradition in which the brass band ensemble is heard as a communal voice. There is the contrasting loss of voice, the silencing of those who are lost. And there is much more. So I resign myself to containing the uncontainable within this triangle of structural violence, interpersonal violence, and musical articulation.

Discussing racial marginalization as *structural violence* in the twenty-first century presents a challenge. Until the end of the twentieth century, race was a determinant of bureaucratic policy; the Emancipation Proclamation, *Plessy v. Ferguson*, and the Civil Rights Act are among numerous legal decisions that had a basis in racial identity. Very recently, however, the juridical, legislative, and executive offices have shifted the terms away from race and toward class; where programs such as public housing, welfare, affirmative action, and public health once had the explicit goal of ameliorating poverty and racial discrimination, the playing field is now assumed to be level and programs are measured exclusively as expenditures. "Public policies have been reframed away from universal access and towards market-based models," write the anthropologists Judith Goode and Jeff Masakovsky in their book *The New Poverty Studies*. "Now, policy debates center on the moral and political imperative to eliminate dependency and the forms of social insurance that encourage it, rather than on programs that are intended to eliminate inequality."[1] In this new order, imbalances in the quality of education, health care, and other services persist, along with the more mundane, concealed, and everyday patterns that have appeared throughout this book: aggressive policing, racial profiling, economic exploitation, urban gentrification, and so on.

The anthropologists Philippe Bourgois and Nancy Scheper-Hughes argue that the "implicit, legitimate, and routinized forms of violence inherent in particular social, economic, and political formations" are a type of everyday violence—structural violence—upon which interpersonal violence flourishes.[2] Incarceration, for example, increased 442 percent between 1970 and 1995 and has disproportionately affected young black men, to the point where one in three will fall under some form of criminal justice supervision.[3] The privatization of prisons coincided with an equally extraordinary reduction of the welfare state that culminated in President Clinton's 1996 Personal Responsibility and Work Opportunity Reconciliation Act.[4] The shrinking of social welfare programs came on the heels of a gradual shift in the market economy, away from unionized and standardized wages in industrial work and toward insecure wage work predominantly in the service sector. Urban school systems remain vastly underfunded compared to their suburban counterparts, despite the stated intentions of President George W. Bush's "No Child Left Behind" program.[5]

The particular risks that structural violence poses for black Americans were evident following Hurricane Katrina, when those who remained in New Orleans were denied assistance while military and law enforcement prioritized the punishment of criminality—both real and imagined—over securing human safety. Thousands were left stranded at the Convention Center without food or water, blocked by police from evacuating to high ground via the Crescent City Connection, at the same time that suspected looters were being jailed and denied their basic rights of citizenship in a sprawling complex constructed by prison labor within days of the flood. The media coverage and public outcry, however, did not open up a serious and sustained discussion of accountability for poverty and racism; instead New Orleans's reputation as an exceptional place, a thing apart from America, combined with unprecedented levels of devastation to define the event as an aberration rather than an exemplary case study.[6]

Long before Katrina, disinvestment had increasingly shrunken opportunities and allowed an informal drug trade to flourish in New Orleans just as in Chicago's South Side, Los Angeles's Watts, and Cincinnati's Over-the-Rhine. In a conversation with Hot 8 bandleader Bennie Pete, he remembered being lured in his youth by the prospect of selling drugs:

> Every day you go to school they laughing at you because of your shoes or this and that. . . . And then you on your way to school and the dealer's saying, "Look at me, man. Hey, you can wear this. You can have one of these for every day of the week." . . . And people be telling you, "What you going to go to school for? What, you going to be a doctor? How you going to be a doctor? What you going to be, the next Michael Jordan? Get real man, come get with me."

The murder rate in New Orleans is approximately ten times the national average and the incarceration rate is the highest of any city in the world, but for Bennie the taunting and the luring were not able to upset his moral compass.[7] His grandfather Willie Lee Thomas, a minister at the Christian Mission Baptist Church where Barbara Frazier ("Mama Rebirth") was the organist, instilled in Bennie a sense of self-certitude grounded in faith. And his mother, Perry Ann Thomas, having followed a medical regimen to control the effects of mental illness, was stable and caring until her death in 2010.

For others, *interpersonal violence* presents itself as a viable, even desirable option to young people operating within illegal drug economies. In the book *In Search of Respect: Selling Crack in El Barrio*, Bourgois observed the "crucial role that public displays of violence play in establishing credibility on the street."[8] Among Puerto Rican drug dealers and users in East Harlem in the 1990s, Bourgois found that individuals were susceptible to "succumb-[ing] to symbolic violence by not only failing to see the structural dynamics oppressing them, but by actually blaming themselves for their failure to achieve the American Dream."[9] Sociologist Loïc Wacquant has written of the concealed relation between structural and interpersonal violence for urban black Americans:

> The massive social disinvestment spelled by the curtailment of state provision (i) accelerates the decomposition of the indigenous institutional infrastructure of the ghetto; (ii) facilitates the spread of pandemic violence and fuels the enveloping climate of fear; and (iii) supplies the

room and impetus for the blossoming of an informal economy dominated by the drug trade. These three processes in turn feed upon each other and become locked into an apparently self-sustaining constellation that presents every outward sign of being internally driven (or "ghetto-specific"), when in reality it is (over)determined and sustained from the outside by the brutal and uneven movement of withdrawal of the semi-welfare state.[10]

The result, Wacquant surmises, is that "violence, from below, in the form of interpersonal aggression and terror, as well as from above, in the guise of state-sponsored discrimination and segregation, has been the preeminent instrument for drawing and imposing the 'color line.'"[11] In media accounts and public discourse, interpersonal violence is linked in a causal relationship not to structural violence but to racial pathology, so that "unless they display the trappings of middle-class culture," black men are "viewed as potential criminals or troublemakers."[12]

The profiles of musicians in this chapter challenge the stereotypes of black men not so much by countering negative images with positive ones as by acknowledging a wider spectrum of possibilities and by situating their agency within the historical context of the post–civil rights era. The three members of the Hot 8 Brass Band who have died by the gun, and the different circumstances of their deaths—an execution-style robbery, a police killing, and the killing of a bystander—demonstrate the multitude of ways that violence, both structural and interpersonal, constitutes the everyday. There are other examples as well, such as that of Brandon Franklin, a twenty-two-year-old saxophonist for the TBC Brass Band, who was shot and killed in 2010 on his ex-girlfriend's front steps while trying to protect her from another suitor. And then there are casualties whose deaths are not a result of physical violence: Hot 8 trombonist Demond Dorsey, twenty-eight, died of a drug-related heart attack in 2004, a year after Rebirth saxophonist James Durant, thirty-one, also died of heart failure after a night of drug use. Calculating a metric of causes and effects is misguided, and pitting structural marginalization against personal responsibility is inadequate; what is verifiable and palpable is the expendability of life, the experience of suffering, and the necessity of overcoming.

"It's real," goes the song by the Hot 8.

"For true," says Bennie.

The deaths of black musicians in New Orleans are not unique to the current moment; in the autobiographies of New Orleans musicians Louis Armstrong, Danny Barker, Pops Foster, and Tom Sancton performances in the streets and clubs are routinely interrupted by gunfire or police raids. Nor is the New Orleans case a particularly unique example of music's entanglement with violence, as recent studies in ethnomusicology demonstrate: Silvia Ramos and Ana María Ochoa write of the mediation of violence through music in the favelas of Rio de Janeiro; Christopher Washburne writes of salsa musicians' encounters with violence in New York City; and Louise Meintjes writes of dominating masculinity in Zulu *ngoma* song and dance.[13] What is notable about music and violence in New Orleans is the explicitness with which musicians have responded to violent death through the composition of new songs and especially through the performances of jazz funerals in honor of their fallen bandmates.

Structural violence, interpersonal violence, and death directly impact the lives of young black musicians in New Orleans because the jazz funeral provides them their basic livelihood, as it has for generations. On the one hand, there is monotony to the funeral business that leaves musicians desensitized to death. Bennie played his first funeral while still a student at Fortier High School, pocketed $20, and thus began a career as a professional musician that has included more funerals than he can remember. Hot 8 snare drummer Dinerral Shavers was only fifteen when his bandmate Jacob Johnson died, but Dinerral's sister Nakita said he already thought of funerals as "just part of his job." On the other hand, the unexpected and tragic loss of someone close managed to break through the monotony. "That was the first traumatizing thing that happened to him," said Nakita of her brother. "You can walk the streets and think, 'Oh, that'll never happen to me,' but that was a reality check." When the life of a friend and bandmate is taken too early, the status of the jazz funeral as the most sacred, profound, and traditional form of local black culture is restored, even for the musician who makes a living playing funerals.

The precariousness of life and the inevitability of death ensure that the jazz funeral tradition remains unbroken; but just as Louis Armstrong and his contemporaries incorporated jazz in the Jim Crow era and Harold Dejan brought in the sound and sentiment of rhythm and blues during the civil rights movement, young musicians have retrofitted the jazz funeral to resonate with present-day experiences. The abandonment of the brass band uniform, the reduction in slow dirges, and other changes to the jazz funeral have offended traditionalists, but young musicians respond that they are simply fulfilling the requests of the deceased's family. "If you play for young people . . . the last thing they want to hear is a funeral dirge," said Keith Frazier of Rebirth. He explained that the dirge is too painful for some mourners: "When we're playing, you just hear crying all the time, and they never want the band to leave." During our interview, as Keith was telling me that Rebirth no longer enters the funeral home or church but waits outside until the service has ended, he glanced at his seven-year-old daughter, Keyantae, sitting on his lap. "I don't want to see a young person [like] that," he paused to search for the right words. "I don't watch. I never. Never . . ." His voice trailed off without finishing the thought.

At the height of the crack epidemic in 1996, New Orleans poet Brenda Marie Osbey wrote an essay about contemporary jazz funerals, which by that time had become so ubiquitous that brass bands were referring to them as "crack funerals." While Osbey mourned the passing of the traditional jazz funeral, she came to see the logic of the changes from the perspective of the young: "I begin to think that perhaps it is not merely all right but appropriate that the very young mourners of the very young dead begin their celebration as soon as the casket is removed to its hearse. Their own lives being so susceptible to the same fate, who knows when they might have the chance to 'do it up right'?"[14]

In the previous chapter, hip-hop's place within the brass band tradition was assessed differently by black New Orleanians with varying subject positions. But when placed in the context of urban criminality, violence, and death as well as new forms of marginalization that have solidified in the post–civil rights period, hip-hop becomes a critical tool for *musical articulation*. The resiliency of the brass band tradition owes much to its currency as a form of popular culture among black New Orleanians who prize hip-hop for its ability to represent their experiences. Hip-hop makes tradition relevant. Jacob Johnson's jazz funeral was not only a timeless communal ritual; it was also a forum to voice highly individualized emotions. In the wake of Jacob's loss, the Hot 8 composed songs such as "Miss My Homies," which modeled its refrain ("I really miss my homies / since you've gone away / Lord, I miss my homies / every single day") on a 1997 song by New Orleans rapper Master P, sending "shout-outs" to fallen "homies" over a propulsive, hip-hop beat and bass line, here played on the traditional tuba and marching drums. "Miss My Homies" exemplifies the congruence between brass band and hip-hop and the way that musicians have modified tradition in response to the most severe problem they face: the loss of young people, especially men, to murder and incarceration.

Structural violence limits the social mobility of the urban poor, constraining agency, while interpersonal violence threatens to void human agency, silencing voices. In jazz funerals and other musical memorials for those who have died tragically young, musicians use iconic instruments in a hip-hop way, conjoining the local and the traditional with the global and the contemporary.

EPISODE 4.2: Joseph "Shotgun" Williams

The odds were stacked against Joseph Williams from an early age. When he was eight, his father shot and killed his mother during a family dinner, and Joseph had to take the witness stand to testify against his father. Joseph and his siblings were raised on Delery Street in the Lower Ninth Ward neighborhood by an extended family that includes several celebrated musicians, among them their grandmother Betty Lastie Williams and uncle Herlin Riley.[15] Lil' Joe, as his friends called him, picked up the trombone, learning to express himself through music. At the same time he was also learning to suppress his feelings through heroin use.

"Joe had caught a real bad rap," said Bennie. "But one thing about him, you never had to worry about him hurting anybody, because the only person he'll hurt is his self. I mean, he'll go at it with his self."

At Lawless High School in the mid-1990s, Lil' Joe became Shotgun Joe, earning his name by skillfully manipulating the long, barrel-like slide of the trombone. He played in the school marching band and teamed up with his classmates Dinerral Shavers and Shamarr Allen to form the Little Jazzmen, a brass band that mostly played for tips in the French Quarter. In 1997, after hearing the Little Jazzmen at a neighborhood block party, Bennie and trombonist Jerome Jones recruited Shamarr to fill Jacob Johnson's place and Dinerral took over for Derrick Tabb, who had left to join Rebirth. When a trombone spot opened in the Hot 8, Dinerral and Shamarr recommended Joe, and over the next few years the band crystallized into a tight-knit unit of musical brothers.

On the afternoon of August 3, 2004, Joe left Delery Street and drove to the Tremé neighborhood to meet the rest of the band for a jazz funeral.

4.2 *I Can Still Hear Buddy Bolden Play.* 2001. 68″ × 48″. © WILLIE BIRCH.

The white Ford F-150 pickup truck that he drove was registered as stolen. Joe's friends claim the truck was a "crack rental," a car that changes hands among drug dealers and users, which would explain why Joe had the original keys. However Joe got the truck, while he was parked outside the Food Store in the Tremé, two police cruisers boxed him in and he was ordered out of the car. When Joe moved toward the passenger door, officers filled his body with bullets. He died at the age of twenty-two, unarmed, with his arms raised upright out of the open passenger window. That evening, NOPD spokesperson Marlon Defillo explained to reporters that Joe had used his truck as a weapon and made reference to Joe's prior arrest as further justification for the shooting. The department classified Joe's death as "justifiable," clearing officers Kevin Scruggs, Jonathan Carroll, and Bruce Little of any wrongdoing. Lawyers informed the family that a criminal trial would be an expensive undertaking and an indictment was a virtual impossibility, so charges were never brought and there was no internal investigation.

As happened with the police killings of unarmed black men in other cities, such as Amadou Diallo's in New York in 1999 and Timothy Thomas's in Cincinnati in 2001, many residents interpreted the death of Joseph Williams as an example of the aggressive policing of young black men. The confrontation certainly turned out differently than one in 2006, when the photographic journalist John McCusker, who was in a state of depression after documenting the devastation of Hurricane Katrina, was pulled over by the police after driving into several parked cars in a wealthy Uptown neighborhood. In this widely reported incident, McCusker begged the officers to shoot him, and when they refused he put his car in reverse, pinning an officer to his cruiser, and then sped off. Police caught up with McCusker again, and cuffed and Tasered him while he resisted and yelled obscenities. McCusker was released from custody for psychiatric observation and eventually was fined $900 and given six months of inactive probation.

On the day of the incident, police commander James Arey described McCusker as a "really fine professional" and noted, "It was to the great credit of the police officers on this scene that they would not do what he wanted and kill him but instead apprehended him alive by Tasering him."[16] McCusker is an exceptional photographer who is also a friend and a colleague; he went on to publish the definitive biography of New Orleans jazz trombonist Edward "Kid" Ory. The officers deserve commendation in his case, which happened to involve apprehending an upstanding white New Orleanian and defusing a crime that took place in a predominantly white and upper-class neighborhood. There are other instances when police securely apprehend black suspects and successfully restore order. Yet any comparison between the police confrontations with John McCusker and Joseph Williams would have to take race into account. In the fleeting moment when the hand reaches for the holster, what criteria are involved in the decision to shoot?

There was not an organized protest of the police killing, though tensions led to a confrontation between residents and the police on May 23, 2005, when friends and family threw a party for Joe on what would have been his twenty-third birthday. Delery Street was blocked off with cars and the Hot 8 was playing for a crowd of three hundred or so when police arrived around 8 p.m. to break it up. People hurled objects and insults at the officers and eleven arrests were made.

Reactions among the band were more severe. Dinerral, who happened to be training as a Civil Sheriff's Office deputy at the time, had heard the shooting incident unfold over his walkie-talkie, and when he arrived on the scene to find his childhood friend was the target, he threw his gun belt to the ground and was taken into custody. Bennie was particularly shaken by the news, having experienced what he says was a premonition on the morning of Joe's killing, when he went to pick up a gun that he carried and a voice spoke to him: "Oh, you want to grab your gun, huh? I'm going to show you what that gun can do." Afterward, Bennie said, "I ain't ever carried my gun again. I'm scared to carry it now, because that thing got spirits with it."

On the night of Joe's viewing, the band gathered outside Tilly's Funeral Home, socializing with Joe's family and friends and waiting to perform. The embalmer at Tilly's, who had developed a relationship with the Hot 8 through the funeral business, began describing the amount of work that was necessary to reconstruct Joe. He had been preparing the body since three o'clock that morning, but an open casket was eventually ruled out. He invited them back to the embalming room to see for themselves. Bennie declined. "I ain't really good with holding that all in my stomach," he said. "Even since I was small, when people get killed, everybody go run and see such-and-such, I run the other way because it just stood with me, and at night it would come get me. I don't want to see that. Have my head hurting."

Even though the plenitude and proximity of death had left Bennie desensitized to a degree, death still managed to leave him nauseated, and the thought of seeing his friend laid out was out of the question. The queasiness was part loss and part anger: the pain of confronting Joe's lifeless body was exacerbated by the events that led to his death. "I was upset he was dead, but I was more upset how he died," Bennie remembered. "It was like he was hunted, man, like he was a deer or something."

Musicians voiced their most explicit response to Joe's death through their instruments and voices. Bennie's clairvoyance at the moment his friend and bandmate was struck down by weapons of state violence is instructive here. Guns and musical instruments are both tools, and in this specific case their functionality is reducible essentially to two options: destructive or productive. They are deployed in public spectacles—a shooting and a musical funeral procession—that take place in the very same streets but differ radically in the way that one stops and silences while the other mobilizes and voices.

As I discussed in episode 1.8, an instrument is simultaneously a material object, a sound, and a traveling symbol, and each of these dimensions can be interpreted in terms of voice. For example, Bennie's instrument, the tuba, has been repurposed from the days of Sousa to sound out riffs that articulate the experiences of the hip-hop generation. This object, which a young Philip Frazier cuddled with in bed, voices the distinctiveness of local black culture whether bouncing down the street at a jazz funeral or wired to an amplifier through a microphone dropped down the bell. The symbolic significance of the brass band in "giving voice" to black New Orleanians is conveyable in a Jazz Fest poster portraying Philip Frazier with his trusty Conn. The gun is also a material object that has come to symbolize blackness and New Orleansness but, in this case, as a thing that disables agency, sounding off an arresting burst of noise followed by silence. Bennie stows away his gun and clutches his tuba ever tighter, making music that merges the ancient voice of black New Orleans with the contemporary voice of black Americans.

EPISODE 4.3: Why Dey Had to Kill Him?

Back when he was known around the Lower Ninth Ward as Lil' Joe, Joseph Williams grew up playing trombone with his schoolmates Dinerral Shavers and Shamarr Allen. Before they were recruited into the Hot 8, Joe partnered with another new band, the Stooges, after many sessions of trading riffs with bandleader Walter Ramsey. "Joe would listen to music all day long," Walter remembered. "And he got that ear. He can hear something and he can play it." When Joe was killed in 2004, the Stooges—including Walter, trombonist Ersel "Garfield" Bogan, and Joe's half-brother Arian Macklin on tuba—composed a song that consolidated the community's emotions surrounding the incident.

"Why Dey Had to Kill Him?" is a song of overt protest with little precedent in the brass band tradition. In fact the first recorded version of the song is not arranged for brass band at all; the marching drums are replaced by drum machines and the vocals trade off between spoken raps and a refrain sung in an R&B style to the accompaniment of keyboard and horns. "Why Dey Had to Kill Him?" is ultimately a hip-hop shout-out or message song played by musicians who happen to be affiliated with a brass band. There are no instrumental passages because the focus is on the story of Joe, beginning with playful memories of childhood, then tough-love descriptions of Joe's pawning his horn for drug money, and a recounting of the murder that makes connections to other incidents of police aggression. "It's just all my thoughts and my feelings about my friend that I don't have here no more," Walter explained. "It's nothing fake, just real shit that happened." Each verse is interspersed with a refrain:

> *Why dey had to kill him?*
> *They have the nerve, to say they protect and serve.*
> *Oh why?*
>
> *Why dey had to kill him?*
> *They need to change their logo, because we can't trust the po-po.*
> *Oh why?*

The musicians in the Stooges grew up listening to hip-hop, soaking up the music of local rappers Soulja Slim, Juvenile, and Lil' Wayne as much as that of local brass band musicians. They make arrangements of commercial hip-hop songs and write new compositions that combine the instrumentation of the brass band with the sounds and lyrical themes of hip-hop. While the produced recording of "Why Dey Had to Kill Him?" has not yet been made commercially available, the live arrangement has become one of the most recognizable songs in the brass band repertoire. Onstage the parts played by electronic instruments are entirely transposed to horns and drums, and in the street the solo vocal parts are eliminated. In all instances, the refrain becomes a participatory chant sung by the Stooges and their audience, culminating in a coda repeating the line "We all gonna miss Joseph."

At the height of their powers, as heard on their 2004 CD *Rock with the Hot 8*, the Hot 8 also included several dedicated composers. Dineral and trumpeter Al Huntley wrote songs initially as hip-hop tracks and then brought them to the band to be rearranged, while Joe and trumpeter Raymond Williams (no relation) preferred to "woodshed" their songs in band rehearsals. Joe's signature composition, "Rastafunk," is based on a reggae beat, a style of music that connotes resistance, and is arranged around two melodic phrases played by the horns in brass band style. After a sequence of instrumental solos, the group chants a refrain that is pure hip-hop:

> *The ghetto!*
> *From the ghetto! [born and raised, probably die right here]*
> *In the ghetto!*
>
> *I smoke weed, drink that gas*
> *Standing on the corner, how you loving that?*
> *It's all about the* HUSTLE.
>
> *I smoke weed, drink that gas*
> *Standing on the corner, how you loving that?*
> *It's all about the* STRUGGLE.

The second and third stanzas are identical except for the final word, linking structural marginalization ("struggle") with tactics of subversion ("hustle") that might include something as mundane yet provocative as a black man smoking, drinking, or loitering on a street corner. Toying with signs of criminality and using wordplay, rhyme, and spoken word ("born and raised, probably die right here in the ghetto") are the tools of the hip-hop emcee who provides a running commentary of social experience. "Rastafunk" exemplifies the affinity between brass band and hip-hop, not to mention reggae, and the way that musicians have modified tradition to resonate with contemporary experience.

The brass band idiom includes a repertoire that every professional musician must know, ranging from the spiritual "Just a Closer Walk with Thee" to the 1950s standard "Joe Avery's Blues" to new-school standards like "Do Whatcha Wanna" and "Let Your Mind Be Free." In terms of religiosity, this repertoire demonstrates the fluidity between sacred and secular domains detectable in many African-derived cultural forms; spirituals and hymns can be heard in events that are not explicitly religious, while secular songs often feature in religious events, such as a jazz funeral.[17] In terms of tradition, brass band music has been propelled forward by key innovators in a scene overflowing with instrumentalists who can play hundreds of traditional songs at a moment's notice. For Joseph, music was not only an expressive outlet but a constructive way of producing the self; his trombone, a seemingly outmoded acoustic instrument from the perspective of a young black man raised to the sounds of drum machines, samplers, and turntables, became in his hands a way of making a centuries-old tradition speak to him and for him. In a city where young black men parade on the same streets where others stand on the corner—some copping drugs, most listening to hip-hop—innovative musicians articulate all of these activities together, making them vibrate at consonant frequencies. Horns and drums become tools for producing subjectivities as much as producing sounds.

For Hot 8 trombonist Jerome Jones the police killing of Joe was the catalyst for a new song, "You Bang, We Bang Bang," that crystalized a lifetime of frustration with the criminal justice system. When he was twenty-seven Jerome spent the night in Orleans Parish Prison because police had mistaken him for a suspect who also had the name Jerome Jones, and the arrest stayed on his criminal record. "Look, if I get killed, are they going to release that I was a Loyola student?" Jerome asked me. "Is they going to release that I own my own floor company? . . . No. What would they release? They might release that record that's not even mine." Jerome contrasts this possibility against what he witnessed at Loyola University, where he took classes and worked installing wall-to-wall carpets. "You have more drugs going on at Tulane University and Loyola University than any ghetto neighborhood. . . . And guess what? They cannot do them college students nothing." As with all of the younger brass bands, the Hot 8 have incorporated qualities associated with hip-hop into their original music as a way of articulating their experiences and fortifying their subject positions.

At the House of Blues nightclub in December 2006, the Hot 8 appeared onstage in matching jeans and T-shirts with the band's logo on the front. Near the end of an exciting set, trumpeter and singer Big Al Huntley introduced "You Bang, We Bang Bang," instructing the crowd, "When we say, 'You bang, we bang bang,' everybody feel that to your heart. I need everybody to sing it right now with me one time."

You bang, we bang bang
You bang, we bang bang
You bang, we bang bang
Why'd they have to kill Lil' Joe?

They gone and killed Joe
Carroll, Scruggs, and Little
Ray Nagin let it go
Why'd they have to kill Lil' Joe?

The music of the Hot 8 condenses the experiences of musicians and audiences: their frustrations, hopes, and aspirations. In "You Bang, We Bang Bang," a song of explicit protest, this is most evident in Jerome's lyrics about the death of his friend, the police officers who shot him, and the mayor who refused public comment on the shooting. However, there are other musical and extramusical cues bundled together with the words that also express emotion. The crowd was singing along, shouting, making vocal imitations of police sirens, and pumping their fists in the air. A man in the audience held up a black T-shirt with the question "Why dey had to kill him?" imprinted in white letters across the front. Shamarr gestured for the man to throw the shirt onstage and then held it up for the audience to see. There were long instrumental sections and horn solos, and the performance reached peak intensity when the song ended with a collision of cymbals and horns, including the recognizable riff from "Joe Avery's Blues."

In the Hot 8's performance of "You Bang, We Bang Bang," musicians and other participants voiced sentiment through sonic, visual, textual, and embodied realms. Musical instruments were deployed as a means of articulating suffering, frustration, and pleasure for audiences who use the music of the brass band to situate themselves as New Orleanians and hip-hop to situate themselves as black Americans. Musical instruments function not as a mere vehicle for expressing agency in some predetermined form but as a generative force that enables action, a material voice in communication with a community of listeners.[18]

EPISODE 4.4: Dinerral Jevone Shavers

The members of the Hot 8 are all black New Orleanians who joined the ranks of the brass band tradition at the end of the twentieth century, but in other ways their experiences vary greatly. Joe's childhood trauma of losing his mother combined with his upbringing in an extended family handed him a life of extremes: heroin use and fits of depression contrasted with intense creativity and musical facility. Trumpeter Raymond Williams is comparatively steady and exacting; he attended conservatory in Hartford, Connecticut, and his compositions are tightly arranged, as heard in the intricate bebop melodies and precise harmonies of his signature song, "Dr. Rackle (the Fine Tuner)." Trumpeter Terrell Batiste was raised in a nurturing musical family in the Lafitte housing projects, but with Katrina came tragedy, first when his grandmother's body was discovered in a makeshift morgue after she had been missing for five months, and second when Terrell was struck by a car in the breakdown lane of the interstate outside Atlanta, where his family had evacuated, and he lost both his legs.

Dinerral Jevone Shavers was raised primarily by his mother, Yolande Adams, who worked for the state and was able to buy a home in the Lower Ninth Ward. All three of Yolande's daughter have graduate degrees, but Dinerral dropped out of Southern University in Baton Rouge in order to return home after his son Dinerral Jr. ("DJ") was born. To support his family he took on a seemingly never-ending string of day jobs: working in the shipyards, substitute teaching, and even delivering the bodies of Katrina victims to the New Orleans coroner's office.

At the start of the 2006 school year, Dinerral began working as a day-to-day substitute teacher at L. E. Rabouin High School. The school was just reopening a year after Katrina, and Principal Kevin George, scrambling to assemble a teaching staff, had hired several substitutes to cover extracurricular classes. "I don't think he knew a lick of French other than *bonjour*," said his sister Nakita, but Dinerral agreed to teach French 1 because he had an ulterior motive: he had wanted to be a marching band director ever since he first played in band at Martin Luther King elementary. Now, at Rabouin, Dinerral sensed an opportunity in the topsy-turvy post-Katrina reshuffling of the school system.

In the classroom where Dinerral taught French, he began recruiting students. "He told me classroom 314, so one day I went up there," remembered

Quincy Bridges, a senior at Rabouin whose friends call him Q. "Then he was like, 'You know bro, I want to get a band started. I don't care what it take, how much it take, I just want to get a band started.' So I was like, 'Well, I'm behind you a hundred percent.'" Having gauged the level of commitment among students, Dinerral began applying pressure to Principal George. "He wanted to know if I wanted a band, and I told him no, I didn't think so," recalled George. "But he was persistent." Dinerral spelled out the benefits of band and demonstrated his knowledge in music notation and performance practices. "And finally I was like, 'You know what, Mr. Shavers, start putting things together.' The first day we announced that we were going to have a band, over eighty-five kids signed up for it!"[19]

Because band had not been added to the official class roster there was no time or space allotted for rehearsal, so Q and the other founding members of the Rabouin band would take lunch in an empty classroom and practice their drum cadences. Instruments were on order from the Tipitina's Foundation, a nonprofit organization that provides instruments to underfunded band programs, but would not arrive until the end of the year. So the students hit textbooks with drumsticks and hummed melodies through horn mouthpieces, which they call "books and humming." Under Dinerral's guidance, they progressed rapidly: "The second day, he called me and said 'Mr. George, I need you to come upstairs, I need you to see something.' So we went up there and he had his drum line set up with desks and with books. And they did a cadence. On books! On the second day! . . . And so I told him, I said, 'Man, give you a couple weeks and some equipment and I hate to see what we could do.'"

Dinerral assigned instrument positions to students even if they had had no prior musical experience and no instrument to practice with. Christopher Lee, a senior in Dinerral's French class, was named drum major: "He thought I should be the band major and he gave me that spot. And I told him he won't regret it and I was going to take care of my business." The drum major, who marches before the band with a tall hat, a marching stick, and a whistle at the ready to signal the musicians, is the most powerful position in marching band. "I had positions in my life, but that was a big step for me," said Christopher, who goes by the nickname Skully. "That's something I always wanted to be, and he was giving me the chance to be it."

The level of personal attention and self-responsibility that Dinerral offered his students is hard to come by in New Orleans public high schools,

4.3 *Playing a Dirge for a Victim of Violence.* 2002. 63″ × 41″. © WILLIE BIRCH.

many of which are categorized as "apartheid schools" because 99 to 100 percent of students are nonwhite.[20] In an environment where security guards troll the hallways and stand imposingly at entranceways to control student flare-ups and confrontations, Dinerral's work helped provide an alternative space for learning, creativity, and social interaction. "Kids that we had serious problems with, after they had band, I saw a total change in them," Principal George told a reporter.[21] But of course, no one person is capable of reaching everyone, and the troubles many students are wrapped in are acute. One problem that arose again and again following Katrina was neighborhood-based conflicts, or "turf wars."

After the flood, public schooling in New Orleans was completely reorganized and most students were reassigned to new schools, both because fewer public schools reopened and because families in devastated neighborhoods relocated to different school districts. In a city where neighborhood identifications are strong and confrontations between those in different neighborhoods can be fierce, placing students from opposite sides of town in the same school is a treacherous undertaking. Dinerral's wife, Tiffany, and her sixteen-year-old son, Thaddeus, were from Uptown, but after the storm Thaddeus was reassigned to John McDonogh High School in the Downtown district. In the hierarchy of neighborhood identities, the Uptown-Downtown divide trumps all, providing the two dominant categories within which narrower geographic delineations are made. Thaddeus was regularly harassed at John McDonogh, to the point where Dinerral and Tiffany considered placing him in another school. Police believe that a feud developed between Thaddeus and David Bonds, a student who stayed near John McDonogh in a house with several other teenagers. Bonds's tattoos signaled his identification with the neighborhood; a letter etched on the fingers of each hand spelled out "D-O-W-N-T-O-W-N" and the "6" on his forehead was short for the Sixth Ward neighborhood where he lived.

The feud came to a head during the holiday break. On the afternoon of December 28, Dinerral left school to play a jazz funeral for Gerald "Mr. Clean" Arthur, a forty-six-year-old man who had been killed in a struggle with a New Orleans police officer outside the Calliope projects. After the funeral, Dinerral hung out with the others in the Hot 8 until it began raining, and then he left to pick up his wife and her son. When Thaddeus emerged from his girlfriend's house on Dumaine Street in the Sixth Ward, a group of teenagers approached the car. As soon as Thaddeus could get inside, Dinerral pulled away as several gunshots broke through the car windows. Four blocks later the car came to a stop. Though he had managed to drive his family to safety, Dinerral was hit. Tiffany called Hot 8's band-leader Bennie Pete, who alerted the rest of the band, but by the time they made it to the Elmwood trauma center Dinerral was gone.

I learned of the murder when the newspaper arrived the next morning with the headline "Prominent Musician Killed While His Family Watched." The report listed a prior arrest of Dinerral's even while speculating that he had not been the intended target. That night I watched the evening news and saw David Bonds being apprehended by police.

**EPISODE 4.5: Voices and Instruments
at Dinerral's Funeral**

"It's like it's a curse on our band, man. It's always our babies," Bennie Pete had told me when we first met a few months before. Now Dinerral, twenty-five, was gone too.

I had decided to file a report on Dinerral's murder with National Public Radio's afternoon news program, *All Things Considered*, and met with Bennie and trombonist Jerome Jones to interview them. I began by asking about some of the songs Dinerral had brought to the Hot 8, and eventually the conversation turned to the preparations for Saturday's funeral.

"Right now, the shock is not wanting to accept it, but learning to accept it once you see him like that and then dealing with that a minute at a time," said Jerome. "After that, knowing—this is the main thing, because he's al-ready dead—is where we go from here as far as pertaining to how he died and how another family don't have to suffer this way. That's where we at right now, because this here, it's got to stop. . . . We play for too many funerals."

I asked Bennie how he had managed to summon the emotional where-withal to perform at the funeral of Joseph Williams. "At first, I was like, 'Man, I can't play this.' But I had to. So I played," he explained. "I felt I had to play, no matter how bad I felt—sad, hurt, wanting to cry, crying—I had to play because I owed him that. . . . I felt and heard his voice saying, 'Man, if I ever go before you, you better bring me down.'"

Bennie and Jerome expressed their role as intermediaries between the dead and the living to me and to an imagined radio audience. In a book this conversation is reduced to words on a page, but the emotion in the room and, to a certain extent, over the airwaves came through in the sound of their voices. When Bennie and Jerome speak they are communicating more than language; they are externalizing the internal by presenting their voices in a certain way. Bennie necessarily uses words to convey the significance of communicating to his lost friend, "bringing him down," but he is referring to nonlinguistic communication through instrumental music. At the funeral service and procession for Dinerral Shavers, many layers and possibilities of voice were detectable.

On the day of Dinerral's funeral, while radio listeners learn about his life and death, I attend the service at the Fifth African Baptist Church in the Central City neighborhood. In the balcony are several Rabouin students, some wearing white T-shirts with pictures of Dinerral and his birth and death dates: "Sunrise: March 19, 1981. Sunset: December 28, 2006." Downstairs, Dinerral's family occupies the first rows in front of the open casket. Onstage are several ministers, including Pastor Malcolm Collins from the Shavers' flooded church in the Lower Ninth Ward and Pastor Sanders of the host church that was rebuilt by the congregation soon after the storm.

The church resounds with spoken sermons, sung spirituals, and instrumental articulations, all juxtaposed and interwoven within a dense soundscape. A student begins sobbing, and Q and another classmate escort her outside. When a member of the chorus begins singing a gospel song accompanied by organ, Dinerral's wife, Tiffany, yells, "No, no, no, no, no. Get up Dinerral." The pastors convene and when the song ends Pastor Sanders steps to the lectern. "I'm going to ask, for the purpose of comfort to this family, we're going to ask that for the remainder of this service we have a closed casket." There are scattered boos and sobs and cries of "Oh, no." Sanders assures the congregation that the casket will be reopened for the viewing following the service.

Pastor Collins sermonizes in a booming voice that echoes off the rafters and stirs the congregation to respond. "There's no cemetery for Dinerral," he intones, and a middle-aged black woman sitting near me calls back, "That's right. He's gone already to be with the Lord." There is a wave of applause and Pastor Collins switches emotional registers from sorrow to anger. His voice, bordering on singing, rises in pitch and intensity, and the organist begins a song underneath the words, filling the spaces in between the proclamations with swelling chords.

"Our gun-slinging partners out there and you pistol-packing-toting fellas and sisters, I want you to know that God's going to send you to hell."

"Bye, bye," says a man in the upper pew.

Collins ends on a note of salvation: "If you follow Jesus, you'll see Dinerral again! Playing in a bigger band! For a greater audience than this!" The drums enter with a crash of the cymbals. "He'll be singing a song the angels can't sing! 'Ain't it good to know one day you'll be washed in the blood of the Lamb!'" Applause builds and the choir stands, first interjecting lines from a contemporary gospel song into the sermon ("You are the source of my strength!") and finally overtaking the pastor with a refrain of melismatic "Amens" that restore a sense of solemnity.

In the ritual of the church service, the voice is fundamental to enlivening the word of God. As the philosopher Mladen Dolar writes, "One cannot perform a religious ritual without resorting to the voice in that sense: one has, for example, to *say* prayers and sacred formulas."[22] At Dinerral's funeral, the emphasis on the voice is underscored by the preacher's stylized vocalizations, the utterances of the congregants, and the singing of the choir. Singing, especially, foregrounds the extralinguistic properties of the voice, enabling it to "turn the tables on the signifier," writes Dolar, "let[ting] the voice take the upper hand, let[ting] the voice be the bearer of what cannot be expressed by words."[23] The voices of those at the Fifth African Baptist Church reside on a vocal continuum in which speech and song not only provide listeners with referential content but also put them into direct contact with one another. This expansive notion of voice, encapsulating a polyphony of spoken, sung, and instrumental voices, is taken a step further when the musicians in Dinerral's band line up beside the pulpit.

"What a Friend We Have in Jesus" begins without the traditional snare drumroll, just three lone beats of the bass drum and a statement of the melody by the horn players in the Hot 8. The familiar sound of the brass band, with the silent snare drum making Dinerral's absence palpable, brings many in the pews to tears before a word is sung. Singer Glen David Andrews then leads us through the refrain, "What a friend we have in Jesus / All our sins and griefs to bear." The choir and audience members join in, and Andrews improvises variations on the melody over top.

After the service ends, the casket is carried to a hearse waiting outside and we hear another spiritual, "Just a Closer Walk with Thee." This time there is no singing, only the sound of the instrumentalists with their horns pointed toward the sky and their drums tapping out a slow rhythm. "When you go to the funeral and the musicians play the slow dirge, that be the time when they mourning the most," Bennie explained. "Because we playing from the heart, all the time, so at this time our heart is feeling that dirge, we expressing that dirge to the dead." Even though the dirge is performed without words, it is the most powerful expression that the living can offer the dead. "We feeling in our mind he could see this some kind of way, but if he can't we don't know, but if he could, he going to see that I brung my best for him on this morning, on this day." Bennie's description of communicating with the dead through his instrument echoes a similar description from the early twentieth century. "If you ever witnessed a funeral in New Orleans and they have one of those brass bands playing this funeral, you really have a bunch of musicians playing from the heart," remembered Louis Armstrong of his youth in New Orleans, "because as they go to the cemetery they play in a funeral march, they play 'Flee as a Bird,' 'Nearer My God to Thee,' and they express themselves in those instruments, *singing those notes the same as a singer would.*"[24]

The accounts of Louis Armstrong and Bennie Pete provide a rich description of the multiple layers of musical meaning embedded in the music of a jazz funeral. The texts of dirges such as "Flee as a Bird" and "Nearer My God to Thee" operate at both literal and metaphorical levels, expressing a universalist message of deliverance from suffering as well as the particular struggles of black Americans who have experienced various forms of bondage. When the singing is substituted with instruments, echoes of these linguistic meanings remain and are supplemented by the sound of the ensemble.[25] Communication among musicians and listeners, the living and the dead, occurs through instruments, a musical dialogue that the ethnomusicologist Ingrid Monson calls "intermusicality," or "a communication process that occurs primarily through musical sound itself, rather than words." Monson continues, "There is a constant interplay among sound, discursivity, language, and representations thereof that takes place when human beings make and listen to music that must be considered with its own particularities in mind."[26]

In the context of the jazz funeral, musicians speak through their instruments, creating a sound that New Orleanians and others interpret as a message to the dead. They conceive of the instrument as a voice, equivalent to yet distinct from the speaking and singing voice. As a wordless voice, the instrument is perhaps less capable of expressing literal meaning, but it gains the capacity to speak more ambiguously and inclusively. The dirge is experienced as a kind of public prayer through music. "At that time we trying to blow," Hot 8 trombonist Jerome Jones said of the dirge, "blow him to heaven."

The instrumental dirge signals the transition from the funeral service to the procession. The change in the atmosphere is also due to the meeting of mourners leaving the church and the second liners waiting outside. Nakita later explained to me that her brother's funeral was "like a reunion of the Ninth Ward" because neighborhood residents and church congregants who were displaced by the destruction of their homes had regrouped for the occasion, and outside they join musicians, acquaintances, and others who may not have known Dinerral but wish to participate in a celebration of his life.

The music organizes the collective suffering of those at the funeral and the collective pleasure that they anticipate in the shift to up-tempo music. During "Just a Closer Walk with Thee," those in the second line march slowly and deliberately, but when the casket is put in the hearse, Bennie sounds out the first notes to the up-tempo spiritual "Over in Gloryland" and the increase in tempo transforms the emotion from mourning to celebration. Rather than merely accompany the funeral procession, the music structures the entire movement and emotional state of the marchers. Bennie said:

> We might be feeling sad or something but that music and that beat's going to lift our spirit along with the happier times we had with that person. Right then and there—the transition, BAM!—from we mourning him and we grieving over him, to we just thinking about the time we was having fun and laughing loud and partying or whatever. The musician dictates that through the music, and that's coming surely from them.

The instruments of the brass band do not only communicate with the dead; they mediate the relationship between the living and the dead.

Behind and alongside the musicians are hundreds of second liners, their dress running the full spectrum from black formalwear to printed T-shirts with images of Dinerral. As the parade winds through the streets of Central City, past abandoned houses, leveled corner stores, and piles of debris that stand as unsettling yet optimistic signs of rebuilding, the band starts the up-tempo hymn "I'll Fly Away." Dinerral's family, friends, and students, as well as familiar faces from the second line community, are voicing the refrain: "I'll fly away, oh Glory, I'll fly away / When I die, Hallelujah bye and bye, I'll fly away."

Bennie, a distant look in his eye, calls out one up-tempo song after another. The music fills the air with jubilation and there is no looking back now, at least not for the Hot 8. The imperative for a brass band musician is to roll with it; after playing for the repast at the Laborer's Union Hall, the band eventually ends the workday by providing entertainment for a birthday party at a daiquiri bar.

EPISODE 4.6: Voices Amplified, Muffled, and Distorted

The brass band, as a material and metaphorical voice, articulated the sentiments of Dinerral's family, friends, bandmates, and others attending his funeral. However, cultural meanings and emotional significance are not containable within the community ritual because the jazz funeral is one in a series of events that, taken together, amount to a kind of public spectacle. This process began with the very public act of violence that took Dinerral's life and wound through a chain of subsequent events, including two protest marches, the arrest of David Bonds, and the murder trial that followed.

The voices that coalesced in the chant of "I'll Fly Away" at Dinerral's funeral, made more poignant by the thunderous blast of dozens of instruments and the contrasting silence of Dinerral's drum, resound in a public sphere that can amplify, muffle, or distort meanings and messages. *Voice* refers to many things here: an act of communication (sermons, lyrics, discourse), a sound (singing, instrumental music), and a symbol of collective agency (the sonic, visual, and physical presence of people occupying public space) (see episode 1.8). But voice encompasses more because each utterance, in the broadest sense, enters into a circulatory system that recontextualizes meanings and recalculates significance, like the echo off the concrete deck of the interstate that slices through a neighborhood, feeding back into the source sound. Just as musicians manipulate their instrumental voices, playing louder and faster to match the noise of the highway, so do we all present our voices in specific ways as we orient ourselves outward, where our voices resonate, entangle, and warp; or are silenced.

The voice of the media echoes loudly and authoritatively in the streets, homes, and other spaces of everyday life. The aim of media outlets is to transform events into spectacles, whether they are perceived as broadly cultural (jazz funerals, community parades, festivals) or explicitly political (crime scenes, trials, peace rallies). The power of media to manipulate voices was abundantly evident during Hurricane Katrina, when reports of rape and murder at city shelters were later determined to be unfounded and racial bias was detectable in many reports of so-called looting.[27] All of the events presented in this chapter in relation to Dinerral's murder were mediated through television news broadcasts and newspaper articles. Within this mediascape, there are informed and sensitive accounts by journalists such as Katy Reckdahl of the *Times-Picayune*, the blogger Deborah "Big Red" Cotton, and the writers of *Treme* crafting drama based on actual events, including Dinerral's murder. Their work, along with my own writings and radio stories, circulates with mainstream media accounts of violence and criminality among urban blacks and their supposed failure to meet social norms.

Dinerral's story took hold of the public imagination partly because of his status as a local musician and teacher and also because his killing coincided with that of Helen Hill, a white filmmaker who was murdered in her home by an intruder. The twin victims—one black, one white; both innocent; and both upstanding citizens and beloved members of sprawling social networks—pained a city suffering from a homicide rate ten times the national average, and stirred anger over the NOPD's abysmal arrest rate (half the national average at 38 percent) and the district attorney's similarly low prosecution rate (13 percent).[28] The *New York Times* ran the story "Storm Left New Orleans Ripe for Violence," while CBS-News produced "Storm of Murder," and NPR aired my segment "Drummer's Funeral Underlines New Orleans Violence."

During the tumult, the community activist group Silence Is Violence was formed by Baty Landis, Nakita Shavers, and others who called for a March against Violence to City Hall on January 11, 2007. When the morning arrives, the Hot 8 position themselves right at the start. But they do not carry instruments, and though the march is a deliberate display of community participation and collective sentiment, it is distinctive from a brass band parade in almost every way. The march begins not on a backstreet in a residential neighborhood but under the high-rise hotels and office buildings along Canal Street in the heart of the Central Business District (CBD). The crowd of approximately five thousand is larger than a community parade, and the majority of participants are white. Most strikingly, there is no music.

The Hot 8 had debated whether to present themselves as citizens calling for reform or performers providing a service, and ultimately they elected not to play. Like many New Orleans musicians, the members of the Hot 8 are public figures who are experienced in dealing with media inquiries and representations, and they recognized the silent parade as a staged media event intended to voice an explicit message of austerity, the intelligibility of which would be compromised by associations with festive music and dance. As we march, parade organizers enforce silence, even going so far as to quiet one musician's attempt to sing the hymn "This Little Light of Mine." Attention is directed toward the signs that silently memorialize Dinerral Shavers, Helen Hill, and even Joseph Williams with messages like "Violent systems create violent people" and "RIP Joseph."

Upon arriving at City Hall, a series of speakers, including Nakita and Hot 8 trombonist Jerome Jones, demand changes in criminal justice, education, and social welfare to an audience that includes Mayor Ray Nagin, Police Chief Warren Riley, and representatives of local and national news media. As speakers at a rally, musicians and activists fulfill the role of community members taking an ideological stance. The loud music, singing, dancing, and collective joy of a brass band parade are antithetical to the politics of protest and would have detracted from these statements, clouding the literalness of sober language with the more ambiguous pleasure of music.

Two weeks later there is another silent parade, this one sponsored by a coalition of parading organizations called the Social Aid and Pleasure Club Task Force. The Task Force began in the immediate aftermath of Katrina as a way of representing the numerous neighborhood clubs and protecting their shared interests. Their inaugural parade in January 2006 was marred by a shooting that incited a media-fueled moral panic over violence at second line parades; on one occasion around this time a clerk at an upscale boutique described the parade to me as a "riot." Sensitive to such associations, the Task Force has organized the March for Peace and Celebration of Hope. Tamara Jackson, president of the Task Force and founder of the VIP Ladies Social Aid and Pleasure Club, outlined their objectives in a press release: "In this historic event, Club members will unite the tradition of the second line and the peace march in the tradition of Dr. Martin Luther King. The Clubs will proceed silently for two miles before brass bands join in to celebrate hope for the full recovery of New Orleans."[29]

As with the march to City Hall, this procession moves silently through the CBD, luring the media with the message that second line parades are safe community events. The organizers lead the march with a banner that states "Save Our Culture—Stop the Violence" to ensure that spectators perceive this as an austere social movement rather than a festive party. This time no one stops the marchers from singing, but the chants of "We sick and tired [of] all that black-on-black crime" and "Shoo fly, don't bother me" leave little room for misinterpretation. The sight of the second liners walking in rigid formation provides a stark contrast to their jubilant second line parades, and the sound of relative silence inspires confused looks on the faces of many bystanders, as well as a few participants. I am walking with the anthropologist Helen Regis, and we discuss the poetics of silence and wonder aloud, "What makes a second line a second line?"

"We made a point, and the city wasn't prepared for that," Tamara later observed. "They didn't think we can all get together with no music, and we did."

Brass band music propels the pleasure of the second line. When people need to make a literal statement that is unequivocally serious, then their most effective option is to silence the music, to remove it and make its absence conspicuous. Making an explicit statement requires disassociation with ambiguous music and the dancing and smiling it inevitably brings. The sound of the brass band was deemed incapable of articulating a political agenda by organizers presenting a unified display of suffering and frustration. "If you're playing music, you can't put out a statement," explained Gerald Platenburg of the Nine Times, one of twenty participating Social Aid and Pleasure Clubs. "You second lining and you dancing, ain't nobody going to be speaking their voice."

When the march leaves the CBD and we make our way toward Central City, a predominantly black residential neighborhood, the remaining media peel off from the route. We turn onto Martin Luther King Boulevard, pass the Guste housing projects, and arrive at Dorothy's Lounge, where the Hot 8, Rebirth, and Free Agents brass bands are waiting outside. Members of the Task Force had disagreed over whether to proceed in silence, so a compromise was reached in which the silent march through the CBD would be followed by a second line through Central City. There is an enormous shift in the emotional register as club members shed their signs and their expressions of seriousness. Dancing comes quickly on the heels of the music, and a middle-aged black woman next to me, evidently recently returned to her hometown, smiles to a friend and says, "I'm home, baby. For good!" The spectacle of protest staged in part for the media has been transformed into a moving block party for the community of parading organizations and their followers. Printed and spoken messages directed to the general public are traded in for personal exchanges and musical voices, the sound resonating off the pavement and the squat, skinny houses packed side by side.

In the news coverage of the Task Force parade, viewers were shown images of club members silently marching and an interview with Tamara explaining the reason for the march, but not the second half of the parade, when the clubs' members met up with the bands and began dancing with unrestrained pleasure. Those scenes feature often enough in news stories, usually programmed as the "feel good" or "cultural" segment at the conclusion of a broadcast, while the peace march and protest march ran as the lead story on the nightly news and were covered on the front page of the *Times-Picayune.*

Locating where voice resides in these events presents a challenge: not only are material, musical, and symbolic voices channeled through the editorial filter of the media, but mediated subjects are aware of how they will be represented and present their voices accordingly.[30] Some are silenced; others are amplified in order to articulate an unambiguous message. This strategy of presenting the self is derived from experiential knowledge of the media's power to shape the perception and discourse of black Americans. Bennie remembered the media response when Joseph Williams was killed: "All the news people came and they felt sorry for us." And so Bennie consented to interviews. But when the stories appeared, they offered a one-dimensional portrait of Joseph as a criminal, inferring that the killing by the police was warranted. "It really opened my eyes to how the news and the media could just blemish a person's personality and character," said Bennie. "They have the control to reach the whole public, so they can say what they want and that's just what they did." Now Bennie self-edits his comments more carefully, contorting his voice in an attempt to ensure that he cannot be misrepresented.

In stories about criminality, the media works in conjunction with that other powerful institution of surveillance and discipline, the criminal justice system. For example, it is police policy to alert the media to the prior arrests of suspects *and* victims. Joseph Williams's identity as a criminal was provided by NOPD spokesperson Marlon Defillo, who was on the crime scene to inform the media of Joseph's arrest record, even though the charges had been dropped. Police also notify the media when suspects will be apprehended so that the arrest creates a news event. Within twenty-four hours after Dinerral's murder, there was some carefully orchestrated footage on the evening news of police officers loading a handcuffed David Bonds into a cruiser. As part of their search for a motive, police informed the media of a previous charge against Dinerral that had been dropped without incident. These instances teach us that voices resound not only in the streets where cultural and violent episodes occur, but also in the virtual spaces of the media that represent them and the authoritative spaces of law and order.

On April 11, 2008, in Section I of the Orleans Parish Criminal Court, I attend David Bonds's trial for Dinerral's murder. Past the security checkpoint and down the hallway with gleaming marble floors and imposing arched ceilings, I inquire at the information desk to find the room number for the trial. "Is that the guy that killed Shavers?" the attendant asks. I nod and am directed to the room. When order is called, I sit in the back and observe the testimonies. Dinerral's stepson, Thaddeus, known as "Lil' Man," recounts the events of the shooting. The story begins with Lil' Man and his friend Guy scrambling into the car amid a barrage of bullets and ends with Lil' Man being questioned in a police trailer. As Lil' Man remembers it, when he asked the interrogating officers if he could see his stepfather, they informed him that Dinerral was dead.

On the podium, Lil' Man seems nervous, or more accurately, fearful. A juror had already expressed concerns to the judge that Bonds was intimidating a witness by making a gun gesture with his hand on the side of his face. Guy had already testified that he could not put Bonds at the scene. When the city attorney asks Lil' Man if he can identify the shooter in the courtroom, he says he cannot.

Testimony must be positively voiced from the witness stand in order to constitute evidence. Witnesses are generally required to appear in person and to take an oath to speak the truth and then verbally testify while facing the accused. Lawyers manipulate their voices to coax witnesses into saying what is best for their client. The voice of the judge presides over all others', the smack of the gavel against the sound block signaling his or her supreme authority. The jury sits in silence and deliberates in isolation before ultimately stealing the final word in a formulaic verbal proclamation of guilt or innocence. The voices in the gallery never rise above the level of a whisper, lest we stand in contempt of court.

When the judge calls for a lunch break, I linger in the hallway to say hello to the family and the members of the Hot 8. Bennie and I talk for a while, and then Nakita introduces me to her mom, Yolande, who thanks me for coming. Everyone looks shell-shocked.

When the trial concludes, Bonds is acquitted. On the local news I see Nakita and Yolande crying as they leave the courtroom. But the sound of their voices, along with that of the accused, is overpowered by the noise of reporters and criminal justice officials sermonizing on the steps of the courthouse. A few days later Guy is shot and killed near his house, in the same block where Dinerral and his family lived briefly after Katrina, just a few blocks from where my own family lives. No one is sure that the killing is related to the trial. Guy was up on charges of cocaine possession, and some of the kids I know in the neighborhood tell me he was dealing drugs. The next month, Bonds is arrested again, this time accused of shooting someone on Canal Street, and in May 2010 he is convicted of attempted murder.

Around this time, the Civil Rights Division of the Department of Justice undertook an investigation of the NOPD, eventually determining that the force "has engaged in patterns of misconduct that violate the Constitution and federal law." The agencies have entered into a Consent Decree to "fundamentally change the culture of the NOPD."[31]

Murders and funerals, parades and protests, arrests and trials, and media representations of these events create a sort of public theater with a script that unfolds in real time, moving from scene to scene and character to character. Amid the calamity can be discerned the sound of voices seeking solidarity, intelligibility, and simply a chance to be heard. These voices, in all their different registers, are amplified, muffled, and distorted as they circulate. Their entanglement creates a polyphony of voices that runs the gamut from silence to cacophony, consonance to dissonance.

EPISODE 4.7: Voices Lost and Found

Death permeates life in New Orleans. If the above-ground cemeteries scattered throughout the city are a permanent reminder that death awaits us all, then the newspaper headlines spell out the specifics for too many young black men: death can arrive at any moment, come from any direction, and strike with absolute precision or indiscriminate blindness.

To the distant or casual observer, the deaths and the victims themselves may seem interchangeable. Newspapers and television news programs might neglect to identify the names of shooting victims unless the killing is deemed noteworthy to the average reader and viewer, such as a police killing or the murder of a celebrated musician and teacher. In either case, providing the arrest records of victims implies that their endings are justified. The security of some relies upon the expendability of others. Root causes are muffled, barely audible, while their aftereffects resonate loudly through the media airwaves and halls of justice.

The funerals also recur with numbing monotony. The end of life sets into motion an unvarying pattern: first the viewing, then the service, then the dirge accompanying the brief moment of public mourning, and finally the grand finale that fills the streets and the banquet halls with celebratory music. For the friends and family of the dead, when the band packs up their instruments and all that is left is to clean up the paper plates and plastic cups, there is the unsettling stillness of absence, the silence of a lost voice. For the musicians, this has all been another day at the office, and more often than not it is time to move on to the next gig. Yet the death of Dinerral Shavers, along with those of Jacob Johnson and Joseph Williams, teaches us that every death amounts to the loss of an individual who impacted others in ways that challenge associations between poverty and pathology. The statistics are revealing, but they can also obscure the fact that the lives of victims intersect with others in positive ways.

"If you look at the news and you just read the paper every day," Bennie Pete warned, "you would be in the mind frame to think that everybody in that age bracket is into killing and crime, and [Dinerral] was just the opposite, you know. He was really striving to be a complete grown man and a musician and just a positive role model, a positive person."

The impact Dinerral made at Rabouin High School was evident in the dazed expressions of his students rehearsing in the band room a week after

4.4 *A Fitting Farewell for Ed Buckner's Son Brandon (Unfinished Piece) [detail].* 2008. Each panel is 54″ × 36″. © WILLIE BIRCH.

his death. "He wasn't just my band teacher," said Skully, "he was like a big brother to me."

Even the brass band musicians desensitized to death by its constant presence are not spared its effects. The closeness of Jacob, Joseph, and Dinerral to their bandmates disrupted the routine of playing funerals. Their deaths demanded recognition and restored the full significance of the jazz funeral tradition, if only temporarily.

I hardly knew Dinerral, but I found myself unable to get my bearings in the immediate aftermath of his death. At the funeral service, sitting in the upper balcony of the Fifth African Baptist Church, I felt like an alien in the black dress clothes I had found tucked away in my closet. Bennie, on the other hand, moved with surefooted determination, even if his facial expression betrayed his grief. He must have worn a black suit like this one a hundred times. It was simply a given from the moment his tuba appeared above the heads of the pallbearers that everything from this point forward was in his large and capable hands. In a moment such as this, the sound emanating from the bell of Bennie's tuba is his voice, and whether his instrument expresses sorrow or joy, it does so with an assuredness matched by the solidity of its low tones.

The commanding presence of Bennie was a counterpoint to the gaping absence of Dinerral, and even an impressive battery of snare drummers could not fill the space left by his silence. Dinerral's cold style—"like an octopus," described Jerome—was his unique voice. You can still hear Dinerral's actual voice on recordings such as the Hot 8's cover of Marvin Gaye's "Sexual Healing," when his soulful singing rises above the voices of his bandmates. And you can still see Dinerral in Spike Lee's *When the Levees Broke*, standing in front of his mother's devastated home in the Lower Ninth Ward, or watch an actor portraying him in the television series *Treme*. But the innovation, improvisation, and motivation Dinerral brought to each Hot 8 performance is no longer present. "He was always pushing, he was always holding me accountable for things," remembered Bennie. It was Dinerral who made the arrangements for the recording sessions that led to the CD *Rock with the Hot 8*, and it was his artwork on the cover. "With his death and stuff, I see like a lot of that force—and pushing—it's kind of gone." Dinerral's approach to drumming was his individual way of making tradition his own, and the songs he composed were his way of extending tradition and, whether he realized it or not, leaving his mark.

On a Sunday evening a few weeks after Dinerral's funeral, the Hot 8 is performing at Stanly U's Lounge in the Uptown neighborhood known as Zion City. After a short break, Bennie launches into the opening of Dinerral's "Get Up" and the band falls into step. The song begins sparsely with tuba and vocals, building in tension until a long snare drumroll leads to the entrance of the full band playing at full volume and energy. Dinerral's absence is jarring. He had hit the snare with a full stroke and added supplemental percussion on wood blocks and cowbell. His replacement plays softer, tapping out a sparse rhythm on the rim of the snare drum. Jerome turns and gestures forcefully with the slide of his trombone to indicate that he should cut loose, but the song remains stagnant, a reminder of Dinerral's loss.

Nakita still asks the Hot 8 to play "Get Up" whenever she sees them perform. She has listened to the recording so many times that she can almost hear Dinerral singing to her. His voice, in reproduction and in memory, continues to testify to his uniqueness. Even now, with Sammy Williams coming into his own in the snare drum role, and many changes in membership—Jerome moved back and forth to Houston, saxophonist Cliff Stewart enrolled in college, and others have come and gone—Dinerral's voice remains audible. Perhaps the lesson for the newer members of the Hot 8 is to carve out their own voice within the group, creating a sonic fingerprint that cannot be duplicated.

CONCLUSION

ENGAGEMENTS

T he people who populate this book and the events that they make happen testify to the vitality of New Orleans culture as well as the predicaments that local musicians share with many other black Americans. The subjective experience of those I have encountered varies greatly, but each of them has exerted agency through words, through action, and, above all, through music. As they navigate uneven terrain, brass band musicians exercise degrees of control over the relations in which they are enmeshed.

In the months after Katrina, while writing grant applications in New York, I projected a study of music, race, and poverty with the Rebirth and Dirty Dozen cast as the triumphant winners who had risen above their humble beginnings and the Hot 8 and Soul Rebels as the proud losers who remained mired in a struggle for money and respect. Though the basic outline of that proposal remains, real people and events turned out to be far more complex. Both Hot 8 and the Soul Rebels, for instance, have achieved relative success since I first met them, and while Rebirth has continued to rise in prominence, their everyday experiences are not free from risk. Local black culture has been a resource for these musicians and their agency does propel their social mobility, even as their movements remain confined to a social and political infrastructure that

c.1 *Two Tubas Playing for the Crowd.* 2003. 70½″ × 36¼″. © WILLIE BIRCH.

consistently marginalizes them by forfeiting the right to a quality public education, ensuring health care remains prohibitively expensive for individuals, and downsizing social welfare programs such as public housing in favor of prisons and other systems of punishment, all while touting universal access to the American dream. A handful of musicians have succeeded, but the odds continue to be stacked against them and their success is an exception to the restaurant workers, hotel maids, workaday musicians, and others whose livelihoods are defined by insecurity. In a state of precarity the only safe bet is to roll with it.

In the years since I moved to New Orleans, entered into domains of local culture, and eventually formalized an academic study, I have become increasingly attuned to music's entanglements with political and economic forces. I came to believe I could write a book about music that was also a book about social justice, and in conclusion I have come to ask what the implications and potential outcomes of such a book might be. At the start of this story I set forth a cluster of themes—voice, agency, subjectivity, mobility—that I was led to explore through my interactions with people and my participation in musical events. As I finish I am compelled to reverse the focus on these interactions, or at least be more forthcoming about my own agency in circulating ideas as the author of this book. One thing about mobility is that you do not always know exactly what direction you are going in or what kind of effect your motion will have. Another thing about voice is that you do not always know the most effective way to present yourself, let alone precisely what you are trying to articulate and how others will receive you.

One evening in April 2007 I went to Rachel Breunlin's house to meet with friends and colleagues, including Helen Regis, Hot 8 bandleader Bennie Pete, and Social Aid and Pleasure Club Task Force members Tamara Jackson and Troy Materre. As I mentioned in the introduction, the purpose of the gathering was to brainstorm in advance of a panel for the Society for the Anthropology of North America's annual conference in New Orleans. The panel was titled "Local Knowledge: New Orleans Artists and Activists Reflect on the State of the City after Katrina," and there was broad agreement that we would discuss, as stated in the abstract, "strategies for confronting multiple challenges facing New Orleanians working in the 'cultural sector,' including a top-heavy culture and tourism industry, urban restructuring, violence, repressive regimes of policing, dispersed family and social networks and personal loss." While we were plotting out talking points for Bennie, Tamara, Troy, and Ronald W. Lewis, curator of the House of Dance and Feathers museum, Bennie asked what the three anthropologists would be contributing to the presentation. Knowing full well that the conference attendees would be most interested in hearing from local artists and activists, Rachel, Helen, and I assumed that we would fulfill the more ancillary roles of moderating discussion and coordinating the audiovisual supplements. But Bennie persisted: What drew us to be active in local culture? Didn't our engagement with New Orleans constitute forms of "local knowledge"?

Bennie's questions resonate with numerous scholarly debates about the appropriation of black music, ethnographic writing as representation, and collaboration and engagement as research methodology. The exploitation of black culture includes not only appropriation by entrepreneurs in the culture industry, as discussed in chapter 2, but also representation by researchers in the academy. "Urban social science," writes Robin Kelley, "has played a key role in marking 'blackness' and defining black culture to the 'outside' world."[1] Studies that have linked poverty and violence to behavior, focusing on individual responsibility while discounting the responsibilities of governmental and private institutions, have unwittingly "provide[d] scholarly ammunition for popular and political efforts to justify and excuse the persistence of poverty," write Goode and Masakovsky.[2] Research critical of this tradition, including Micaela di Leonardo's *Exotics at Home: Anthropologies, Others, American Modernity*, has revealed the liberal left's complicity with conservative "blame the victim" narratives that attribute poverty to "social disorganization."[3]

In the catalogue for the House of Dance and Feathers museum, published in collaboration with Rachel and Helen by the Neighborhood Story Project, Ronald Lewis writes, "A lot of them came around with that education—PhDs and stuff—and stole a lot. They're just repeating what they done heard and using the extravagant words."[4] Herreast Harrison, the wife of Mardi Gras Indian chief Donald Harrison Sr., calls the interlopers "talking heads of tradition." These comments demonstrate how the appropriation of black culture is linked to the representation of black people in local discourse. But Bennie's question went beyond race to intersect more broadly with the politics of representation. His request to make our participation in the production of local knowledge transparent is consistent with a reflexive turn in ethnography associated with the book *Writing Culture: The Poetics and Politics of Ethnography*.[5] Increasingly since the 1980s, anthropologists have come to recognize their role in constituting subjects and to reflect upon their own entanglements with those they represent. In *Anthropology as Cultural Critique*, George Marcus and Michael Fischer suggest that "efforts to make ethnographic writing more sensitive to its broader political, historical, and philosophical implications" have the potential to "place anthropology at the vortex of the debate about the problems of representing society in contemporary discourses."[6] In their formulation, which helped to revise the genre of anthropological monographs both in narrative position and purpose, ethnographic inquiry is presented subjectively with the goal of cultural critique.

But again, Bennie's question was not limited to the problem of representing culture in writing or repurposing ethnographic research for cultural critique, because he was asking the anthropologists to be explicit about their everyday engagements as New Orleanians. Bennie knows me not only as an ethnographer but also as a radio reporter, curator, client, musician, and listener, not to mention adopted New Orleanian, father, white man, antiracist, and secular humanist. The stories in this book emanated from my entanglements with New Orleans musicians and others invested in local culture: helping to organize community workshops with Rebirth; collaborating on panels at academic conferences; conducting an interview with the Soul Rebels at Jazz Fest; producing public radio stories on the Hot 8 and Black Men of Labor; hiring the New Birth Brass Band to play at my wedding; and publishing articles in scholarly journals. This book is part of an ensemble of activities in which I not only represent others but engage with them in multiple scenarios.

Bennie's question was a challenge that also offered a possible way forward: of reflecting on my position as a white author representing predominantly black subjects, composing a narrative about my interactions with him and others. "We do not have 'informants,'" Michael Taussig writes of ethnographers. "We live with storytellers, whom too often we have betrayed for the sake of an illusory science. The task before us, then, is to cross the divide, scary as it may be, and become storytellers as well."[7] By imposing order on events in an attempt to create coherence, we are all active narrators of subjective knowledge, not passive conveyors of objective truths. The anthropologist Michael Jackson writes, "To reconstitute events in a story is no

c.2 *Brother with Straw Hat, Sunglasses, and Cross.* 2003. 49″ × 42″.
© WILLIE BIRCH.

longer to live those events impassively, but to actively rework them, both in dialogue with others and within one's own imagination."[8] My collaborations with Bennie and others became a methodological model for writing culture.

Bennie was not the only one advising the anthropologists that evening. Tamara followed up by inquiring about the intended outcome of our efforts. As the director of the Social Aid and Pleasure Club Task Force, she was in the final stages of a successful lawsuit against the NOPD to lower the permit fees for community parades (see episode 1.4). She would go on to become the director of victim and community outreach for Silence Is Violence, organizing press conferences and neighborhood "peace walks" to stem violence and hold the criminal justice system accountable for negligence (see episode 4.6). She is an activist whose purpose is not only to critique but to utilize critique for the purpose of action, and she was justifiably perplexed over the purported aims of ethnographic research.

Tamara's question is in step with scholarly discourse about cultural critique and its limits. Reflexive ethnography and cultural critique have transformed the discipline of anthropology but it is not clear to what ends. Marcus and Fischer's intervention, as they state, was fundamentally about addressing the problems of *representing* society without necessarily being concerned with the subsequent step of addressing society's problems. Anthropologist Kim Fortun has made a call to ethnographers to deploy critique as one part of an ensemble of "design logics" that are "directed at transformation": "Ethnography thus becomes creative—setting language games in motion, provoking different orderings of things, having patience for what we cannot yet imagine."[9] Other ethnographers have extended beyond critique by being more explicit about their engagements with research subjects and their role not only as critics but as activists. In the foreword to Victoria Sanford and Asale Angel-Ajani's *Engaged Observer: Anthropology, Advocacy, and Activism*, Philippe Bourgois urges anthropologists who have been "jolted emotionally by the human face of their research topics" to "engage with political stakes that matter to the people who bear a disproportionate toll for suffering caused by the inequalities that power imposes."[10] Sanford writes of the contributors to the volume:

> Violence, experience, access, representation, witnessing and analysis are not abstract theoretical issues for these authors. On the contrary, they are tangible and immediate to the lives of those who live in communities where we work and they are as much markers for our practice as researchers as they are a framework in which we each try to build an intellectual context in territories where survivors are often denied not only agency but their very subjectivity.[11]

The subjects of this book live in the most prosperous country in the world, but they have been subjected to forms of structural violence that threaten their rights to full citizenship. Without making a grand claim for the power of academic writing to transform society, there is potential for ethnographers who make uniquely intimate engagements with people to open up more possibilities for social justice. In this story, there are models for overcoming vulnerability provided by the astute members of the Rebirth Brass Band, and there is the confounding opportunity for economic stability offered to musicians working in, of all places, a massive casino franchise. There is a multisited study of the cultural economy that includes analysis of a state-sponsored report outlining steps to compensate cultural workers more equitably. There is an open discussion about the current relevance of traditional cultural practices, surveying two sides of a thorny debate, and noting that each side has utilized tradition productively to stake out a viable subject position. And there is a portrayal of victims of interpersonal violence as individuals who impacted those around them in ways that challenge uncritical associations between poverty and pathology. In relating these stories, I face my own received limitations as a talking head of tradition, an interloper and expropriator, but I have tried to make the most of this anxious, in-between position to orient my writing toward social justice.

In November 2010, when the American Anthropological Association held its annual meeting in New Orleans, Rachel, Helen, and I again collaborated with local artists and activists on a series of panels titled "Engaging New Orleans." This time around we each took a seat at the table, alongside a larger and more diverse set of panelists, and joined in the discussion. Tamara Jackson and Ronald W. Lewis returned, and Gerald Platenburg was there to represent the Nine Times, but Bennie was not able to make it. The Hot 8 was on tour, bringing New Orleans music to an appreciative audience in the Culp Auditorium at East Tennessee State University. Earlier in the day, the band had presented a demonstration of brass band and parading traditions to students, discussing local culture, playing representative material, and orienting themselves within a proud legacy. For the moment, the band has managed to thrive by tapping into the resourcefulness of culture, expertly maneuvering a course that has presented them with more than their share of obstacles. Bennie wants to write a book about it all. We have been meeting with Rachel at Neighborhood Story Project, and Bennie is going forward with the book, though his busy schedule makes it hard to pin him down. Experience has taught him it is best to keep moving.

IMAGE AND MUSIC IN
THE ART OF WILLIE BIRCH

The presence of Willie Birch's art goes beyond illustration, to embody the ideas proposed in Matt Sakakeeny's text. Images and words play with and against each other, much the same way musicians play with each other's voices to create something greater than their own.

The process began with a series of conversations between the artist and the author in New Orleans during the hot summer months of 2012. Matt would come from Uptown on his bike with his tape recorder and sit with Birch in his downtown studio in the Seventh Ward, a shotgun house with walls covered in large black-and-white works in progress. Finished paintings are stacked side by side like books, while actual books — about art, philosophy, and culture — are packed onto shelves or arranged in piles on end tables. Although Birch owns an old air-conditioner, he usually prefers to leave it off and work in the heat, letting the sounds from the backyard and street come through the open windows, into the workspace and, ultimately, into the art.

In 2008 Matt attended the Prospect.1 exhibition of Birch's work at the New Orleans Museum of Art and was struck by a life-size painting of a second line parade in seven panels. The layers of charcoal, applied with acrylic washes in a process called *grisaille*, somehow created an event rather than a representation of an event; somehow the static figures were in rhythmic motion, dancing beyond the limits of their two-dimensional confines; somehow the passive spectator was transformed into an active participant. The sense of motion was further reinforced by the fact that each panel

A.2 *The Second Liner.* 2000. 72³/₄" × 36". © WILLIE BIRCH.

connected to the next, vertically and horizontally, capturing the feel of the procession as it meanders through the streets.

It was not until two years later that we crossed paths. While attending a lecture by the cultural historian Robin Kelley, Birch listened to Matt introduce the renowned guest speaker and then sought him out afterward. We spoke about music, particularly New Orleans music, and, as the saying goes, one thing led to another. Matt eventually shared the manuscript of this book with Birch, which he returned marked profusely with comments and suggestions. Birch was excited about Matt's ability to transport the reader out of an abstract word space onto solid ground where real people create actual events. He encouraged Matt to reveal more of himself as a real person writing a story that would, in itself, constitute an actual event. As Matt worked on the manuscript, Birch selected works that he felt best expressed the spirit of the text and invited Matt back to his studio to continue the conversation.

Matt arrived to find that Birch had loaded the projector with slides that he beamed onto a blank spot on the wall in his back room. The first slide was *Black Men of Labor (Labor Day Parade)*.

> **MATT:** I mean, that's a straight correspondence to my book, I would say.
> **BIRCH:** (Smiles) Yeah. Your book has already dictated the rhythm. I just want to give you enough variations where you can see that there is a rhythm that we can create together.

Going through the slides we began to see our work in parallel. In the paintings, Matt recognized faces and places that he knew and events that he had attended; reading the text, Birch came to the realization that he had shared experiences with Matt. The possibility arose that our mutual understanding could create a book in which the visual and written layering would re-create the rhythms of the musicians, second liners, and bystanders who created the experiences described.

Matt, forty-one, white, and from the Northeast, came into his own in New Orleans, where his professional and social activities are all entangled. A friend once gave him the nickname "Professor Second Line," but the name has not stuck. Birch, sixty-nine, black, was born and raised in New Orleans, then left for academic training and travel—to Amsterdam, Baltimore, Harlem, Nairobi, and elsewhere—before he returned to the city in 1994. The young people who watch him riding his bike through the neighborhood, snapping photographs of ordinary scenes, call him "Mr. Willie."

We are two very different people with dissimilar experiences, and our perspectives reflect this; for instance, while the brass band musicians in Birch's work often appear in traditional uniform, those in Matt's work favor everyday clothes. But where we separate in terms of racial, geographic, and generational identity we reconnect in terms of subjectivity: our perspectives are complementary. First and foremost, we are both awestruck by culture—especially musical, culinary, and visual culture—as a set of entwined processes that speak to collective experience (identity) as well as individuality (subjectivity).

> **BIRCH:** So here we have cultural manifestations that transcend food, that transcend dance, that transcend visual art, that transcend music—all coming from the same place. From the outside you may see these as different things, but to somebody born to the culture like me, the connectedness is taken for granted. When I listen to Ms. Chase [a Creole chef in New Orleans] talk about the preparations of her food—her concerns about how it's going to look; commenting on the different colors or textures of the ingredients—there is a direct parallel to how we can talk about music. New Orleans music is melodic, easy not only to listen to but to dance to as well. It should feel good and talk to you, otherwise most people won't participate in it. Connections are everywhere; all you have to do is open your window and look and listen. Just look at the way we dress! These cultural manifestations are in the lifestyle and express who we are collectively.
>
> The problem in American culture is that we tend to put labels on everything: music, culture, art. We tend to characterize and departmentalize everything, attempting to distance it from whatever has come before or will come after. But that's not the artist's or musician's concern. Our role is to define and participate in the moment that we live in, and that means that the new generation of New Orleans musicians is going to look at hip-hop, for example, and take from it what they feel fits into who they are and make it their own and build on it. In the same way, my generation is going to have to learn to speak to it, or move out to the side.

New Orleanians such as chef Leah Chase emerge out of a collective and historical past to actively reshape the present. Cultural forms such as a plate of food, a hand-painted sign for a barbershop, or a jazz funeral are simultaneously manifestations of deep histories and the grounds for new creative innovation. Matt and Birch are in that mix also: in Matt's writing just as in Birch's paintings, public culture provides a template for creating work undertaken with the various specialized tools inherent in the medium. Rather than generate abstract theory, Matt's ethnographic research yields a text modeled on the complex rhythms and dynamic interactions of a brass band parade. Birch compares his use of technique—composition, scale, contrast, perspective—to that of a musician training, composing, and improvising toward an end of personal expression, social commentary, and public art making.

Although his formal training allows him to be part of a community whose language came out of a European sensibility, Birch's upbringing in New Orleans helps him understand that it is not the only tradition by which he could create. Like the musicians in New Orleans, whose music has been shaped by both European and African sensibilities, Birch realizes that the audience is critical to what is expressed; if the music does not reflect the aspirations and concerns of its audience, it will be rejected. Ideally the people who follow the processions become collaborators in creating the music. When Birch lived in New York in the 1970s and 1980s, he struggled with defining who his audience was. The answer that finally came to him was his people, beginning with his mother and continuing outward to his community.

The visual traditions most reflected in the culture of New Orleans are not formal, but folkloric. The most glaring example of this can be seen in the making, wearing, and performing of Mardi Gras Indian suits. Recently some Mardi Gras Indians have embraced other forms of artistic expression. At the same time, young, formally trained visual artists are creating imagery about what it means to live in this part of the world and how place consciously or unconsciously defines how they create.

> **BIRCH:** The uncertainty of the Louisiana environment, its susceptibility to hurricanes, floods, humidity, heat, and rain, makes for different visual imagery. The will to survive among the people of New Orleans is part of our improvisational nature, allowing us to create art forms that are unique to our environment.

One day, standing around the kitchen table in the studio, Matt was guzzling water after a particularly grueling bike ride while Birch was speaking of a documentary film he had seen the night before, *Gilles Deleuze from A to Z*, about the French philosopher. Birch was excited by Deleuze's radical claim that philosophers actively create new realities rather than passively analyze existing ones. For Deleuze, the tools of the philosopher—or those of the musician, artist, or writer—are constructive. Birch related this to his realization, upon his return to New Orleans years back, that he no longer had to deal with the issue of art as being either representational or abstract. It was a philosophical affirmation of his belief that as an artist, the definition followed your creation, not the other way around.

While there are obvious differences in the properties of music, art, writing, and philosophy (such as materiality and temporality), in our conversations we spoke of them only as complements. How exciting to arrange a meeting of written words and visual art and music! The spark arises from the conjoining of the mediums, produced differently but toward the same end; that, following Deleuze, is as much a matter of the artist's *intent* as of artistic *content*.

Against the momentum of so much contemporary art and so much current academic writing, we are not picking up the tools of our trades to deconstruct the real or to fabricate an abstraction of the real, but to create other manifestations of the real. In both of our cases (and often for Deleuze as well), we apply them in targeted ways to reveal the politics that enliven culture, even (or especially) when it is not explicitly about politics at all.

> **BIRCH:** How do I get race and class into my work? At this point in my career I have come to realize that the imagery I choose will denote class and race by the very nature of the things that I'm depicting. That liberating insight has freed me to concentrate on painting or sculpture itself.
>
> Since the year 2000, most of my work has been life-size. This was a very conscious decision; I wanted the viewer to experience the work as an equal, to allow him or her to enter the piece physically. Drawing the parallel of the second line, I wanted the viewer to feel part of the procession, transforming them from a spectator to a participant, being of equal importance and responsibility in making the ritual meaningful.

As New Orleans musicians, dancers, and cooks have been celebrated as tradition-bearers they have also been compartmentalized within these identities. As a black artist and a white anthropologist, we know something about being compartmentalized. What we have each attempted to do is follow the lead of our subjects—Leah Chase, Philip Frazier, or Gerald Platenburg—in creating new cultural forms from their assumed positions. We both intentionally make stories as subjective creators rather than as objective documentarians.

> **BIRCH:** I'm not trying to record. I mean, I am a recorder—the work can be dismissed as documentation—but that is not my emphasis. When all is said and done, I'm trying to create something that comes out of the history of visual mark-making, and that's where process becomes very important.
>
> I'm not trying to make a traditional painting. I'm not interested in making works that duplicate whatever came before. I have a grasp of art history, not only from a Western point of view but also from the African and African American points of view. All this informs my work. Yes, I want you to see my visual connection to Romare Bearden. I want you to see my visual connection to Jacob Lawrence. I want you to see my visual connection to Charles White. But it will be through Willie Birch. Like jazz musicians, I believe in the personal voice. Our musicians are not trying to play like Armstrong or Buddy Bolden or whomever. It's about adding your own stamp to the history of your art form based on your time and place on earth, to create something unique.
>
> **MATT:** Which is what drew me to your work, this documentarian aspect that was so clearly a personal statement. And it's interesting because the first thing you said when you read me was "Well, I like the documentarian aspect, but I want to understand you and where you're coming from. Why are you so shy? Why don't you be more upfront that this is your book and your interpretation?" You pushed me there.
>
> **BIRCH:** Right! I had to push you there if I was going to continue with you on this project. Because I feel that, in the end, we are creating for this time. And since art is a process, this is our only moment to get it right. Not tomorrow, but now.

ACKNOWLEDGMENTS

This book is full of the words, thoughts, and ideas of musicians and others I have come to know in New Orleans, and I want to thank everyone who took the time to speak with me, including Shamarr Allen, Lee Arnold, Bethany Bultman, Johann Bultman, Tyrus Chapman, Ariana Hall, Glen Hall Jr., Marcus Hubbard, Tamara Jackson, Fred Johnson, Benny Jones, Jerome Jones, Ellis Joseph, Baty Landis, Cherice Harrison Nelson, Gerald Platenburg, Walter Ramsey, Nakita Shavers, Gregg Stafford, Joseph Torregano, and Winston Turner. Among this group I want to give special thanks to those who blurred the line between work and friendship: Keith Frazer, Philip Frazier, Lumar LeBlanc, Bennie Pete, and Derrick Tabb. Thanks also to the students and teachers I met at L. E. Rabouin and John McDonogh high schools as well as the Roots of Music afterschool program, whose founders, Derrick Tabb and Allison Reinhardt, have advised dozens of my student volunteers. To Jason Brettel, Dan Cutler, Anthony DelRosario, Jonathan Goldman, Dave Greengold, Pableaux Johnson, Caitlin Keily and Peter Leonard, David Kunian, Diego Larguia and Kelly Sherman, Bethany Rogers, Joel Rose, and Stephen Rose: thanks for your great company.

In New Orleans a community of scholars has embraced me and offered me invaluable insight. At Tulane I've had exchanges with Thomas Adams, Joel Dinerstein, Chris Dunn, Kevin Gotham, Carole Haber, Larry Powell, and Felipe Smith that influenced my research, along with my colleagues in the Department of Music,

John Baron, John Joyce, and Dan Sharp. Nick Spitzer first invited me to New Orleans years ago and taught me to listen carefully and critically to the words and music of musicians. Bruce Raeburn launched my graduate studies and has been an invaluable resource ever since, along with Lynn Abbott at the Hogan Archive of New Orleans Jazz. Chandler Moore assisted with the index and website for the book. Helen Regis has been an advisor, collaborator, and friend since I sought her out after returning to New Orleans in 2006, and her ideas appear throughout. And so much in this book and my life would be less interesting without Rachel Breunlin, who is a model public anthropologist, activist, teacher, and editor, and (along with her husband, Dan, and son, Max) a great friend. Rachel and Helen provided extensive discussion and comments on the manuscript.

This book started as a dissertation at Columbia University, where my committee—Aaron Fox, George Lewis, Ana Ochoa, Michael Taussig, and Chris Washburne—oversaw a more fulfilling educational experience than I could ever have imagined. John Szwed never failed to share his wisdom and encyclopedic knowledge. Robin Kelley gave me critical direction at key moments. I am grateful to have been a part of an amazing group of students in the music department at Columbia, including Tyler Bickford, Andy Eisenberg, Melissa Gonzalez, Farzi Hemmasi, Niko Higgins, Anita Hoyvik, Brian Karl, Toby King, Morgan Luker, Mandy Minks, Ben Piekut, Ryan Skinner, Maria Sonevytsky, and Anna Stirr. Special thanks to Lauren Ninoshvili for her comments on voice. And gratitude forever to Dave Novak, who has based our friendship from day one on unrestrained dialogue based on mutual respect and admiration. In the wider world, Steve Feld, Charlie Keil, Maureen Loughran, Louise Meintjes, and Amanda Weidman have all offered comments that are reflected in the book.

My fieldwork from 2006 to 2007 was supported by a National Science Foundation Doctoral Dissertation Improvement Grant in Cultural Anthropology. The writing of the dissertation from 2007 to 2008 was supported by a Giles Whiting Foundation Dissertation Writing Fellowship. At Tulane I received a Committee on Research Summer Research Fellowship grant in 2009 and a Study of the Global South fellowship in 2010. I finished the manuscript with an Awards to Louisiana Artists and Scholars (ATLAS) fellowship in 2011. A subvention grant from Tulane University in 2013 assisted with publication and especially the inclusion of Willie Birch's artwork.

Portions of the book are based upon previous publications. Episode 1.2

borrows selectively from "New Orleans Music as a Circulatory System" in *Black Music Research Journal* 31, no. 2 (2011). Episodes 1.3 and 1.4 are distillations of my article "Under the Bridge: An Orientation to Soundscapes in New Orleans" in *Ethnomusicology* 54, no. 1 (2010). Episodes 3.2 and 3.3 are drawn from my chapter "The Representational Power of the New Orleans Brass Band" in *Brass Bands of the World: Militarism, Colonialism, and Local Music Making,* edited by Suzel Reily and Kate Brucher (forthcoming).

My relationships with many of my friends have revolved around music: thanks to Melissa Cusick, Mark DiClaudio, Ric Edinberg, Todd Hulslander, Chris Kirsch, Jake Pine, Mat Rappaport, Billy Simms and Kate Stevens, Lisa Stump, Doug Vey, and Reginald Williams. Finally, and most significantly, love to my family for their unending support: my mother, Rebecca Nourse; father, Robert Sakakeeny; stepmother, Gale Nigrosh; and stepsister, Maya Nigrosh.

Alexis Annis started this adventure with me as my girlfriend, became my wife along the way, and was with me through good times and bad, until we came to the end. To our daughter, Ella: your presence in my life makes me whole. I love you.

APPENDIX

LIST OF INTERVIEWS AND PUBLIC EVENTS

This list reflects the interviews and public events from which most of the quotes in the book were drawn.

9/12/06 Gregg Stafford interview at my house
(Excerpted for WWOZ *Street Talk*, "Black Men of Labor Parade 2006," http://www.wwoz.org/programs/street-talk/2006/09/black-men-of -labor-parade-2006)

9/17/06 Fred Johnson interview at his Neighborhood Development Foundation office
(Excerpted for WWOZ *Street Talk*, "Black Men of Labor Parade 2006")

10/22/06 Joseph Torregano interview at Harrah's Casino

11/07/06 Philip Frazier interview at my house
(Excerpted for *American Routes* segment, "New Orleans Brass Bands," http://americanroutes.wwno.org/player/playlist/24385)

11/07/06 Bennie Pete interview at *American Routes* studios
(Excerpted for *American Routes* segment, "New Orleans Brass Bands")

11/29/06 Kerwin James benefit at Tipitina's (includes Philip Frazier's monologue)

12/15/06 Lumar LeBlanc and Marcus Hubbard interview at *American Routes* studios
(Excerpted for *American Routes* segment, "New Orleans Brass Bands")

01/03/07 Interviews with principal and students at Rabouin High School (Kevin George and Christopher "Skully" Lee)

APPENDIX.1 *Saxaphone Player (Waiting for Parade).* 2002. 60″ × 44″.
© WILLIE BIRCH.

(Excerpted for wwoz *Street Talk*, "Rabouin High School Remembers Teacher Dinerral Shavers," http://www.wwoz.org/programs/street -talk/2007/01/rabouin-high-school-remembers-teacher-dinerral -shavers)

01/03/07   Bethany and Johann Bultman interview at Wicker Elementary School

01/03/07   Bennie Pete and Jerome Jones interview at *American Routes* studios (Excerpted for NPR *All Things Considered* segment, "Drummer's Funeral Underlines New Orleans Violence," http://www.npr.org /templates/story/story.php?storyId=6735417)

01/10/07   Gregg Stafford meeting at his home

2/02/07   Lumar LeBlanc meeting in his car

4/03/07   Benny Jones interview near the Backstreet Museum

4/12/07   Keith Frazier interview at *American Routes* studios

4/19/07   Lee Arnold conversation at Rock n Bowl

4/21/07   Society for the Anthropology of North America panel "Local Knowledge: New Orleans Artists and Activists Reflect on the State of the City After Katrina" (includes comments by Tamara Jackson and Bennie Pete)

8/1/07   Nakita Shavers interview at Sound Café

10/04/07   Press conference regarding the arrests at Kerwin's memorial (includes quotes by Ellis Joseph and Joe Blakk)

11/6/07   "Brass Band Music across the Generations" workshop with Rebirth at Musicians' Union Hall (includes comments from Keith Frazier and Philip Frazier)

05/03/09   Soul Rebels interview at Jazz Fest (Lumar LeBlanc, Winston Turner, Derrick Moss)

10/02/09   Drum workshop with Keith Frazier and Derrick Tabb of Rebirth at Tulane University

06/30/10   Gerald Platenburg interview in his apartment

NOTES

Prologue

1. The Prince of Wales Social Aid and Pleasure Club was the subject of a Tulane University documentary project and an *American Routes* radio segment in 2009. See http://tulane.edu/americanroutes/pow/index.cfm, accessed June 12, 2012. Joel Dinerstein (2009) has written an article on the club, and his interactions with club member Joe Stern, known as "white Joe," as well as Dinerstein's subsequent joining of the club, indicate that black membership in clubs is not without exception. See also Dinerstein 2013.

2. Nine Times Social and Pleasure Club 2006: 118.

3. Salaam 2008.

4. On "assemblage," see Deleuze and Guattari (1987: 342–86). Though I do not reference Deleuze and Guattari, throughout the text I approach the brass band as an assemblage, along the lines of Deleuze's (2007: 176) description: "In assemblages you find states of things, bodies, various combinations of bodies, hodgepodges; but you also find utterances, modes of expression, and whole regimes of signs."

5. There are brass band traditions in many African and diasporic cultures, and evidence suggests that they developed in dialogue with recordings of American jazz and popular Caribbean styles. For an overview of brass bands in former colonial territories, see Flaes 2000; Reily and Brucher forthcoming.

6. The clarinet was the original reed instrument used in marching bands but was gradually supplanted by the tenor saxophone starting in the 1920s. However, since the clarinet became associated with the traditional New Orleans style, it continues to be used in explicitly traditionalist jazz and brass bands (as well as school marching bands). See Hazeldine (1984: 22) regarding the debate among musicians about the traditional use of the clarinet.

7. *Precarity* is a term encompassing the effects of the neoliberal state on its subjects. See, for example, Neilson and Rossiter (2008).

Introduction

1. Studies of black American music explicitly situated in the context of race and power include Jones 1963; Keil 1966; Murray 1976; Floyd 1995; Radano 2003. For anthropological studies of the politics of pleasurable music and dance, see Meintjes 2004; B. White 2008.

2. Studies of the New Orleans brass band tradition include Schafer 1977; Knowles 1996; White 2001; Burns 2006.

3. I am referring to three strands of scholarship: (1) the sociology of the ghetto pioneered by members of the Chicago School such as Louis Wirth (1928), carried forward in the "culture of poverty" studies initiated by Oscar Lewis (1961), and then theories of the underclass proposed by William Julius Wilson (1987), which have been formidably critiqued by Robin Kelley (1997), Micaela di Leonardo (1998: 112–27), and Loïc Wacquant (2002), even as they continue to reappear (Small, Harding, and Lamont 2010); (2) the anthropology of black American expressive culture, led by Franz Boas's students Zora Neale Hurston (1935) and Melville Herskovits (1941), reaching peak activity in the civil rights era with Roger Abrahams (1964) and other anthropologists (Whitten and Szwed 1971); and (3) the ethnographic, ethnomusicological study of black music in U.S. cities, launched by Keil (1966) and then virtually abandoned (Sakakeeny 2005: 144–47), with exceptions including Gaunt (2006), Sakakeeny (2010), and T. Jackson (2012).

4. Foundational studies of New Orleans music include Ramsey and Smith (1939) on jazz and Berry, Foose, and Jones (1986) on rhythm and blues and subsequent styles. The critical reevaluation of New Orleans music has so far been limited to historical studies of traditional jazz by Lawrence Gushee (2005), Thomas Brothers (2006), and Bruce Raeburn (2009).

5. On the "problem" of the black American male, see Mincy 2006; National Urban League 2007. I recognize that my focus on black men perpetuates the marginalization of black women in scholarly studies, though I make references on occasion to the intersection of racial and gender inequalities. On black feminism, see Collins 1990.

6. Here and throughout I follow musicians in using "horn" as a covering term for any wind instrument, including brass and reeds.

7. Sewell 1992: 20.

8. Ortner 2006: 133.

9. Biehl, Good, and Kleinman 2007: 14. For critiques of musicology's "great men" narratives, see McClary 1991; Goehr 1994. For critiques of folklore's romanticization of the folk, see Bendix 1997; Filene 2000.

10. Biehl et al. 2007: 8–9.

11. Rachel and Helen have cowritten two articles about collaborative ethnography (Breunlin and Regis 2009; Breunlin, Regis, and Lewis 2011). Their ethnographic study of the Nine Times Social Aid and Pleasure Club is a companion piece to the Nine Times book (Breunlin and Regis 2006).

12. On "ethnography at home," see Peirano (1998) and the introduction and case studies in Amit (2000).
13. So far I have had the pleasure of taking academics and friends Marïe Abe, Steve Feld, Jocelyne Guilbault, Anne Lovell, Dave Novak, Ana María Ochoa, Ryan Skinner, and Mick Taussig to brass band parades.
14. Falk Moore 1987: 730. See also Falk Moore 2005.
15. Falk Moore 1987: 735.
16. Too often, southern blackness is equated with stasis or slowness, the counterpoint to migration from South to North, which is nearly always equated with upward social mobility, as evidenced by the titles of the best-selling books *The Promised Land: The Great Black Migration and How It Changed America*, and *The Warmth of Other Suns: The Epic Story of America's Great Migration*. In formulations such as these, movement in the South can only be accommodated in terms of "return" and/or "redemption," but as someone who migrated from North to South many years ago I have witnessed much motion, and I have come to evaluate movement in terms of circulation rather than unidirectional migration.
17. Baker 2001: 69.
18. Benjamin 1999: 720–22.
19. Events I witnessed firsthand, for example, are written in the present tense in an attempt to retain the sense of immediacy that accompanied their emergence. Quotes are in the past tense, corresponding to dates of interviews and events listed in the appendix. In general, I use first names for people I have interviewed and otherwise interacted with personally and last names for those I have not been in direct contact with.
20. The experimental ethnographic writings of Taussig (2004), Stewart (2007), and M. Jackson (1998) serve as models.
21. Spoken words appear throughout the text in standard English. Though many black New Orleanians are capable of speaking in a dialect known colloquially as "Ebonics" or "Black English," I have decided against attempting to capture these spoken subtleties in writing, choosing to present speech in denaturalized form rather than as naturalized text or "eye-dialect" (Bucholtz 2000). I made this choice for two reasons. First, on transcribing interviews there was very rarely consistent use of "Black English"; for example, speakers, including myself, would sometimes drop the *g* at the end of a gerund and sometimes not (i.e., *going* and *goin*). Second, this book is of course a written text containing quotations from written sources (including musicians' autobiographies) in which authors had some agency in determining how their words appeared in written form, and in the vast majority of cases the sources were composed in standard English, so I decided to present verbal quotations appearing alongside those quotations in standard English to maintain consistency. That said, I have not made grammatical or syntactical "corrections" to nonstandard English (i.e., "you gotta go" would be written "you got to go" and not "you've got to go"), though I recognize that this occasionally presents awkward phrasing. The few occasions where "Black English" appears in the text are quotations of published song titles and lyrics.

Chapter 1

1. Armstrong 1954: 219.
2. For a comprehensive history of black American burials, see Holloway 2001.
3.

(HEY!)

TRUMPET RIFF FROM "JOE AVERY'S BLUES."

4. Floyd 1995: 95.
5. Hazen and Hazen 1987.
6. There is debate as to whether historians and geographers have overstated the concentration of Creoles Downtown and African and Anglo Americans Uptown. See Campanella 2007.
7. On the local consequences of *Plessy v. Ferguson*, see Logsdon and Cossé Bell 1992; Roach 1996: 179–237. On how racial mixing has been represented in the United States, see Sollors 1997.
8. Murray 1976: 45.
9. Flaes 2000: 10.
10. Flaes 2000: 22–31; see also McNeill 1995.
11. Brothers 2006: 22.
12. Floyd 1991: 267–68.
13. Latrobe 1819/1980: 203.
14. Latrobe 1819/1980: 203; Floyd 1991: 266.
15. Gomez 1998: 271.
16. Hall 1992: 59. Historical studies of the New Orleans brass band tradition include Schafer 1977; Knowles 1996; White 2001; Burns 2006; Sakakeeny 2011b.
17. Bourdieu 1986.
18. Membership in the majority of brass bands fluctuates greatly from year to year and even day to day. For instance, between the time of my fieldwork and the publication of this book, Gregory Veals replaced Corey Henry on trombone and Chad Honore joined Rebirth on trumpet.
19. There are white musicians, such as Matt Perrine on tuba, Craig Klein on trombone, Chuck Brackman on clarinet, and Bell Ellman on saxophone, who have consistently performed with black brass bands.
20. On the television show *Treme* as it relates to New Orleans exceptionalism, see Sakakeeny 2011a, 2012.
21. Crutcher 2010: 38.
22. Shearouse 1971.
23. Fairclough 1995: 244.
24. See Hirsch 2000; Hayden 2003.
25. Souther 2006: 64–72.
26. Samuels 2000: 85.

27. Crutcher 2010: 96–113.
28. Nine Times Social and Pleasure Club 2006: 210.
29. See Hirsch 2000; Hayden 2003.
30. Lipsitz 2011: 28.
31. Lipsitz 2011: 32. On gentrification, see also Smith 2006.
32. From the café's website, www.cafetreme.com, accessed December 14, 2011.
33. Eggler 2010.
34. The attempt to secure an exception to the Residential Development Overlay caused a flap, and Naydja resigned from the neighborhood association she had founded. See Webster 2012.
35. Breunlin 2004: 10. On the social uses of neighborhood bars in New Orleans, see Rogers 2010.
36. Regis 1999: 473.
37. Low 1996: 862.
38. Regis 1999: 480.
39. Sanders quotes taken from *Social Aid and Pleasure Club Task Force et al. v. City of New Orleans et al.* 2006: 9.
40. Reckdahl 2006; Troeh 2006.
41. *Social Aid and Pleasure Club Task Force et al. v. City of New Orleans et al.* 2006: 1.
42. This discussion builds upon the literature of resistance studies, beginning with James Scott's (1985, 1990) emphasis on small and covert acts of resistance, and including productive critiques of resistance and accommodation by Lila Abu-Lughod (1990), Achille Mbembe and Janet Roitman (1994), and Sherry Ortner (1995).
43. For more on "tuning" tradition, see Sakakeeny (2010), which extends Feld's (1996) theory of acoustemology.
44. On the history of New Orleans music as a culture of circulation, see Sakakeeny (2011b). The theory of cultural "feedback" is based on Novak (2013).
45. The Olympia Brass Band included white musicians such as Tom Sancton on clarinet and Alan Jaffe and Woody Penouilh on sousaphone.
46. Lipset and Bendix 1959: 6.
47. Lipset and Bendix 1959: 3.
48. Du Bois 1903b: 33.
49. Berliner 1994.
50. The Young Leadership Council had chosen *Coming Out the Door for the Ninth Ward*, written by members of the Nine Times, for a citywide reading campaign in 2007, and Rachel Breunlin with Neighborhood Story Project asked me to moderate a workshop with Rebirth, who figured prominently in the book as the band that often played the annual Nine Times parade. A transcript of the event was accessed on March 4, 2013, at http://www.docstoc.com/docs/52309311/Brass-Band-Across-the-Generations.
51. On female participation in jazz, see Tucker 2000. For a discussion of the study of black American music and gender, see the introduction to Kyra Gaunt's (2006) book about black girls' games and songs. For a comparative study of how

musical instruments articulate with gender in a variety of cultures, see Doubleday (2008).

52. Morton 1938/2005: 104. On the Latin tinge in New Orleans music, see Washburne 1997; Hiroshi-Garret 2008.

53. On continuity in "African rhythm," see Chernoff 1979. On the "virtual time" of musical events, see Blacking 1973: 27, 52. On deejay techniques, see Schloss 2004.

54. There are multiple recordings of "Do Whatcha Wanna." The original, recorded in approximately 1987 for Dubat Records, was eventually released on the album *Do Whatcha Wanna* by Mardi Gras Records in 1997. "Do Whatcha Wanna (Part 2)" featured new lyrics by Kermit Ruffins about Mardi Gras day and a new introductory section; it was released on *Feel Like Funkin' It Up* on Rounder Records in 1989. A similar version, shortened and with additional vocals, was released as "Do Whatcha Wanna (Part 3)" as a single and then issued on several compilations by Rounder. This is the version analyzed here.

55. On authoritarian bandleaders, see B. White 2008: 225–52.

56. McClary 1991: 136.

57. See the conclusion for my discussion of engagement and public anthropology. This episode draws on methodologies of representing ethnographic subjects in the aftermath of the *Writing Culture* critique, especially Michael Jackson's take on intersubjectivity in *Minima Ethnographica* (1998) and Kathleen Stewart's take on the inherent partiality of ethnographic knowledge in *Ordinary Affects* (2007).

58. Medical anthropologists have argued that the links between race and health are more complex than heredity and biology. For a study of health care among black New Orleanians, see Lovell 2011.

59. Joe Blakk became part of Philip and Keith's family when he married their sister Nicole.

60. Lipset and Bendix 1959: 5–6. On the sturdiness of racial identity as a virtually immobile barrier, see Omi and Winant 1994.

61. The song "A. P. Tureaud" is named for a street in the Seventh Ward neighborhood that is home to many bars and the site of many parades. The street itself is named after the famed civil rights attorney.

62. *Polyphony* here refers both to the actual musical texture of voices and instruments making sound together and to the metaphorical usage by the literary theorist Mikhail Bakhtin (1984), meaning the "many voices" brought together in dialogue in a novel.

63. Douglass 1845: 13–14.

64. Du Bois 1903a: 250. See also Weheliye 2005.

65. In *Blackness and Value*, the literary theorist Lindon Barrett argues that the voice has been "a primary means by which African Americans may exchange an expended, valueless self in the New World for a productive, recognized self" (1999: 57). See also Radano 1996; Cruz 1999; Moten 2003.

66. Douglass 1845: 13; Du Bois 1903a: 250.

67. Weidman 2007: 131.

68. Feld, Fox, Porcello, and Samuels 2004: 61.

69. Fox 2004: 34.
70. On Homer's Sirens, see Cavarero (2005: 103–16). On the sound of the shofar, see Dolar (2006: 52–56) with reference to Jacques Lacan.
71. Cavarero 2005: 69, 71.
72. Cavarero 2005: 75. I would argue that meanings of instrumental sound surpass language not only for individuals, as Cavarero emphasizes, but also for communities of listeners and practitioners, as in the jazz funeral for Kerwin James.
73. See especially Feld 1982, 1986, 1996.
74. Weidman 2006: 57.
75. Qureshi 2000: 815.
76. Qureshi 2000: 812.
77. On drums as speech surrogates, see Herzog 1945; Villepastour 2010.
78. Haraway 1988.

Chapter 2

1. A video of the incident is available at http://www.youtube.com/watch?v=tG6Fk7CbLLI.
2. Video of Sean Roberts is available at http://www.youtube.com/watch?v=laaoUFJvyjA.
3. Video of protest is available at http://www.youtube.com/watch?v=ooOk3EZVi-g. This song was composed by Derrick Tabb and has been recorded by the Rebirth Brass Band.
4. Video of testimony is available at http://www.youtube.com/watch?v=A2CfNnGxTeE.
5. Reckdahl 2010.
6. Vieux Carré Property Owners, Residents, and Associates, Inc. mission statement, available at www.vcpora.org/index.php?topic=about, accessed April 17, 2012.
7. For a critical history of preservation efforts in the French Quarter, see Souther 2006: 38–72. For a political science study of entertainment zones in New Orleans, see Passavant 2011.
8. Quoted on company's website, http://www.bbcdmc.com/noFlavor.html, accessed May 12, 2011.
9. Yúdice 2003.
10. Gotham 2006.
11. Grazian 2003.
12. On urban entertainment destinations, see Hannigan 1998; Passavant 2011.
13. Geertz 1973; Turner 1969.
14. The Habitat for Humanity quote is taken from a print advertisement soliciting donations for Musician's Village. The Glen Andrews photo is referenced in Reckdahl 2007.
15. Hebdige 1979: 90–99.
16. Kirschenblatt-Gimblett 1998: 52.
17. Regis 1999: 473.
18. Comaroff and Comaroff 2009: 2, emphasis in original.

19. Comaroff and Comaroff 2009: 32.
20. On the utility of ritual as a resource, see García Canclini (1993) and research that extends his theories by Yúdice (2001, 2004).
21. Ochoa 2003: 71.
22. Comaroff and Comaroff 2009: 21. On self-commodification, see also Bunten 2008.
23. Comaroff and Comaroff 2009: 71.
24. Kelley 2002: 12.
25. Davis 2005.
26. Figures taken from Sweet Home New Orleans (2010: 9) and Logan (2005).
27. Data from the 2000 and 2010 censuses relating specifically to New Orleans is available from the Greater New Orleans Community Data Center, www.gnocdc .org.
28. Benjamin 1968: 257.
29. "Jass and Jassism" 1918/1995: 231–32. On Eurocentric evaluations of early jazz, see Levine 1989; Ogren 1989.
30. Myers 1958.
31. Mt. Auburn Associates 2005: 4.
32. Mt. Auburn Associates 2005: 14.
33. Louisiana Department of Culture, Recreation and Tourism 2005: 14. At an urban planning conference soon after Katrina, Nick Spitzer (2006) cautioned that culture should not be marginalized as "window dressing" to the infrastructural rebuilding of New Orleans because the city's economic restabilization hinged on the return of culture workers.
34. Mt. Auburn Associates 2005: 35.
35. Louisiana Department of Culture, Recreation and Tourism 2006: 8.
36. Roach 1996: 180.
37. I am referring here, again, to Kirschenblatt-Gimblett 1998.
38. Atkinson 1996: 152.
39. Mt. Auburn Associates 2005: 36.
40. The "art world" reference is to Howard Becker 1982.
41. Black Men of Labor Social Aid and Pleasure Club 2006.
42. Spitzer 2003.
43. According to the Louisiana Department of Culture, Recreation and Tourism (2006: 8), before Katrina the tourism and hospitality industry accounted for eighty-five thousand jobs in the metro area.
44. For an ethnographic study of jazz musicians providing a service by playing familiar standards, see Faulkner and Becker 2009. The redefinition of musicians as service workers would call into question Richard Florida's (2002: 71) distinction between the "Creative Class" (which is generally "well compensated") and the "Service Class" (which is filled with "low-end, typically low-wage and low-autonomy occupations").
45. Stokes 1999: 144.
46. Mt. Auburn Associates 2005: 60.

47. Mt. Auburn Associates 2005: 59.
48. Mt. Auburn Associates 2005: 59.
49. Mt. Auburn Associates 2005: 4.
50. Mt. Auburn Associates 2005: 62–63.
51. "Paula Zahn Now" 2005.
52. "Presidential Address" 2005.
53. Jackson 2001: 60.
54. Price 2005.
55. Souther 2006: 119.
56. Schiro 1964.
57. Raeburn 2009: 245.
58. Regis and Walton 2008: 401. See Powell (2007) for a discussion that situates post-Katrina Jazz Fest within a longer history of boosterism.
59. Regis and Walton 2008: 401.
60. Regis and Walton 2008: 415.
61. Rothman 2002.
62. The white "colonizers" reference is to Memmi (1965); the white "mainstream" reference is to Jones (1963).
63. Krupa 2011: 105.

Chapter 3

1. As mentioned in the introduction, this book encompasses my experiences in New Orleans from 1997 to 2013, which includes but is not focused on the aftermath of Hurricane Katrina. I consider "post-Katrina New Orleans" to refer to the years immediately after the flood when the city was collectively focused on the rebuilding effort, a specific period of time which has now passed. This puts me at odds with the bulk of scholarly and media accounts of contemporary New Orleans, which often attribute longstanding problems to the rupture of the disaster. For exceptions, see Breunlin and Regis 2006; Johnson 2011; Sakakeeny 2011a.
2. I am using the categorical term *hip-hop* expansively to refer to a cluster of subgenres including R&B, rap, and hip-hop.
3. Studies of gangsta rap in the 1980s and 1990s include Kelley 1994; Quinn 2005. For a journalistic account of southern hip-hop in this period, see Sarig (2007).
4. Quotes taken from Jordan 2003, emphasis added.
5. See the station's website, wwoz.org/about, accessed December 2006.
6. M. White 2001: 81, 92.
7. M. White 2001: 90.
8. M. White 2004.
9. Neville et al. 2000: 9.
10. Wacquant 2009: xv.
11. Alexander 2010: 12.
12. M. White 2001: 19; Rose 1994: 21.
13. Jones 1967; Boyd 2003: 10. For an example of the "changing same" as a research model for the study of hip-hop, see Keyes (1996).

14. M. White 2001: 91.
15. Barker 1986, 1998. Barker's materials are collected at the Hogan Archive of New Orleans Jazz.
16. Danielsen 2006: 43. Danielsen relates funk's cyclical grooves to many African traditions of music and dance in a long tradition of analyzing "African rhythm" by musicologists such as J. H. Kwabena Nketia, Simha Aron, and John Chernoff. Kofi Agawu (1995) has critiqued this analytical tradition for essentializing "African rhythm."
17. Kelley 1994: 50–51.
18. Regis 2001: 767.
19. Gates 1992: 75.
20. Julien and Mercer 1988/1996: 197.
21. Wallace 1990: 1.
22. Boyd 1997: 17.
23. West 1993: 289.
24. The Sudan Social Aid and Pleasure Club is another parading organization that incorporates West African fabrics and symbols into their annual parade. Several men are members of both clubs.
25. Lumar's lyric "music by any means necessary," from the Soul Rebels "Intro" that begins the album *Rebelution*, is a reference to a speech by Malcolm X, later reformulated by the political rap group Boogie Down Productions for their 1987 album *By All Means Necessary*.
26. Bauman 2001: 15819.
27. Urban 2001: 20.
28. Soul Rebels 2006.
29. Soul Rebels 2009.
30. Kitwana 2002: 10.
31. Rose 2008: 8.
32. Boyd 2003: xxi.
33. "Knock with Me — Rock with Me" by the Lil' Rascals Brass Band on *Buck It Like a Horse* (2003). The lyrics are by Glen David Andrews, while the rhythm section part is derived from Rebirth's arrangement of "Casanova."
34. Salaam 2008.
35. Tsing 2005: 5.

Chapter 4

1. Goode and Masakovsky 2001: 9.
2. The term *everyday violence* is taken from Scheper-Hughes and Bourgois (2004: 21). The term *structural violence* is taken from Farmer (2004).
3. Wacquant 2009: xv, 61. On the incarceration of black Americans, see also Alexander 2010. While statistics on crime have remained relatively static over time, Wacquant identifies an increasingly alarmist "gaze that society trains on certain street illegalities, . . . [on] their presumed perpetrators, on the place they occupy in the

city, and on the uses to which these populations can be subjected in the political and journalistic fields" (2009: 4).

4. On welfare "reform," see Piven 1998.

5. Orfield et al. 2004.

6. There has been a deluge of post-Katrina scholarship evaluating the racial dimensions of the disaster. See especially the chapters in Johnson (2011) and the articles in the special issue of *American Quarterly*, "In the Wake of Katrina: New Paradigms and Social Visions," edited by Clyde Woods (2009). On the exceptionalism of New Orleans and Hurricane Katrina, see Sakakeeny 2011a, 2012.

7. See Federal Bureau of Investigation (2012). Regarding incarceration in Louisiana, see C. Chang (2012).

8. Bourgois 1995: 171.

9. Bourgois 2004: 307.

10. Wacquant 2004: 115.

11. Wacquant 2004: 112.

12. Wacquant 2007: 57.

13. Meintjes 2004; Washburne 2008; Ramos and Ochoa 2009.

14. Osbey 1996: 101.

15. See Berry et al. (1986: 40–50) for a portrait of Joseph Williams's relatives in the Lastie family.

16. "N.O. Man Arrested after Chase" 2006.

17. Some of the musicians in this book are practicing Christians, many more would describe themselves as believers, and all are experienced in playing religious music at Christian burials. Their experiences exemplify the ongoing role that the church plays in the lives of many black Americans as well as the fluidity between the (imposed) categories of sacred and secular. See, for example, Guthrie Ramsey's discussion of "hip-hop hybridity and the black church muse" (2003: 190–215).

18. I am picking up here where Amanda Weidman's (2007) work on the politics of voice and instrumentality in Karnatic music leaves off. See episodes 1.8 and 4.5.

19. Interviews with L. E. Rabouin principal and students were conducted on the first day of school after Dinerral's death, January 3, 2007, and excerpted for a WWOZ *Street Talk* segment.

20. Kozol 2005: 19. See also Orfield et al. 2004.

21. Reckdahl 2007.

22. Dolar 2006: 107, emphasis added.

23. Dolar 2006: 30.

24. *Satchmo the Great* 1957, emphasis added.

25. Amanda Weidman (2006: 57) writes of the violin in Karnatic music, "It is precisely the capacity of the instrument to be heard as a voice, to sound almost human while remaining nonhuman and to sound Indian while remaining foreign, which makes it powerful."

26. Monson 1996: 127, 209.

27. In two Associated Press photos published the day after Katrina, a black man carrying a soft drink and a garbage bag is described as "walk[ing] through chest-deep flood water after looting a grocery store," while a photo of a white couple carrying food and drinks refers to "two residents wad[ing] through chest-deep water after finding bread and soda from a local grocery store." The only apparent distinction between the subjects of the photographs is their race. See Sommers et al. 2006.
28. Metropolitan Crime Commission 2012.
29. Social Aid and Pleasure Club Task Force 2007.
30. This episode's emphasis on collective, mediated, and mediatized voices could be read as a critique of Cavarero's (2005) interpretation of voice as the unmediated expression of the individual.
31. The press release for the consent decree is at http://www.justice.gov/opa/pr/2012/July/12-ag-917.html, accessed October 25, 2012.

Conclusion

1. Kelley 1997: 16.
2. Goode and Masakovsky 2001: xi.
3. di Leonardo 1998.
4. Lewis and Breunlin 2009: 17.
5. Clifford and Marcus 1986.
6. Marcus and Fischer 1986: vii.
7. Taussig 2004: 314.
8. Jackson 2002: 15.
9. Fortun 2012: 450, 459.
10. Bourgois 2006: x.
11. Sanford and Angel-Ajani 2006: 6. For an overview of the anthropology of engagement, see Low and Merry 2010; for a call for activist ethnography, see Hale 2006.

BIBLIOGRAPHY

Abrahams, Roger D. 1964. *Deep Down in the Jungle: Negro Narrative Folklore from the Streets of Philadelphia*. Hatboro, Pa.: Folklore Associates.

Abu-Lughod, Lila. 1990. "The Romance of Resistance: Tracing Transformations of Power through Bedouin Women." *American Ethnologist* 17(1): 41–55.

Agawu, Kofi. 1995. "The Invention of African Rhythm." *Journal of the American Musicological Society* 48(3): 380–95.

Alexander, Michelle. 2010. *The New Jim Crow: Mass Incarceration in the Age of Colorblindness*. New York: New Press.

Amit, Vered, ed. 2000. *Constructing the Field: Ethnographic Fieldwork in the Contemporary World*. New York: Routledge.

Anderson, Elijah. 1990. *Streetwise: Race, Class, and Change in an Urban Community*. Chicago: University of Chicago Press.

———. 2008. *Against the Wall: Poor, Young, Black, and Male*. Philadelphia: University of Pennsylvania Press.

Armstrong, Louis. 1954. *Satchmo: My Life in New Orleans*. New York: Prentice Hall.

Atkinson, Connie. 1996. "Creativity, Compromise, and the Tourist Industry in New Orleans." In *Dixie Debates: Perspectives on Southern Cultures*, edited by Helen Taylor and Richard Wilde, 150–64. New York: New York University Press.

Baker, Houston A. 2001. *Turning South Again: Re-thinking Modernism/Re-reading Booker T.* Durham: Duke University Press.

Bakhtin, Mikhail. 1984. *Problems of Dostoevsky's Poetics*. Edited and translated by Caryl Emerson. Minneapolis: University of Minnesota Press.

Barker, Danny. 1986. *A Life in Jazz*. New York: Oxford University Press.

———. 1998. *Buddy Bolden and the Last Days of Storyville*. Edited by Alyn Shipton. New York: Continuum.

Baron, Robert, and Nick Spitzer, eds. 1992. *Public Folklore*. Washington, D.C.: Smithsonian Press.

Barrett, Lindon. 1999. *Blackness and Value: Seeing Double*. New York: Cambridge University Press.

Bataille, Georges. 1991. *The Accursed Share*. Vol. 1: *Consumption*. Cambridge: MIT Press.

Bauman, Richard. 2001. "Anthropology of Tradition." In *International Encyclopedia of the Social and Behavioral Sciences*, edited by Neil J. Smelser and Paul B. Baltes, 15819–24. London: Elsevier.

Becker, Howard S. 1982. *Art Worlds*. Berkeley: University of California Press.

Bendix, Regina. 1997. *In Search of Authenticity: The Formation of Folklore Studies*. Madison: University of Wisconsin Press.

Benjamin, Walter. 1968. "Theses on the Philosophy of History." In *Illuminations: Essays and Reflections*. Edited by Hannah Arendt and translated by Harry Zohn, 253–64. New York: Schocken Books.

———. 1986. "On the Mimetic Faculty." In *Reflections: Essays, Aphorisms, Autobiographical Writings*. Edited by Peter Demetz and translated by Edmund Jephcott, 333–36. New York: Schocken Books. Cambridge: Harvard University Press.

Berliner, Paul. 1994. *Thinking in Jazz: The Infinite Art of Improvisation*. Chicago: University of Chicago Press.

Berry, Jason. 1995. "New Orleans Brass Band Revival." *Reckon* 1–2: 28–39.

Berry, Jason, Jonathan Foose, and Tad Jones. 1986. *Up from the Cradle of Jazz: New Orleans Music Since World War II*. Athens: University of Georgia Press.

Biehl, João, Byron Good, and Arthur Kleinman, eds. 2007. *Subjectivity: Ethnographic Investigations*. Berkeley: University of California Press.

Black Men of Labor Social Aid and Pleasure Club. 2006. "A Message to the Citizens of New Orleans." Press release.

Blacking, John. 1973. *How Musical Is Man?* Seattle: University of Washington Press.

Bourdieu, Pierre. 1986. "The Forms of Capital." In *Handbook of Theory and Research for the Sociology of Education*, edited by J. Richardson, 241–58. New York: Greenwood Press.

Bourgois, Philippe I. 1995. *In Search of Respect: Selling Crack in El Barrio*. New York: Cambridge University Press.

———. 2004. "U.S. Inner-city Apartheid: The Contours of Structural and Interpersonal Violence." In *Violence in War and Peace: An Anthology*. Edited by Nancy Scheper-Hughes and Philippe I. Bourgois, 301–7. Oxford: Blackwell.

———. 2006. Foreword to *Engaged Observer: Anthropology, Advocacy, and Activism*, edited by Victoria Sanford and Asale Angel-Ajani, ix–xii. New Brunswick, N.J.: Rutgers University Press.

Boyd, Todd. 1997. *Am I Black Enough for You: Popular Culture from the 'Hood and Beyond*. Bloomington: Indiana University Press.

———. 2003. *The New H.N.I.C.: The Death of Civil Rights and the Reign of Hip Hop*. New York: New York University Press.

Breunlin, Rachel. 2004. "Papa Joe Glasper and Joe's Cozy Corner: Downtown Development, Displacement, and the Creation of Community." MA thesis, University of New Orleans.

Breunlin, Rachel, and Helen Regis. 2006. "Putting the Ninth Ward on the Map: Race,

Place, and Transformation in Desire, New Orleans." *American Anthropologist* 108(4): 744–64.

———. 2009. "Can There Be a Critical Collaborative Ethnography? Creativity and Activism in the Seventh Ward, New Orleans." *Collaborative Anthropologies* 2: 115–46.

Breunlin, Rachel, Helen Regis, and Ronald W. Lewis. 2011. "Building Collaborative Partnerships through a Lower Ninth Ward Museum." *Practicing Anthropology* 33(2): 4–10.

Brothers, Thomas David. 2006. *Louis Armstrong's New Orleans*. New York: W. W. Norton.

Bucholtz, Mary. 2000. "The Politics of Transcription." *Journal of Pragmatics* 32: 1439–65.

Bunten, Alexis Celeste. 2008. "Sharing Culture or Selling Out? Developing the Commodified Persona in the Heritage Industry." *American Ethnologist* 35(3): 380–95.

Burns, Mick. 2006. *Keeping the Beat on the Street: The New Orleans Brass Band Renaissance*. Baton Rouge: Louisiana State University Press.

Campanella, Richard. 2007. "An Ethnic Geography of New Orleans." *Journal of American History* 94: 704–15.

Cavarero, Adriana. 2005. *For More Than One Voice: Toward a Philosophy of Vocal Expression*. Stanford: Stanford University Press.

Chang, Cindy. 2012. "Louisiana Is the World's Prison Capital." (New Orleans) *Times-Picayune*, May 13.

Chang, Jeff. 2005. *Can't Stop Won't Stop: A History of the Hip-Hop Generation*. New York: St. Martin's Press.

Chernoff, John M. 1979. *African Rhythm and African Sensibility: Aesthetics and Social Action in African Musical Idioms*. Chicago: University of Chicago Press.

Chude-Sokei, Louis. 2006. *The Last "Darky": Bert Williams, Black-on-Black Minstrelsy, and the African Diaspora*. Durham: Duke University Press.

Clifford, James, and George E. Marcus. 1986. *Writing Culture: The Poetics and Politics of Ethnography*. Berkeley: University of California Press.

Collins, Patricia Hill. 1990. *Black Feminist Thought: Knowledge, Consciousness and the Politics of Empowerment*. Boston: Unwin Hyman.

Comaroff, John L., and Jean Comaroff. 2009. *Ethnicity, Inc.* Chicago: University of Chicago Press.

Crutcher, Michael E., Jr. 2010. *Tremé: Race and Place in a New Orleans Neighborhood*. Athens: University of Georgia Press.

Cruz, Jon. 1999. *The Black Spiritual and the Rise of American Cultural Interpretation*. Princeton: Princeton University Press.

Danielsen, Anne. 2006. *Presence and Pleasure: The Funk Grooves of James Brown and Parliament*. Middleton, Conn.: Wesleyan University Press.

Davis, Mike. 2005. "Catastrophic Economics: The Predators of New Orleans." *Le Monde Diplomatique* (English edition). Accessed March 19, 2013, at http://mondediplo.com/2005/10/02katrina.

Deleuze, Gilles. 2007. *Two Regimes of Madness: Texts and Interviews, 1975–1995*. New York: Semiotext(e).

Deleuze, Gilles, and Félix Guattari. 1987. *A Thousand Plateaus: Capitalism and Schizophrenia*. Minneapolis: University of Minnesota Press.

di Leonardo, Micaela. 1998. "The Three Bears, the Great Goddess, and the American Temperament: Anthropology without Anthropologists." In *Exotics at Home: Anthropologies, Others, American Modernity*, 79–144. Chicago: University of Chicago Press.

Dinerstein, Joel. 2009. "Second Lining Post-Katrina: Learning Community from the Prince of Wales Social Aid and Pleasure Club." *American Quarterly* 61(3): 615–37.

———. 2013. "39 Sundays: Rollin' Wid It." In *Unfathomable City: A New Orleans Atlas*, edited by Rebeca Solnit and Rebecca Snedeker. Berkeley: University of California Press.

Dolar, Mladen. 2006. *A Voice and Nothing More*. Cambridge: MIT Press.

Doubleday, Veronica. 2008. "Sounds of Power: An Overview of Musical Instruments and Gender." *Ethnomusicology Forum* 17(1): 3–39.

Douglass, Frederick. 1845. *Narrative of the Life of Frederick Douglass, an American Slave. Written by Himself*. Boston: Anti-Slavery Office.

Du Bois, W. E. B. 1903a. *The Souls of Black Folk*. Chicago: A. C. McClurg.

———. 1903b. "The Talented Tenth." In *The Negro Problem: A Series of Articles by Representative Negroes of To-day*, edited by Booker T. Washington, 31–75. New York: James Pott.

Eckstein, Barbara. 2005. *Sustaining New Orleans: Postwar Literature and the Fate of An American City*. New York: Routledge.

Eggler, Bruce. 2010. "Treme Commercial Opportunities Increase under Zoning Change Approved by City Council." (New Orleans) *Times-Picayune*, August 18.

Fairclough, Adam. 1995. *Race and Democracy: The Civil Rights Struggle in Louisiana, 1915–1972*. Athens: University of Georgia Press.

Falk Moore, Sally. 1987. "Explaining the Present: Theoretical Dilemmas in Processual Ethnography." *American Ethnologist* 14: 727–36.

———. 2005. "From Tribes and Traditions to Composites and Conjunctures." *Social Analysis* 49(3): 254–72.

Farmer, Paul. 2004. "An Anthropology of Structural Violence." *Current Anthropology* 45(3): 305–25.

Faulkner, Robert R., and Howard S. Becker. 2009. *Do You Know—? The Jazz Repertoire in Action*. Chicago: University of Chicago Press.

Federal Bureau of Investigation. 2012. *Uniform Crime Report, January–December 2011*. Accessed February 23, 2013, at http://www.fbi.gov/about-us/cjis/ucr/crime-in-the-u.s/2011/preliminary-annual-ucr-jan-dec-2011.

Feld, Steven. 1974. "Linguistic Models in Ethnomusicology." *Ethnomusicology* 18(2): 197–217.

———. 1982. *Sound and Sentiment: Birds, Weeping, Poetics, and Song in Kaluli Expression*. Philadelphia: University of Pennsylvania Press.

———. 1984a. "Communication, Music, and Speech about Music." *Yearbook for Traditional Music* 16: 1–18.

———. 1984b. "Sound Structure as Social Structure." *Ethnomusicology* 28(3): 383–409.

———. 1986. "Sound as a Symbolic System: The Kaluli Drum." In *Explorations in Ethnomusicology: Essays in Honor of David P. McAllester*, edited by Charlotte Frisbie, 147–58. Detroit: Information Coordinators.

———. 1996. "Waterfalls of Song: An Acoustemology of Place Resounding in Bosavi, Papua New Guinea." In *Senses of Place*, edited by Steven Feld and Keith Basso, 91–136. Santa Fe, N.M.: School of American Research Press.

Feld, Steven, and Aaron A. Fox. 1994. "Music and Language." *Annual Review of Anthropology* 23: 25–53.

Feld, Steven, Aaron A. Fox, Thomas Porcello, and David Samuels. 2004. "Vocal Anthropology: From the Music of Language to the Language of Song." In *A Companion to Linguistic Anthropology*, edited by Alessandro Duranti, 321–45. Oxford: Blackwell.

Filene, Benjamin. 2000. *Romancing the Folk: Public Memory and American Roots Music*. Chapel Hill: University of North Carolina Press.

Flaes, Rob Boonzajer. 2000. *Brass Unbound: Secret Children of the Colonial Brass Band*. Amsterdam: Royal Tropical Institute.

Florida, Richard. 2002. *The Rise of the Creative Class*. New York: Basic Books.

Floyd, Samuel. 1991. "Ring Shout! Literary Studies, Historical Studies, and Black Music Inquiry." *Black Music Research Journal* 11(2): 265–87.

———. 1995. *The Power of Black Music*. Oxford: Oxford University Press.

Fortun, Kim. 2001. *Advocacy after Bhopal: Environmentalism, Disaster, New Global Orders*. Chicago: University of Chicago Press.

———. 2012. "Ethnography in Late Industrialism." *Cultural Anthropology* 27(3): 446–64.

Fox, Aaron A. 2004. *Real Country: Music and Language in Working-Class Culture*. Durham: Duke University Press.

García Canclini, Néstor. 1993. *Transforming Modernity: Popular Culture in Mexico*. Austin: University of Texas Press.

Gates, Henry Louis, Jr. 1992. "The Black Man's Burden." In *Black Popular Culture*, edited by Gina Dent, 75–83. Seattle: Bay Press.

Gaunt, Kyra Danielle. 2006. *The Games Black Girls Play: Learning the Ropes from Double-Dutch to Hip-Hop*. New York: New York University Press.

Geertz, Clifford. 1973. "Deep Play: Notes on the Balinese Cockfight." In *The Interpretation of Cultures*, 412–53. New York: Basic Books.

Goehr, Lydia. 1994. *The Imaginary Museum of Musical Works: An Essay in the Philosophy of Music*. New York: Oxford University Press.

Gomez, Michael A. 1998. *Exchanging Our Country Marks: The Transformation of African Identities in the Colonial and Antebellum South*. Chapel Hill: University of North Carolina Press.

Goode, Judith, and Jeff Masakovsky. 2001. *The New Poverty Studies: The Ethnography of Power, Politics, and Impoverished People in the United States*. New York: New York University Press.

Gotham, Kevin. 2007. *Authentic New Orleans: Tourism, Culture, and Race in the Big Easy*. New York: New York University Press.

Grazian, David. 2003. *Blue Chicago: The Search for Authenticity in Urban Blues Clubs*. Chicago: University of Chicago Press.

Gushee, Lawrence. 2005. *Pioneers of Jazz: The Story of the Creole Band*. Oxford: Oxford University Press.

Hale, Charles. 2006. "Activist Research v. Cultural Critique: Indigenous Land Rights and the Contradictions of Politically Engaged Anthropology." *Cultural Anthropology* 21(1): 96–120.

Hall, Gwendolyn Midlo. 1992. "The Formation of Afro-Creole Culture." In *Creole New Orleans: Race and Americanization*, edited by Arnold R. Hirsch and Joseph Logsdon, 58–87. Baton Rouge: Louisiana State University Press.

Hall, Stuart. 1990. "Cultural Identity and Diaspora." In *Identity: Community, Culture, Difference*, edited by Jonathan Rutherford, 223–37. London: Lawrence and Wishart.

Hannigan, John. 1998. *Fantasy City: Pleasure and Profit in the Postmodern Metropolis*. New York: Routledge.

Haraway, Donna. 1988. "Situated Knowledges: The Science Question in Feminism and the Privilege of Partial Perspective." *Feminist Studies* 14(3): 575–99.

Hayden, Dolores. 2003. *Building Suburbia: Green Fields and Urban Growth, 1820–2000*. New York: Pantheon Books.

Hazeldine, Mike. 1984. "Dear Wynne." *Footnote* 15: 4–29.

Hazen, Margaret, and Robert Hazen. 1987. *The Music Men: An Illustrated History of Brass Bands in America 1800–1920*. Washington, D.C.: Smithsonian Institution.

Hebdige, Dick. 1979. *Subculture: The Meaning of Style*. New York: Routledge.

Herskovits, Melville. 1941. *Myth of the Negro Past*. New York: Harper and Brothers.

Herzog, George. 1934. "Speech Melody and Primitive Music." *Music Quarterly* 20: 452–66.

———. 1945. "Drum Signaling in a West African Tribe." *Word* 1: 217–38.

Hiroshi-Garret, Charles. 2008. "Jelly Roll Morton and the Spanish Tinge." In *Struggling to Define a Nation: American Music and the Twentieth Century*, 48–82. Berkeley: University of California Press.

Hirsch, Arnold R. 1992. "Simply a Matter of Black and White: The Transformation of Race and Politics in Twentieth-Century New Orleans." In *Creole New Orleans: Race and Americanization*, edited by Arnold R. Hirsch and Joseph Logsdon, 262–319. Baton Rouge: Louisiana State University Press.

———. 2000. "'Containment' on the Home Front: Race and Federal Housing Policy from the New Deal to the Cold War." *Journal of Urban History* 26(2): 158–89.

Holloway, Karla F. C. 2001. *Passed On: African American Mourning Stories*. Durham: Duke University Press.

Hurston, Zora Neale. 1935. *Mules and Men*. New York: HarperCollins.

Jackson, John L., Jr. 2001. *Harlemworld: Doing Race and Class in Contemporary Black America*. Chicago: University of Chicago Press.

Jackson, Michael. 1998. *Minima Ethnographica: Intersubjectivity and the Anthropological Project*. Chicago: University of Chicago Press.

————. 2002. *The Politics of Storytelling: Violence, Transgression and Intersubjectivity*. Copenhagen: Museum Tusculanum Press.

Jackson, Travis. 2012. *Blowin' the Blues Away: Performance and Meaning on the New York Jazz Scene*. Berkeley: University of California Press.

"Jass and Jassism." (1918) 1995. (New Orleans) *Times-Picayune*, June 20. Reprinted in *African American Review* (29)2: 231–32.

Johnson, Cedric, ed. 2011. *Neoliberal Deluge: Hurricane Katrina, Late Capitalism, and the Remaking of New Orleans*. Minneapolis: University of Minnesota Press.

Jones, LeRoi (Amiri Baraka). 1963. *Blues People: The Negro Experience in White America and the Music That Developed from It*. New York: Morrow.

————. 1967. "The Changing Same (R&B and New Black Music)." In *Black Music*, 180–211. New York: Morrow.

Jordan, Scott. 2003. "The Rap on WWOZ." *Gambit Weekly*, August 19.

Julien, Isaac, and Kobena Mercer. (1988) 1996. "Introduction: De Margin and de Centre." *Screen* 29(4): 2–10. Reprinted in *Black British Cultural Studies: A Reader*, edited by Houston A. Baker Jr., Manthia Diawara, and Ruth H. Lindeborg. Chicago: University of Chicago Press.

Keil, Charles. 1966. *Urban Blues*. Chicago: University of Chicago Press.

Kelley, Norman, ed. 2002. *R&B (Rhythm and Business): The Political Economy of Black Music*. New York: Akashic.

Kelley, Robin D. G. 1994. "Kickin' Reality, Kickin' Ballistics: 'Gangsta Rap' and Post-Industrial Los Angeles." In *Race Rebels: Culture, Politics, and the Black Working Class*, 183–228. New York: Free Press.

————. 1997. "Looking for the 'Real' Nigga: Social Scientists Construct the Ghetto." In *Yo' Mama's Disfunktional! Fighting the Culture Wars in Urban America*, 15–42. Boston: Beacon Press.

Keyes, Cheryl L. 1996. "At the Crossroads: Rap Music and Its African Nexus." *Ethnomusicology* 40(2): 223–48.

Kirschenblatt-Gimblett, Barbara. 1998. *Destination Culture: Tourism, Museums, and Heritage*. Berkeley: University of California Press.

Kitwana, Bakari. 2002. *The Hip Hop Generation: Young Blacks and the Crisis in African American Culture*. New York: Basic Civitas Books.

Knowles, Richard. 1996. *Fallen Heroes: A History of New Orleans Brass Bands*. New Orleans: Jazzology Press.

Kozol, Jonathan. 2005. *The Shame of the Nation: The Restoration of Apartheid Schooling in America*. New York: Crown.

Krupa, Michelle. 2011. "New Orleans City Hall Dysfunction Leaves Specialist 'Shocked.'" (New Orleans) *Times-Picayune*, March 3. Accessed July 11, 2013, at

http://www.nola.com/politics/index.ssf/2011/03/new_orleans_city_hall_dysfunct
.html.

Lassiter, Eric Luke. 2005. *The Chicago Guide to Collaborative Ethnography*. Chicago:
University of Chicago Press.

Latrobe, Benjamin Henry. (1819) 1980. *The Journals of Benjamin Henry Latrobe, 1799–
1820*. Vol. 3: *From Philadelphia to New Orleans*. New Haven: Yale University Press.

Levine, Lawrence. 1989. "Jazz and American Culture." *Journal of American Folklore*
102(403): 6–22.

Levitin, Daniel J. 2007. *This Is Your Brain on Music: The Science of a Human Obsession*.
New York: Penguin.

Lewis, Oscar. 1961. *Children of Sánchez: Autobiography of a Mexican Family*. New
York: Random House.

Lewis, Ronald W., and Rachel Breunlin. 2009. *The House of Dance and Feathers:
A Museum*. New Orleans: University of New Orleans Press.

Lipset, Seymour Martin, and Reinhard Bendix. 1959. *Social Mobility in Industrial
Society*. Berkeley: University of California Press.

Lipsitz, George. 2011. *How Racism Takes Place*. Philadelphia: Temple University Press.

Logan, John. 2005. *The Impact of Katrina: Race and Class in Storm-Damaged Neighborhoods*. Study published by Brown University. Accessed March 24, 2008, at www
.s4.brown.edu/Katrina/report.pdf.

Logsdon, Joseph, and Caryn Cossé Bell. 1992. "The Americanization of Black New
Orleans, 1850–1900." In *Creole New Orleans: Race and Americanization*, edited by
Arnold R. Hirsch and Joseph Logsdon, 201–261. Baton Rouge: Louisiana State Uni-
versity Press.

Louisiana Department of Culture, Recreation and Tourism. 2005. "Louisiana Rebirth:
Restoring the Soul of America." Accessed April 1, 2011, at www.cbsnews.com/ht
docs/pdf/rebirthPlan.pdf.

———. 2006. "2006–2007 Marketing Plan." Accessed March 19, 2013, at http://www
.docstoc.com/docs/5925625/new-orleans-department-of-tourism.

Lovell, Anne. 2011. "Debating Life after Disaster: Charity Hospital Babies and Bio-
scientific Futures in Post-Katrina New Orleans." *Medical Anthropology Quarterly*
25(2): 254–77.

Low, Setha M. 1996. "Spatializing Culture: The Social Production and Social Construction of Public Space." *American Ethnologist* 23(4): 861–79.

Low, Setha M., and Sally Engle Merry. 2010. "Engaged Anthropology: Diversity and
Dilemmas." *Current Anthropology* 51 (Supplement 2): S203–S226.

Marcus, George E., and Michael M. J. Fischer. 1986. *Anthropology as Cultural Critique:
An Experimental Moment in the Human Sciences*. Chicago: University of Chicago
Press.

Mbembe, Achille, and Janet Roitman. 1994. "Figures of the Subject in Times of
Crisis." In *The Geography of Identity*, edited by Patricia Yaeger, 153–86. Ann Arbor:
University of Michigan Press.

McClary, Susan. 1991. *Feminine Endings: Music, Gender, and Sexuality*. Minneapolis: University of Minnesota Press.

McNeill, William H. 1995. *Keeping Together in Time: Dance and Drill in Human History*. Cambridge: Harvard University Press.

Meintjes, Louise. 2004. "Shoot the Sergeant, Shatter the Mountain: The Production of Masculinity in Zulu Ngoma Song and Dance in Post-Apartheid South Africa." *Ethnomusicology Forum* 13(2): 173–201.

Memmi, Albert. 1965. *The Colonizer and the Colonized*. Boston: Beacon Press.

Metropolitan Crime Commission. 2012. *Orleans Parish Criminal Justice System Accountability Report*. Accessed March 1, 2013, at http://www.metropolitancrime commission.org/html/documents/NOCJSOversightProjectDecember2012Report -final.pdf.

Mincy, Ronald, ed. 2006. *Black Males Left Behind*. Washington, D.C.: Urban Institute Press.

Monson, Ingrid. 1996. *Saying Something: Jazz Improvisation and Interaction*. Chicago: University of Chicago Press.

Morton, Jelly Roll. (1938) 2005. *The Complete Library of Congress Recordings*. Rounder Records. CD boxed set.

Moten, Fred. 2003. *In the Break: The Aesthetics of the Black Radical Tradition*. Minneapolis: University of Minnesota Press.

Mt. Auburn Associates. 2005. *Louisiana: Where Culture Means Business*. Accessed March 19, 2013, at http://www.crt.state.la.us/culturaldistricts/Documents/cultural economyreport.pdf.

———. 2007. *The Louisiana Cultural Economy: 2007 Status Report*. Accessed April 1, 2011, at http://www.crt.state.la.us/CulturalDistricts/Documents/CulturalEconomy 2007StatusReport.pdf.

Mullings, Leith. 2005. "Interrogating Racism: Toward an Antiracist Anthropology." *Annual Review of Anthropology* 34: 667–93.

Murray, Albert. 1976. "Blues Music as Such." In *Stomping the Blues*, 57–76. New York: McGraw-Hill.

Myers, Sim. 1958. Editorial. (New Orleans) *Times-Picayune*.

"N.O. Man Arrested after Chase; He Asked Cops to Shoot Him, Police Say." 2006. (New Orleans) *Times-Picayune*, August 6.

National Urban League. 2007. *The State of Black America 2007: Portrait of the Black Male*. Silver Spring, Md.: Beckham.

Nealy, Michelle. 2007. "Living Legacy." (New Orleans) *Times-Picayune*, September 4.

Neilson, Brett, and Ned Rossiter. 2008. "Precarity as a Political Concept, or, Fordism as Exception." *Theory, Culture & Society* 25(7–8): 51–72.

Neville, Art, Aaron Neville, Charles Neville, Cyril Neville, and David Ritz. 2000. *The Brothers: An Autobiography*. Boston: Little, Brown.

Nine Times Social and Pleasure Club. 2006. *Coming Out the Door for the Ninth Ward*. New Orleans: Neighborhood Story Project.

Novak, David. 2013. *Japanoise: Music at the Edge of Circulation.* Durham: Duke University Press.

Ochoa, Ana María. 2003. *Entre los Deseos y los Derechos: Un Ensayo Critico sobre Politicas Culturales.* Bogota: Colombian Institute of Anthropology and History.

Ogren, Kathy. 1989. *The Jazz Revolution: Twenties America and the Meaning of Jazz.* New York: Oxford University Press.

Oliver-Smith, Anthony. 1996. "Anthropological Research on Hazards and Disasters." *Annual Review of Anthropology* 25: 303–28.

Omi, Michael, and Howard Winant. 1994. "Racial Formation." In *Racial Formation in the United States: From the 1960s to the 1990s*, 53–76. New York: Routledge.

Orfield, Gary, Daniel Losen, Johanna Wald, and Christopher Swanson. 2004. *Losing Our Future: How Minority Youth Are Being Left Behind by the Graduation Rate Crisis.* Civil Rights Project at Harvard University, Urban Institute, Advocates for Children of New York, and Civil Society Institute. Accessed online January 14, 2008, at www.urban.org/url.cfm?ID=410936.

Ortner, Sherry. 1995. "Resistance and the Problem of Ethnographic Refusal." *Comparative Studies in Society and History* 37(1): 173–93.

———. 2006. *Anthropology and Social Theory: Culture, Power, and the Acting Subject.* Durham: Duke University Press.

Osbey, Brenda Marie. 1996. "One More Last Dance: Ritual and the Jazz Funeral." *Georgia Review* 50(1): 97–107.

Passavant, Paul. 2011. "Mega-Events, the Superdome, and the Return of the Repressed in New Orleans." In *The Neoliberal Deluge: Hurricane Katrina, Late Capitalism, and the Remaking of New Orleans*, edited by Cedric Johnson, 87–129. Minneapolis: University of Minnesota Press.

"Paula Zahn Now." 2005. CNN, September 19. Transcript accessed March 24, 2008, at http://transcripts.cnn.com/TRANSCRIPTS/0509/19/pzn.01.html.

Peirano, Mariza G. S. 1998. "When Anthropology Is at Home: The Different Contexts of a Single Discipline." *Annual Review of Anthropology* 27: 105–28.

Petryna, Adriana. 2002. *Life Exposed: Biological Citizens after Chernobyl.* Princeton: Princeton University Press.

Piven, Frances Fox. 1998. "Welfare Reform and the Economic and Cultural Reconstruction of Low Wage Labor Markets." *City and Society Annual Review* 10: 21–36.

Powell, Lawrence N. 2007. "New Orleans: Chasing the Blues Away." *American Scholar* 76(3): 9–13.

"Presidential Address to the Nation, September 15, 2005." 2005. Accessed March 19, 2008, at http://www.whitehouse.gov/news/releases/2005/09/20050915-8.html.

Price, Chris. 2005. "New Orleans's Jazz Fest Organizers Expect up to $500M Boost." *New Orleans CityBusiness*, April 25.

Quinn, Eithne. 2005. *Nuthin' but a 'G' Thang: The Culture and Commerce of Gangsta Rap.* New York: Columbia University Press.

Qureshi, Regula. 2000. "How Does Music Mean? Embodied Memories and the Politics of Affect in the Indian Sarangi." *American Ethnologist* 27(4): 805–38.

Rabinow, Paul. 2003. *Anthropos Today: Reflections on Modern Equipment*. Princeton: Princeton University Press.

———. 2007. *Marking Time: On the Anthropology of the Contemporary*. Princeton: Princeton University Press.

Rabinow, Paul, and George E. Marcus, with James D. Faubion and Tobias Rees. 2008. *Designs for an Anthropology of the Contemporary*. Durham: Duke University Press.

Radano, Ronald. 1996. "Denoting Difference: The Writing of the Slave Spirituals." *Critical Inquiry* 22: 506–44.

———. 2003. *Lying Up a Nation: Race and Black Music*. Chicago: University of Chicago Press.

Raeburn, Bruce. 2009. *New Orleans Style and the Writing of American Jazz History*. Ann Arbor: University of Michigan Press.

Ramos, Silvia, and Ana María Ochoa. 2009. "Music and Human Rights, AfroReggae and the Youth from the Favelas as Responses to Violence in Brazil." In *Music and Cultural Rights*, edited by Andrew Weintraub, 219–40. Urbana: University of Illinois Press.

Ramsey, Frederic, Jr., and Charles Edward Smith, eds. 1939. *Jazzmen: The Story of Hot Jazz Told in the Lives of the Men Who Created It*. New York: Harcourt Brace.

Ramsey, Guthrie P., Jr. 2003. *Race Music: Black Cultures from Be-Bop to Hip-Hop*. Berkeley: University of California Press.

Reckdahl, Katy. 2006. "The Price of Parading." *Offbeat*. November. Accessed March 19, 2013, at http://www.offbeat.com/2006/11/01/the-price-of-parading.

———. 2007. "Feeling His Spirit." (New Orleans) *Times-Picayune*. January 1.

———. 2010. "Bourbon Street Music Curfew Enforcement Draws Complaints." (New Orleans) *Times-Picayune*, June 17.

Regis, Helen. 1999. "Second Lines, Minstrelsy, and the Contested Landscapes of New Orleans Afro-Creole Festivals." *Cultural Anthropology* 14(4): 472–504.

———. 2001. "Blackness and the Politics of Memory in the New Orleans Second Line." *American Ethnologist* 28(4): 752–77.

Regis, Helen, and Shana Walton. 2008. "Producing the Folk at the New Orleans Jazz and Heritage Festival." *Journal of American Folklore* 121(482): 400–440.

Reily, Suzel, and Kate Brucher, eds. Forthcoming. *Brass Bands of the World: Militarism, Colonialism, and Local Music Making*. London: Ashgate.

Roach, Joseph. 1996. *Cities of the Dead: Circum-Atlantic Performance*. New York: Columbia University Press.

Rogers, Bethany W. 2010. "'It's Not Just about the Buildings, It's about the People': Architecture, Practice, and Preservation in Post-Katrina New Orleans." PhD dissertation, Louisiana State University.

Rose, Tricia. 1994. *Black Noise: Rap Music and Black Culture in Contemporary America*. Middletown, Conn.: Wesleyan University Press.

———. 2008. *The Hip-Hop Wars*. New York: Free Press.

Rothman, Hal. 2002. *Neon Metropolis: How Las Vegas Started the Twenty-first Century*. New York: Routledge.

Sakakeeny, Matt. 2005. "Disciplinary Movements, the Civil Rights Movement, and Charles Keil's 'Urban Blues.'" *Current Musicology* 79–80: 143–68.

———. 2010. "'Under the Bridge': An Orientation to Soundscapes in New Orleans." *Ethnomusicology* 54(1): 1–27.

———. 2011a. "'New Orleans, Louisiana, USA': Critical Exchange on David Simon's Treme." *Contemporary Political Theory* 10(3): 395–98.

———. 2011b. "New Orleans Music as a Circulatory System." *Black Music Research Journal* 31(2): 291–325.

———. 2012. "New Orleans Exceptionalism: Culture and Complicity." *Perspective on Politics* 10(3): 723–26.

Salaam, Kalamu ya. 2008. "Lil' Rascals Brass Band: 'Knock with Me—Rock with Me.'" Accessed June 11, 2012, at http://www.kalamu.com/bol/2008/06/02/lil'-rascals-brass-band-"knock-with-me---rock-with-me".

Samuels, Daniel. 2000. "Remembering North Claiborne: Community and Place in Downtown New Orleans." MA thesis, University of New Orleans.

Sanford, Victoria, and Asale Angel-Ajani, eds. 2006. *Engaged Observer: Anthropology, Advocacy, and Activism.* New Brunswick, N.J.: Rutgers University Press.

Sarig, Roni. 2007. *Third Coast: OutKast, Timbaland, and How Hip-Hop Became a Southern Thing.* New York: Da Capo Press.

Satchmo the Great. 1957. CBS television documentary, Edward R. Murrow, producer.

Schafer, William J. 1977. *Brass Bands and New Orleans Jazz.* Baton Rouge: Louisiana State University Press.

Scheper-Hughes, Nancy, and Philippe Bourgois, eds. 2004. *Violence in War and Peace.* London: Blackwell.

Schiro, Victor. 1964. Letter to International Jazz Festival organizers, December 11. Hogan Archive of New Orleans Jazz, Tulane University.

Schloss, Joseph. 2004. *Making Beats: The Art of Sample-based Hip-hop.* Middletown, Conn.: Wesleyan University Press.

Scott, James C. 1985. *Weapons of the Weak: Everyday Forms of Peasant Resistance.* New Haven: Yale University Press.

———. 1990. *Hidden Transcripts: Domination and the Arts of Resistance.* New Haven: Yale University Press.

Sewell, William F. 1992. "A Theory of Structure: Duality, Agency, and Transformation." *American Journal of Sociology* 98(1): 1–29.

Shearouse, Chris. 1971. "Blacks in Treme Area Pay Price of Progress." *New Orleans States-Item,* July 16.

Small, Mario Luis, David J. Harding, and Michele Lamont. 2010. "Reconsidering Culture and Poverty." *Annals of the American Academy of Political and Social Science* 629: 6–27.

Smith, Michael P. 1994. *Mardi Gras Indians.* Gretna, La.: Pelican.

Smith, Neil. 2006. "Gentrification Generalized: From Local Anomaly to Urban 'Regeneration' as Global Urban Strategy." In *Frontiers of Capital: Ethnographic*

Reflections on the New Economy, edited by Melissa S. Fisher and Greg Downey, 191–208. Durham: Duke University Press.

Social Aid and Pleasure Club Task Force. 2007. "March for Peace and Celebration of Hope." Press release.

Social Aid and Pleasure Club Task Force et al. v. City of New Orleans et al. 2006. "Memorandum." Filed November 16.

Sollors, Werner. 1997. *Neither Black nor White yet Both: Thematic Explorations of Interracial Literature*. New York: Oxford University Press.

Sommers, Samuel R., Evan P. Apfelbaum, Kristin N. Dukes, Negin Toosi, and Elsie J. Wang. 2006. "Race and Media Coverage of Hurricane Katrina: Analysis, Implications, and Future Research Questions." *Analyses of Social Issues and Public Policy* 6(1): 39–55.

Soul Rebels Brass Band. 2006. Liner notes to *Urban Legend*. Barn Burner Music.

———. 2009. Liner notes to *No Place Like Home*. Independent release.

Souther, Marc. 2006. *New Orleans on Parade: Tourism and the Transformation of the Crescent City*. Baton Rouge: Louisiana State University Press.

Spitzer, Nick. 2003. "The Aesthetics of Work and Play in Creole New Orleans." In *Raised to the Trade: Creole Building Arts of New Orleans*, edited by John Ethan Hankins, 96–130. New Orleans: New Orleans Museum of Art.

———. 2006. "Rebuilding the 'Land of Dreams' with Music." In *Rebuilding Urban Places after Disaster: Lessons from Hurricane Katrina*, edited by Eugenie L. Birch and Susan M. Wachter, 305–28. Philadelphia: University of Pennsylvania Press.

Stewart, Kathleen. 2007. *Ordinary Affects*. Durham: Duke University Press.

Stokes, Martin. 1999. "Music, Travel, and Tourism: An Afterword." *World of Music* (41)3: 141–55.

Sweet Home New Orleans. 2010. *State of the New Orleans Music Community Report*. Accessed April 1, 2011, at www.sweethomeneworleans.org.

Taussig, Michael. 2004. *My Cocaine Museum*. Chicago: University of Chicago Press.

Toll, Robert C. 1974. *Blacking Up: The Minstrel Show in Nineteenth-Century America*. New York: Oxford University Press.

Troeh, Eve. 2006. "Secondline Fees." *Gambit Weekly*. June 27.

Tsing, Anna. 2005. *Friction: An Ethnography of Global Connection*. Princeton: Princeton University Press.

Tucker, Sherrie. 2000. *Swing Shift: "All-Girl" Bands of the 1940s*. Durham: Duke University Press.

Turner, Victor. 1969. *Ritual Process: Structure and Anti-Structure*. New York: Aldine de Gruyter.

Urban, Greg. 2001. *Metaculture: How Culture Moves through the World*. Minneapolis: University of Minnesota Press.

Villepastour, Amanda. 2010. *Ancient Text Messages of the Yorùbá Bàtá Drum: Cracking the Code*. London: Ashgate.

Wacquant, Loïc. 2002. "Scrutinizing the Street: Poverty, Morality, and the Pitfalls of Urban Ethnography." *American Journal of Sociology* 107(6): 1468–1532.

———. 2004. "Decivilizing and Demonizing: The Remaking of the Black American Ghetto." In *The Sociology of Norbert Elias*, edited by Steven Loyal and Stephen Quilley, 95–121. Cambridge: Cambridge University Press.

———. 2007. *Urban Outcasts: A Comparative Sociology of Advanced Marginality*. Malden, Mass.: Polity Press.

———. 2009. *Punishing the Poor: The Neoliberal Government of Social Insecurity*. Durham: Duke University Press.

Wallace, Michele. 1990. *Invisibility Blues: From Pop to Theory*. New York: Verso.

Washburne, Christopher. 1997. "The Clave of Jazz: A Caribbean Contribution to the Rhythmic Foundation of an African-American Music." *Black Music Research Journal* 17: 59–80.

———. 2008. *Sounding Salsa: Performing Latin Music in New York City*. Philadelphia: Temple University Press.

Webster, Richard. 2012. "Treme Divided over Couple's Restaurant, Live Music Plans." *New Orleans City Business*, May 17.

Weheliye, Alexander G. 2005. "The Grooves of Temporality." *Public Culture* 17(2): 319–38.

Weidman, Amanda. 2006. *Singing the Classical, Voicing the Modern: The Postcolonial Politics of Music in South India*. Durham: Duke University Press.

———. 2007. "Stage Goddesses and Studio Divas: Agency and the Politics of Voice." In *Words, Worlds, and Material Girls: Essays on Language, Gender, Globalization*, edited by Bonnie McElhinny, 131–56. The Hague: Mouton de Gruyter Press.

West, Cornel. 1993. "The Paradox of the African American Rebellion." In *Keeping Faith: Philosophy and Race in America*, 271–92. New York: Routledge.

White, Bob. 2008. *Rumba Rules: The Politics of Dance Music in Mobutu's Zaire*. Durham: Duke University Press.

White, Michael. 2001. "The New Orleans Brass Band: A Cultural Tradition." In *The Triumph of the Soul: Cultural and Psychological Aspects of African American Music*, edited by Ferdinand Jones and Arthur C. Jones, 69–96. Westport, Conn.: Praeger.

———. 2004. Liner notes to *Dancing in the Sky*. Basin Street Records CD503.

———. 2008. Liner notes to *Blue Crescent*. Basin Street Records CD5042.

Whitten, Norman E., and John F. Szwed. 1971. *Afro-American Anthropology*. New York: Free Press.

Wilson, William Julius. 1987. *The Truly Disadvantaged: The Inner City, the Underclass, and Public Policy*. Chicago: University of Chicago Press.

Wirth, Louis. 1928. *The Ghetto*. Chicago: University of Chicago Press.

Woods, Clyde, ed. 2009. "In the Wake of Katrina: New Paradigms and Social Visions." Special issue of *American Quarterly* 61(3).

Yúdice, George. 2001. "From Hybridity to Policy: For a Purposeful Cultural Studies." In *Consumers and Citizens: Globalization and Multicultural Conflicts*, edited by Néstor García Canclini, ix–xxxviii. Minneapolis: University of Minnesota Press.

———. 2004. *The Expediency of Culture: Uses of Culture in the Global Era*. Durham: Duke University Press.

INDEX